SACRED GEOGRAPHY:
CONVERSATIONS WITH PLACE

SACRED GEOGRAPHY:
CONVERSATIONS WITH PLACE

Edited by
Bernadette Brady
Jack Hunter

SOPHIA CENTRE PRESS
Ceredigion, Wales
2024

Sacred Geography: Conversations with Place
edited by Bernadette Brady and Jack Hunter

© Sophia Centre Press 2024

First published in 2024.

All rights reserved. No part of this publication may be reproduced
or utilised in any form or by any means, electronic or mechanical,
including photocopying, recording, or by any information storage
and retrieval system, without permission in writing from the Publishers.

Sophia Centre Press
University of Wales Trinity Saint David
Ceredigion, Wales SA48 7ED, United Kingdom.
www.sophiacentrepress.com

Typeset by Daniela Puia
Cover design: Jenn Zahrt

ISBN: 978-1-907767-16-6

Names: Brady, Bernadette, 1950- editor. | Hunter, Jack, 1986- editor.
Title: Sacred geography : conversations with place / edited by Bernadette Brady [and] Jack Hunter.
Description: Ceredigion, Wales : Sophia Centre Press, 2024. | Includes bibliographical references and index.
Identifiers: ISBN: 978-1-907767-16-6 (paperback) | 978-1-907767-56-2 (ebook)
Subjects: LCSH: Sacred space. | Religion and geography. | Landscapes--Religious aspects. | Nature--Religious aspects.
Classification: LCC: BL580 .S33 2024 | DDC: 203.5--dc23

Printed by Lightning Source.

CONTENTS

FOREWORD   XI
Bernadette Brady and Jack Hunter

INTRODUCTIONS
I   SACRED GEOGRAPHY: CONVERSATIONS WITH PLACE   1
    Bernadette Brady

II   SACRED GEOGRAPHY: COVERSATIONS WITH THE OTHER   11
    Jack Hunter

THE VOLUME

OVERVIEW OF SACREDNESS

1   SITTING WITH A DANDELION:
    PLANTS AS DOORWAYS TO THE SACRED   25
    Amanda-Jane Page

SECTION ONE – SACREDNESS THROUGH ENCOUNTERING THE ANCIENT

2   THE LAPIS NIGER OF ANCIENT ROME:
    HIEROPHANY OR SOCIAL CONSTRUCT?   39
    Sarah Bisby

3   A CAVE OF STORIES: FINDING SACRED SPACE AT
    WAYLAND'S SMITHY LONG BARROW   55
    Amy R. Mercy

SECTION TWO – JOURNEYS AS SACRED

4   AN UNEXPECTED PILGRIMAGE TO SEOUL'S NAMSAN MOUNTAIN   73
    Holly McNiven

5   WINDY BANK: A JOURNEY INTO A SECLUDED WOODLAND   89
    Karen Hanson

SECTION THREE – ENGAGING WITH GARDENS AS SACREDNES

6   THE ART OF LISTENING TO STONES:
    ENCOUNTERING A JAPANESE GARDEN   111
    Berna Lee 李映晴

7   GATHERINGS, LINES AND ENCHANTMENT:
    ENGAGEMENT WITH A BUTTERFLY GARDEN   127
    Kim Corrall

8	THE GNOME, THE ROCK AND THE POOL – SACREDNESS IN A DOMESTIC GARDEN *Wendy Fey*	143

Section Four - Dark Sacredness

9	A WAR MEMORIAL IN THE NEW FOREST: LOOKING TOWARDS HOME *Kathy Vinton*	157 157
10	THE HIROSHIMA PEACE PARK; IS IT POSSIBLE FOR A NUCLEAR WEAPON TO CREATE A SACRED SPACE? *Andrew Spencer*	173
11	A LIMINAL HAVEN: EXPLORING THE SACRED GEOGRAPHY OF AN ENGLISH DROSSCAPE *Daniel Broadbent*	185

Section Five – Sacredness and the Other

12	HIVE MINDS: EXPLORING THE SPIRITUAL CONNECTIONS BETWEEN BEEKEEPERS AND BEES *Jake Eshelman*	203

INDEX	219

FOREWORD

Bernadette Brady and Jack Hunter

The papers in this volume explore the various issues concerning our understanding of sacred place, such as whether sacredness spontaneously emerges from place, or how sacredness may be part of an interweaving between place and surrounding life.

The individual chapters are organized in sections, beginning with an examination of encounters with place. The first section, *Overview of Sacredness*, Amanda-Jane Page's chapter, , 'Sitting with a Dandelion: Plants as doorways to the sacred'. Page gives an overview of the nature of the human experience of the sacred and spiritual. She argues for the acknowledgement of the role of plants as active agents in building bridges between humans and nature. Going beyond notions of psychedelic plants, or plants for healing, she suggests that the simple act of sitting with a dandelion can begin to open the doors to another world. For Page, plants can be gate-keepers giving access to a deeper link with nature, moving human perception from seeing plants simply in terms of food or drugs for human consumption towards a more personal relationship, an essential union that is not just one way.

The next two chapters both focus on how encountering a many-layered place produces an experience of sacredness. Sarah Bisby's chapter, 'The Lapis Niger of Ancient Rome: Hierophany or Social Construct?',' unpacks the ontology of sacredness in a particular place, the ancient Roman omphalos, the Lapis Niger. Located in the Roman Forum, this is today under canvas and hidden from view. Bisby tells its story through its history and her own experience in order to reveal - through layers of myth, ritual and events - the power of that place and its link to Rome. Chapter 3, by Amy Mercy, is titled, 'A cave of stories: finding sacred space at Wayland's Smithy Long Barrow.' Mercy takes a similar approach to Bisby to show how vastly different cultures have placed layers of meaning and myth onto an ancient site in southern England. She paints a palimpsest of myths and meaning over time, from the neolithic builders and early users of the site, through the medieval period and on to consider the attitudes of today's visitors. Mercy draws on Michel Foucault's notion of *heterochrony*, a type of other-time where time exists in complex multiplicity - built by layers of diversity.

Section two, *Journeys as Sacred*, consists of two chapters. The first, Chapter 4, is by Holly McNiven and titled 'An unexpected pilgrimage to Seoul's Namsan mountain'. McNiven took a rambling walk one morning in Seoul, the capital of South Korea, but was unconsciously pulled towards the mountain, which overlooks the city. The chapter tells McNiven's story of alienation in a culture, of unexpectedly finding a part of her family's story and then finally encountering a sense of her own proper place in the world. McNiven reminds us of the need for 'place' by quoting Simone Weil's comment that 'to be rooted is perhaps the most important and least recognized need of the human soul'.[1]

Chapter 5 by Karen Hanson, is titled 'Windy Bank, a journey into a secluded woodland.' Hanson recounts a different type of journey, through Windy Bank, a Woodland Trust walk consisting of mature deciduous trees, situated in in Culcheth in the north-west of England. Visiting it by day and by night Hanson ponders the sense of sacredness that grows slowly from frequent visits, and explores the sense of ownership that arises from leaving a mark, whether this is placing a stone or carving a name into a tree, or even leaving litter. All these are ways that humans claim ownership of a place and Hanson suggests that such actions of ownership can be pathways to building sacredness into a place.

The third section is titled *Engaging with gardens as sacredness*. Berna Lee 李映晴, opens this section with Chapter 6, 'The Art of Listening to Stones: Encountering a Japanese Garden'. The garden is Portland Japanese Garden, situated on top of a hill in Washington Park in Portland, Oregon USA. Lee steps into the Japanese concept of space and time, known as *ma*, which is the presence of stillness, a pause or a space. It is through this stillness that Lee experiences a sense of sacredness that has been intentionally 'planted' in the garden. Lee also draws on Levy-Bruhl's notion of participation. The combination enabled her to engage with the garden and, even as a visitor from Hong Kong, allowed for her to experience a sense of belonging and of being grounded in this particular place. She argues that this feeling of connectedness, or sacredness, was only encountered when she personally strove to be present in the garden - to know its story and listen to the stones.

Kim Corrall's Chapter 7 follows and is titled 'Gatherings, Lines and Enchantment: Engagement with a Butterfly Garden.' Corrall focuses on the gathering of things, such as rocks, plants, local wildlife, humans and lines. Corrall's Butterfly Garden is the desert botanical garden in Palm Desert, Riverside County, California, and is known as the Living Desert. Unlike Lee's Japanese Garden in Portland, this garden has governed itself, drawing into itself the plants and wildlife that see it as their proper place. To this complexity of life Corrall notes the soundscape - the song of the place - and through the combination of all of these threads she finds another version of sacredness, one that comes directly out of nature.

Chapter 8, by Wendy Fey, is titled 'The Gnome, the Rock and the Pool – sacredness in a domestic garden', and reveals sacredness in the ordinary and everyday. Fey encounters wonder by participating with an unloved area of her own garden, a rockery. A garden gnome sheepishly engaged with by Fey becomes the guardian of a place which had been set apart from the rest of the surroundings, and to a large extent forgotten. However, Fey found that it was not only full of memories and family stories but also contained pathways and habitats for others. Fey shows us that, by taking the rockery's perspective, a different world is viewed!

The fourth section, *Dark Sacredness*, consists of three chapters. Chapter 9, by Kathy Vinton, is titled, 'A War Memorial in The New Forest - looking towards home'. The war memorial in question is the Canadian War Memorial, located near Burley, in The New Forest National Park, on the south coast of the UK, close to the coast of France. The memorial is isolated as it is placed in the location where services were held for the Canadian airmen gathering to be a part of the D-Day landings in June 1944. It consists of a small natural amphitheatre, which was protected from westerly wind and with a tree line which provided cover from the view of German planes. Vinton visited every day for fourteen days and, in keeping with the activities held there in the past, she offered prayers on each day to help her engage with the site. By the end of her fourteen days, she had become deeply aware of the natural sacredness of the site, a natural place for the chaplain of the Canadian airmen to choose to offer services to those who were facing possible death.

Chapter 10 is by Andrew Spencer and stays within the period of World War Two. His chapter, 'The Hiroshima Peace Park: Is it possible for a nuclear weapon to create a sacred space?' considers the ways in which a sense of the sacred may emerge out of destruction. Spencer visited the Peace Park, which is located within a few hundred metres radius of the hypocentre of the world's first use of a nuclear weapon, in August 2018, and was deeply moved by its stillness and power. Spencer's recounting of his visit is a journey into dark sacredness, and what might be considered the ultimate Eliadian eruption of a dark hierophany - a nuclear explosion. Spencer also pointed to the nature of the place itself, as it was also the site of the main entrance to one of the most important Shinto shrines in Japan, which had been established in 1869 and dedicated to the *Han* victims of the *Boshin* War, the Japanese civil war. Additionally, since the seventeenth century the site had also been the location of the Pure Land Buddhist temple, Jisen-ji.

Spencer makes the case that the place itself held the story of wars and peace across generations. Sadly, Spencer died in 2022 so was not able to expand on his thinking for this current volume.

Moving forward from World War Two, Daniel Broadbent offers a different perspective on sacredness through death and liminality. In Chapter 11, 'A Liminal Haven: exploring the sacred geography of an English drosscape,' Broadbent recounts a morning run on which he encountered a liminal landscape and a commemoration of one of the UK's worst motor accidents, which occurred in 2011. Both are embraced in a concrete motorway flyover located on the edge of the town of Taunton, Somerset, in the southwest of England. Broadbent considers Bjørn Thomasson's ideas on inbetweenness and Alan Berger's concept of a 'drosscape' defined as 'a largely ignored place of land which exists only as a by-product of industrial or economic activity'.[2] He explores this drosscape, which is revealed to have its own stories of ancient sacred swords found in the river, as well as lives lost in the motor crash, and discovers the power of a liminal place.

The final section of the volume is themed around the *Sacred and the Other*. It contains just one chapter, Chapter 12, by Jake Eshelman, 'Hive Minds: Exploring the Spiritual Connections Between Beekeepers and Bees'. Eshelman takes the reader into the world of a hive, a superorganism. In his ethnographic research project Eshelman interviewed beekeepers and their thoughts on the nature of sacred beekeeping and discovered that concepts of speaking to the bees and the notion of bee-breath are important features of the beekeepers' worldviews. He found that the beekeepers had developed a heightened sense of ecological consciousness, a greater awareness of the sacredness of the bees and their world. Eshelman reminds us of the fact that engagement with the other is a central part of the recognition of sacredness in a place.

The volume thus comes in full circle, from its beginning by engaging with the other, either by sitting down with a dandelion, and it ends in talking to bees. In between these two chapters each author engages in an exploration of how to engage with place and its many layers of intersecting conversations: hence our title, *Conversations with Place*. Each chapter focuses on different faces of the same theme - sacredness embedded into place, moving from the acknowledgement of layered history and memories, to the taking of journeys, engaging with gardens and finally exploring the sacredness that erupts from terror or loss.

Notes

1   Simone Weil, *The Need for Roots: Prelude to a Declaration of Duties towards Mankind*, trans. by Arthur Wills (Taylor & Francis e-Library: Routledge, 2005), p. 40.
2   Alan Berger, 'Drosscape In The Landscape', in *The Urbanism Reader*, ed. by Charles Waldheim (Princeton: Princeton University Press, 2006), pp. 197-217.

INTRODUCTION PART I

SACRED GEOGRAPHY: CONVERSATIONS WITH PLACE

Bernadette Brady

Sacred Geography

Sacred Geography played a foundational role in the early stages of the MA programme in Cultural Astronomy and Astrology within the Sophia Centre for the Study of Cosmology in Culture. This innovative programme was conceived at Bath Spa University College, and launched in October 2002 with Michael York, Nicholas Campion, and Patrick Curry as the original teaching team. The Sacred Geography module itself was part of the MA in the Study of Religions, the tutor for which was Michael York, who was also the Programme Director of the MA in Cultural Astronomy and Astrology, so it was felt appropriate to include it as an option for those students. The earth-based study of Sacred Geography brought the vital ingredient of earthing cosmologies to the sky-based study of Cultural Astronomy and Astrology. When Michael York retired in 2004 the topic was briefly taught by Nicholas Campion (2005-6) and when the MA transferred to the University of Wales, Lampeter (now the University of Wales Trinity Saint David), it was taken over by Anthony Thorley, who taught it from 2010 to 2017. When Anthony retired, he was succeeded by Bernadette Brady.

What is Sacred Geography?

In 1851, the term 'Sacred Geography' was used in a report published in *Scientific American*. This report discussed a lecture given by Col. Rowlinson at the Royal Geographical Society in London, centred on the Biblical cities of Assyria. The lecture primarily focused on the Tigris River, its dynamic flow, and the cities it influenced. Adding the adjective 'sacred' to the noun 'geography' stemmed from the fact that this landscape held profound religious significance within the context of Christianity.[1] While some might view this definition of sacred geography as superficial, it points to a crucial basic concept. This landscape carried immense spiritual significance to Col. Rowlinson and his audience at the Royal Geographical Society as it was deeply rooted in the Christian narrative.

Indeed, Bergmann in 2009, adhered to this idea of a landscape's sacredness when he suggested that 'religions can be analysed as ritualisations which depend on space and reshape it'.[2] Bergmann et al. used the term 'earthing sacredness' to describe how Christianity and other religions were embedded in places, places well beyond Col. Rowlinson's view of the Holy Land.[3]

Sacred places, however, are not limited to religious narratives. In 1936, with the emergence of aviation technology, aerial perspectives of landscapes became available, and René Guénon made airborne observations of Glastonbury, United Kingdom. These observations suggested to him that Iron Age humans had intentionally shaped the natural topography of Glastonbury to resemble an 'image of the vault of the sky', hinting at an ancient, and maybe sacred, hidden message in the landscape.[4] This notion of ancient arranged landscapes holding power was also a theme of J. Heinsch, a German town planner. He delivered a paper during the 1938 International Congress of Geography titled 'Principles of Prehistoric Sacred Geography' where he discussed the benefits of aligning contemporary urban planning with any orientations established by nearby ancient sites. Heinsch viewed these ancient sites as holding an intricate geometry binding the different architectural elements together. He proposed that these ancient arrangements contained a deliberate design that imbued the entire environment with a sense of power or sacredness, one that was not weakened by the current lack of understanding of its original purpose. Heinsch described this idea as:

> Therefore these principles of an ancient geometrical landscape arrangement, which are imprinted everywhere and which seemed like natural laws to the 'natural insight' of their originators, must not be treated merely as the antique hieroglyphs of a vast 'primitive handwriting', still legible, with the help of measure and angle, in the landscape today. They should above all be recognised and evaluated as the ground-plans for a certain configuration of land and people, which with its geometric proportions – 'pleasing to God' as well as man – works today as effectively on our natural human feeling for our homeland as do the same proportions in Gothic cathedrals and other old buildings reflecting the cosmic order, which even now somehow put the silent beholder in harmony with the infinite, impressing him spiritually and thus influencing him 'magically'.[5]

For Heinsch, to align a town or structure to an ancient orientation made use of this unknown or undefined power. By incorporating the ancient sacred ratios and alignments into contemporary urban planning, he believed that modern structures could partake of ancient sacredness. This idea of an archaicising approach to architecture was not new. John Wood, the eighteenth century Georgian town planner who designed the city of Bath in England, drew on Stonehenge to design the Bath Royal Circus. He matched the diameter of the Circus to that of Stonehenge and reflected the layout of the inner stones with horse hitching rails in order to draw on the 'magic' of the older, and what he considered to be Druidic, design.[6]

By the mid-20th century, followers of Heinsch's belief in the sacredness of ancient landscapes were known as the 'Straight Track Club'. These researchers approached a site or landscape to explore the presence of alignments and considered these alignments to hold hidden intentions and meaning. This meaning extended to the units of measurement believed to be instrumental in the creation of the ancient sites, Alexander Thom's megalithic yard (0.83 cm in length) being a notable example.[7] Using this approach, researchers sought to comprehend the relationships between prehistoric landscapes and the constructed elements within them, such as, for example, temples, stone circles, dolmens, or burial mounds. Followers of the Straight Track Club are today viewed as adopting a form of green sacred geography where the label of 'green' can be borrowed from archaeoastronomy.

Green archaeoastronomy was defined by Anthony Aveni as being focused on the orientations and alignments that a structure may have to a sky object. In Britain in the 1970s a rigorous and statistical methodology was developed for working with green archaeoastronomy which allowed for judging whether any orientation within a pre-historical site was intentional or occurred by chance. In contrast, 'brown' archaeoastronomy emerged from North American research into pre-Columbian Mesoamerican structures and their relationship to each other and the sky. Brown archaeoastronomy integrates techniques and data from a broad range of humanities, history, cultural anthropology, art history, folklore studies and the history of religions.[8] With this distinction in mind, researchers adopting a green sacred geography approach tend to speak of decoding landscapes to reveal a hidden message of an ancient cosmology embedded into the land and sky. With this approach place itself is viewed as a canvas on which ancient humanity built or amplified a message in shape, orientation, ratios, and measurements. In contrast, brown sacred geography draws heavily on the aforementioned humanities and studies the human, and at times non-human, relationships within a living landscape. Jack Hunter's introduction to this volume focuses on the non-human relationships in a landscape but whether human or non-human relationships, a brown approach allows place to gain agency. Researchers seek conversations with place. Its central methodology is phenomenology rather than measurement, 'placefulness' rather than alignments.

Hence Bergmann's idea of 'earthing sacredness' can be broadened beyond religions to where sacredness can be both allocated or pre-existing in a physical place. Green sacred geography tends to focus on ancient earthed cosmologies, while brown sacred geography can turn its eye to contemporary cultures. The two approaches can be blended: the former privileging orientations and measurements and the latter privileging phenomenology and narratives. Both seek to discover a sacredness or specialness to place. How and why this specialness occurs and what is its nature and purpose are where the two styles of sacred geography diverge. Green sacred geography is orientated largely around the activities of humans in a landscape, while brown sacred geography broadens the research question into a landscape having a dialogue with itself without the need for humans. The papers in this volume all approach their subject matter leaning towards a brown sacred geography viewpoint.

Thinking through Place

Edward Casey stated that society's view of place is dominated by the modern neutrality of 'space'.[9] This domination of space in the West was fuelled by medieval Christian theology. In the thirteenth century, the Italian theologian Saint Thomas Aquinas (1225-1274) inserted Aristotelian philosophy into Christian theology.[10] Aristotelian order, however, required that God, the divine unmover who instigated all causation, needed to be located somewhere within the cosmos.[11] God, however, needed to exist without boundaries, so God existed in infinite space. With God allocated to space, the idea of a place, with its sense of limits, became inferior. In discussing the split between a universal God existing in space and humanity existing in place, Bergmann pointed to Johann Wolfgang Goethe's (1749-1832) argument that when humanity splits from place, there is a loss of self as self-awareness only comes from an awareness of one's place in the world.[12] The home-place is where the individual or group holds their status, and that place is embedded with their stories and memories. Humanity has always fought for the right to be in 'one's place'. At a local level, Tilley suggested that a group's stories or memories embedded in place humanises and encultures a place. The landscape becomes saturated with place names which in turn are intertwined with topography, human intentionality and even mythological characters.[13] Lane pointed out that the greater the number of stories or the cultural importance of the stories, the greater the place is valued and held as sacred.[14] Place may have stopped being the location of an infinite God, but, nevertheless, place is central to life, for all life must live in a place.

To approach the complexity of place, it is helpful to return to the Classical period and the ideas of Aristotle (384 BCE–322 BCE). He viewed place as a vessel which gave shape to its contents and also had a certain power to attract objects towards itself.[15] Aristotle drew on his theory of elements (fire, earth, air, and water) to explain the drawing power of place. He argued that the elements sought to move to their proper place: fire and air upwards, earth and water downwards. He maintained that all bodies consist of a mixture of these elements, and hence the motion of a body was caused by the elements seeking their preferred place. He concluded that this, 'show[s] that not only that place is something, but also that it exerts a certain influence'.[16] Aristotle considered this a type of 'gravity'. Additionally, when a body finally reached such a place, Aristotle considered that it was in its 'proper place' for 'the movement of each body to its own place is motion towards its own form'.[17] Aristotle reasoned that the location of a body in its proper place was where the body experienced a sense of wholeness and a form of stillness.[18] Casey summed up Aristotle's notion of place as a 'unique and nonreducible feature of the physical world, something with its own inherent powers'.[19]

Today, Aristotle's view of place falls outside the sciences, but it does speak of the human experience of place. For humans and non-humans, place holds, as I have previously stated, a type of phenomenological gravity, the power of place to draw towards itself that which finds comfort in the qualities of that place.[20] To be in one's Aristotelian proper place is to feel a sense of wholeness, a form of completeness, and to experience the stillness of a centre. On a human level, such a place provides a sense of ease and satisfaction with one's environment, whether that is in one's membership of a community, the peace of one's living room, or a local coffee shop. The experience of being in one's proper place leads to a person attributing levels of sacredness to that place. This sacredness is mundane, generated by the instinctual urge to safeguard the place. Whether on a personal level or within a community, there is a natural inclination to oppose any alterations to a cherished location. The longer a place accumulates its history, distinctive names, and personal narratives, the stronger 'its' community becomes driven to preserve and safeguard it. Place is like a weight on a canvas. Place causes a 'dip' in the fabric, which then attracts nearby lighter objects. The more place draws in, the heavier it becomes and so the more it draws. Hence, sacredness or cultural specialness grows in influence and produces its own 'gravity'. What causes the initial 'dip' in the fabric is debatable. For Mircea Eliade the initial 'dip' was what he defined as a hierophany. Eliade wrote, 'For religious man, space is not homogeneous; he experiences interruption, breaks in it; some parts of space are qualitatively different from others'.[21] In an Aristotelian sense, a hierophany is an unexpected encounter with the power of a place. By contrast, for Émile Durkheim, culture may not create the initial 'dip' but it certainty enlarges it, as Durkheim viewed sacred places as cultural artefacts.[22] Whatever position one adopts, the Aristotelian influence of a place, is the power that a place exerts on humans and non-humans – the power of place.

The power of place is central to sacred geography. In particular, a brown sacred geography researcher tries to think through place. In this regard the researcher lets 'place' present itself to them and attempts to see the view of a place by that place. This is the argument of Amiria Henare, Martin Holbraad and Sari Wastell who argued:

> With purpose naïveté, the aim of this method is to take 'things' encountered in the field as they present themselves, rather than immediately assuming that they signify, represent, or stand for something else.[23]

To apply this idea to sacred geography is to allow place to have its own quality, rather than existing as a blank canvas for the activity of another. To seek the quality of a place the researcher can ask questions about how a place regards itself. To think through place, or to see through place's eyes is to adopt a 'placefulness' perception. To help gain this perception, the researcher can ask questions about a place which are informed by Aristotle's arguments such questions as:

- What is in this place? What is drawn to this place? What are the bodies in this place which consider it their 'proper place'?
- What is alien in this place? What avoids this place? What would be 'out-of-place' in this place?
- What supports this place? What does the place need to be supported? If a forest, it needs biodiversity, if an airport, it needs transient people and planes.
- How does the place maintain itself? How does it resist change? Is this resistance through the topography and environment, or does commercial activity maintain it? Is this commercial activity by humans or is it organic activities by other life forms?
- What happens in this place? What are the activities that are observed here? Is it a habitat for some but a transient place for others? For example, if it is a river, it contains flow and comings and goings; if it is a mountain, it holds ideas of ascent and descent, weather and clouds.

- Who or what could hold this place as sacred? What is barren for one group can be a paradise for another.

These types of questions asked in quiet observation of the place can give rise to an image of a place beyond the human gaze.

Place, Time and the Sacred

As Tilley and Lane both argued, places hold memories. Thus place also becomes a time-holder. When place links to memory, it captures a moment and wraps it in visuals and sensations ready to be delivered back to the individual at any future time. Hence, place not only holds time it can fold time, juxtaposing memories with the present, layer upon layer. Such multi-layers held by place can be experienced, for example, in returning to a place of one's childhood, which has years of memories all layered on top of each other, giving the sense that these moments in time are only separated by the thinnest of dimensions. These memory layers may be dark and turbulent, they may be about sporting victories or defeats, or times of personal joy. Whatever their nature, memories (moments of time) do not exist without a place, they are held by place. Even for global events, we ask each other, 'where were you when you heard the news of.... ?' Indeed, a method to help remember things is to build a mental place and locate each item in its proper place within the imagined place - recalling the place is to recall the item, recalling the item is to also recall the place.

As place holds our memories, it displays tenseless time. Thinking in tenseless time was addressed by the Dutch philosopher Barcuh de Spinoza (1632–1677). He claimed that reason saw the world *sub specie aeternitatis*, without reference to time. He wrote, 'In so far as the mind conceives a thing under the dictates of reason, it is affected equally, whether the idea be of a thing future, past, or present'.[24] He pointed out that reason was affected just as much by events in the past as those in the present and future, so personal history and memories all existed in the present, they were timeless. Martin Lin noted that in this idea Spinoza did not mean eternity, time without end, but rather he was referring to a form of 'atemporal timelessness'.[25] Spinoza's extended this idea into any instrument that could hold tenseless time and argued that such an instrument promoted a level of reflection.[26] Hence if a place contains stories and memories, it becomes a personal instrument of *sub speci aeternitatis*. Place offers and indeed almost insists upon moments of reflection and inner contemplation as the person encounters their history as mental images, sounds, smells, emotions, events and words. This is the stillness of Aristotle's proper place, not stillness of motion but stillness of mind.

Granted such building up of layers of which can produce sacredness can be viewed as Durkheimian, but if so, then place becomes the neutral recipient of such layers. However, as already stated, Aristotle's view of place is that place holds qualities in its own right, for it shapes what it contains. An example of place shaping its own layers can be found in a simple story from the history of Bath, UK. In the late seventeenth century, a young French refugee arrived in Bath, England. Her name was Solange Luyon, today known as Sally Lunn. Being a baker by trade she bought a small house in order to open a bakery. The house stands on what is now known as North Parade Passage. In her house she baked her family's secret recipe for buns, which proved so popular that the house and bakery still operate to this day. For over three hundred years the owners of the house have produced her famous buns. The secret recipe is linked to the title of the house and whoever owns the house also owns the recipe. In recent times, the owners were repairing the foundations of the house and found that it had been built on the location of two other inns and kitchens, one in the twelfth century as the site of the kitchens for the monks of Bath Abbey and an earlier inn and kitchen of the Roman period, 100 CE – 500 CE. Hence, for nearly 2,000 years, this small patch of ground, this place, has been a place of baking and cooking. It is easy to dismiss this story as not that unusual or just a curiosity. However, it does hint at the power of place, the agency of place to draw towards itself what suits it, activities and events that 'fit' into the place, in this case a place of yeast and flour, fire and food.

Place may slowly reveal itself, as in the case of the Bath bakery, but if the power of place suddenly erupts into one's awareness, it is a hierophany. In 1903, the children's author Kenneth Grahame described such a hierophany in his work, *Wind in the Willows*. The book initially received negative reviews, as it was one of the earliest works that anthropomorphised animals – Louis Wain's cats a decade earlier, probably being the first. In Grahame's work, the world was viewed through the eyes of humanised animals. Two of his central characters, Mole and Ratty, search for a lost baby otter and in their search Grahame has them encountering a hierophany. The story describes how Mole and Ratty have spent a long night searching for the missing otter. As dawn approaches, they moor their boat on a tiny island in the river. Ratty feels drawn to the island by the sound of music caused by the wind in the river reeds. Grahame builds the environment for the experience of a hierophany: the two animals are tired and searching for something, the time is liminal as night gives way to day, and the place is set apart from the rest of the river world, a tiny island. Grahame wrote,

In silence they landed, and pushed through the blossom and scented herbage and undergrowth that led up to the level ground, till they stood on a little lawn of a marvellous green, set round with Nature's own orchard-trees—crab-apple, wild cherry, and sloe.

'This is the place of my song-dream, the place the music played to me,' whispered the Rat, as if in a trance. 'Here, in this holy place, here if anywhere, surely we shall find Him!'[27]

The 'Him' referred to by Ratty is a divine presence. The two friends experience a heightening of colours and sounds and, suddenly, a great awe falls upon Mole, 'an awe that turned his muscles to water' as they both encounter the animal god, called by Grahame, 'the Helper'. This chapter, 'The Piper at the Gates of Dawn' was often left out of later editions of the book as it was felt to be too pagan, for Grahame wove into his children's book an animal sacredness based on the Greek god Pan. Notably, for this discussion, Grahame painted a sacred eruption rooted in a place that had no obvious layers of memories or experience for his two characters. To paint this scene he used the features, later described by Eliade, as an experience occurring at a liminal time mixed with a place set apart. This is a different form of sacredness; it comes directly from place rather than emerging due to accrued cultural layers. Both these origins of sacredness of place are considered in this volume, for all of the papers in this volume are about place.

We are born into place, we live in place, we die in place, we keep our memories in place, we story ourselves in place. Everywhere is 'place'. We can ignore it and use it like a holder, a location for living or we can think about it from a different perspective. Granted, place grows in importance as we attribute layers to it, nevertheless, place is not a blank canvas. Place has a 'voice' and how one engages with this voice and what that voice 'says' is the focus of this volume.

In this context, Sacred Geography becomes the study of the activities *of place*.

Notes

1   'Sacred Geography', *Scientific American* 7, no. 6 (1851): pp. 43–43.

2   Sigurd Bergmann et al., eds, *Nature, Space and the Sacred : Transdisciplinary Perspectives* (Aldershot: Ashgate, 2009), p. 11.

3   See *Nature, Space and the Sacred: Transdisciplinary Perspectives* (Aldershot: Ashgate, 2021 [2009]).

4   René Guénon, 'The Land of the Sun', *Studies in Comparative Religion* 14, no. 3 & 4 ([1936] 1980), http://www.studiesincomparativereligion.com/Public/articles/The_Land_of_the_Sun-by_Ren%C3%A9_Gu%C3%A9non.aspx.

5   Josef Heinsch, 'Principles of Prehistoric Sacred Geography', (1938), https://www.cantab.net/users/michael.behrend/repubs/ggw/heinsch_gvkg/pages/gvkg_en.html.
6   Jo Odgers, 'The Emblematic City: John Wood and the Refounding of Bath', in *Primitive: Original Matters in Architecture*, ed. Jo Odgers, Flora Samuel, and Adam Sharr (London and New York: Routledge, 2006), p. 162.
7   Alexander Thom, 'The Megalithic Unit of Length', *Journal of the Royal Statistical Society* A 125 (1962): pp. 243–51.
8   Anthony F. Aveni, 'Archaeoastronomy in the Ancient Americas', *Journal of archaeological research* 11, no. 2 (2003): pp. 149–91: p. 155.
9   Edward S. Casey, *The Fate of Place, a Philosophical History* (Berkeley, CA: University of California Press, 1998), p. xii.
10 F. Earle Fox, 'Biblical Theology and Pelagianism', *The Journal of Religion* 41, no. 3 (1961): pp. 169–81: p. 172.
11 Aristotle, *Metaphysics*, ed. Jonathan Barnes, trans. R. P. Hardie and R. K. Gaye, *The Complete Works of Aristotle* (Princeton, NJ: Princeton University Press, 1984), 1072b 3-4.
12 Bergmann et al., *Nature, Space and the Sacred: Transdisciplinary Perspectives*, p. 9.
13 Tilley, *A Phenomenology of Landscape*, p. 24.
14 Lane, *Landscapes*, p. 15.
15 Aristotle, 'Physics', in *The Complete Works of Aristotle* Volume 1, ed. Jonathan Barnes, trans. R. P. Hardie and R. K. Gaye (Princeton, NJ: Princeton University Press, 1984), 315–446: 4.2, 209a 8-9, at 32–33.
16 Aristotle, 'Physics', 208b11.
17 Aristotle, 'On the Heavens', in *The Complete Works of Aristotle* Volume 1, ed. Jonathan Barnes, trans. J. L. Stocks (Princeton, NJ: Princeton University Press, 1984), 447-511: IV 3, 310a, at 35.
18 Aristotle, 'Metaphysics', in *The Complete Works of Aristotle* Volume 2, ed. Jonathan Barnes, trans. R. P.Hardie and R. K. Gaye (Princeton, NJ: Princeton University Press, 1984), 1552-1728: IV, 1014b, at 16-26.
19 Casey, *The Fate of Place*, 70.
20 Bernadette Brady, 'Mountains Talk of Kings and Dragons, the Brecon Beacons', in *Space, Place and Religious Landscapes, Living Mountains* ed. Darrelyn Gunzburg and Bernadette Brady (London and NY: Oxford Bloomsbury 2020): pp. 173-90, p. 183.
21 Mircea Eliade, *The Sacred and the Profane, the Nature of Religion*, trans. Willard R. Trask (London: Harcourt, Inc., [1957] 1987), p. 20.
22 Émile Durkheim, *The Elementary Forms of Religious Life*, trans. Karen E. Fields (New York: Free Press, 1995 [1912]), Field's introduction p. xlvi–v.
23 Amiria J. M. Henare, Martin Holbraad, and Sari Wastell, *Thinking through Things: Theorising Artefacts Ethnographically* (London: Routledge, 2007), p. 2.
24 Barcuh de Spinoza, *The Ethics*, trans. R.H.M. Elwes (Forgotten Books, [1883] 2008), Part 4. Prop. 62 also expanded in Part 2. Prop.44. Corollary 2.
25 Martin Lin, 'Teleology and Human Action in Spinoza', *The Philosophical Review* 115, no. 3 (2006): 317-54: p. 340-41.
26 Spinoza, *The Ethics*, Part 2, Prop. 44, corollary 2 and Part 5, Prop 2 and 4.
27 Kenneth Grahame, *Wind in the Willows* (New York: Charles Scribner's Sons, 1929 {1903]), pp. 179–80.

INTRODUCTION PART II

SACRED GEOGRAPHY: COVERSATIONS WITH THE OTHER

Jack Hunter

A significant current running through the field of sacred geography – as it is conceived and taught at the Sophia Centre – is an emphasis on the human experience of interaction with what is variously referred to as 'the other', the 'non-human', and the 'other-than-human'. These are ideas that will be unpacked and re-entangled in the following pages to provide some further conceptual context for the chapters that follow.

Social Construction and Hierophany

As Brady has already explained, there are, broadly speaking, two dominant approaches to understanding the nature of the sacred in the academic study of spirituality and religion. The sociological perspective suggests that the sacred is something that is socially constructed. In other words, that it is essentially human-made – manifested and maintained by human activity alone, and not by anything 'supernatural'. Émile Durkheim (1858–1917), the originator of this approach, for example, suggested that the sacred is created by human societies through a conceptual separation of the profane (the everyday world of mundane matter and experience), from those things held to be somehow special by any particular human social group. Once this distinction is established in the form of culture, the special or sacred character of objects or places is reinforced through collective rituals and taboos, which alter human behaviour around the object or place, further differentiating it from its surroundings.[1] Taken in its extreme form, then, the Durkheimian position suggests that there is nothing that is inherently sacred in itself, rather objects, places and people are *made sacred* by human beings and the things that they do in their vicinity. This is essentially the dominant perspective in most of the social sciences, and might be understood as a form of social and cultural constructivism.

On the other hand, for those who believe – or experience – a place to be sacred, its sanctity is often understood as something that *actually exists* in the world, so that it is not so much created or projected by human beings as experienced by them in particular places, pre-existing any kind of social construction or cultural elaboration. This is the view that the sacred is an ontologically distinct reality, and is clearly expressed in the writings of the controversial Romanian historian of religion Mircea Eliade (1907–1986), who argued in favour of understanding the sacred through the lens of what he termed *hierophany* – as a 'manifestation of the sacred', or an eruption of 'the other'. He explains:

> When the sacred manifests itself in any hierophany, there is not only a break in the homogeneity of space; there is also revelation of an absolute reality, opposed to the nonreality of the vast surrounding expanse. The manifestation of the sacred ontologically founds the world.[2]

The idea here is that there is something external to human beings in the very fabric of the world that we can encounter and experience directly, and which bursts through the profane reality of the natural world from a 'supernatural' origin. In his *Patterns in Comparative Religion*, Eliade also discusses the concept of Kratophany, literally defined as 'an emanation of power'.[3] Notions of power, place and the sacred are often intimately connected. This sacred power dwells, or perhaps even pools in particular locations, seeping through cracks in reality, and awaiting human interaction.

Haunted Places and the Numinous

The German theologian Rudolf Otto's (1869–1937) perspective provides a sort of compromise between the two strong positions of Durkheimian social construction of the sacred and Eliadean ontological hierophany. He argued that there is a distinct kind of feeling-response that human beings experience when we encounter what he called the 'wholly other', which – like Eliade's notion of hierophany – may erupt through the mundane fabric of the everyday world into human experience. He called this feeling response the *numinous*, and suggested that it might arise when we move into particular places where the 'wholly other' seeps through. These locations might be understood as 'thin places', to use the terminology of Celtic Spirituality, which are places where there is thought to be a 'thinness of the boundary between this world and the spiritual world'.[4] The experience of the numinous may then go on to serve as the basis for further social and cultural elaboration (social construction in the Durkheimian sense).

In addition to the possibility of an external supernatural reality seeping through into the natural world, Otto also suggests that there might be an 'implicit meaning' in place that can be 'rendered explicit' through human engagement. He explains:

> It is already the beginning of this explicative process [...] when a [person] says: '*It* is not quite right here'; '*It* is uncanny' [...] 'This place is haunted' [...] Here we have the obscure basis of meaning and idea rising into greater clarity and beginning to make itself explicit as the notion [...] of a transcendent Something, a real operative entity of a numinous kind, which later [...] assumes concrete form as a *'numen loci,'* a daemon, an 'El,' a Baal, or the like.[5]

This 'implicit meaning' might be understood to suggest that, like the deep ecologist Arne Naess' (1912–2009) notion of 'intrinsic value, the place itself – the matter and substance of the environment – has an inherent sacred quality of its own (i.e., not dependent on an external supernatural source), that may be unpacked by human observation'.[6] The hierophantic experience comes first – experienced through the body's innate numinous feeling-response – and is followed by the proliferation of stories, rituals, taboos and further cultural elaborations that personify the intrinsic, or implicit, sense of place.[7] As Otto suggests, the idea that particular places are haunted by ancestors, spirits, or other entities may be rooted in numinous experiences had by people in particular locations, transmitted in the form of what folklorists call *memorates* (stories told and believed to be true), that are later incorporated into cultural and religious traditions.[8] Indeed, the parapsychologists Neil Dagnall and colleagues have suggested that hauntings are one of the 'oldest problems in environmental psychology', raising important questions about the different ways that people experience, relate to and interpret their surrounding environments.[9]

Sacred geography research is therefore especially concerned with the different ways in which a sense of the - - and the numinous – is manifested in particular places through a combination of human (psychological, social and cultural) and non-human (other, extra-human) factors.

Extraordinary Experience

The twentieth century philosopher and scholar of mysticism Walter T. Stace (1886–1967) identified nature mysticism as one of the two fundamental forms of mystical experience more generally. .He suggested that nature-mystical experiences be referred to as 'extrovertive' – as distinct from much more interior forms of 'introvertive' mystical experiences, which are usually occasioned by dedicated meditation, prayer, or other forms of contemplative and ritual practice. Extrovertive experiences, by contrast, are often spontaneously triggered by the *external* physical environment, frequently inducing in the experiencer a sense of the underlying unity of the natural world, which is revealed through a transfiguration of the surrounding environment:

> The extrovertive mystic with his physical senses continues to perceive the same world of trees and hills and tables and chairs as the rest of us. But he sees these objects transfigured in such manner that the Unity shines through them [...] the extroversive experience is sensory-intellectual in so far as it still perceives physical objects but is nonsensuous and nonintellectual in so far as it perceives them as 'all one'.[10]

In addition to feelings of unity, connection and oneness, mystical experiences in nature may also take the form of a 'sudden flash' of animistic insight – that is, of a highly *personal* natural world. The scholar of religion Graham Harvey defines animism as a recognition that 'the world is full of persons, only some of whom are human'.[11] Animism implies a personal cosmos consisting of multiple perspectives – a world of many different points of view, some of which are human and most of which are not (see discussion below). The following experience – taken from the archives of the Alister Hardy Religious Experience Research Centre – took place in April 1917, during the traumatic events of the First World War, while the author was serving in the British army in France. The account gives a particularly vivid impression of what it might be like to undergo a spontaneous extrovertive mystical experience in which an animated and personalised cosmos is seemingly revealed:

> While spending an afternoon hour alone in my hilltop wood, a mood of depression had come down. We were due to move in a few days [...] After supper in the mess I felt restless. I wondered if the full moon shining down from a cloudless sky had anything to do with my mood. A walk by the canal might make it easier to sleep. I walked eastward for about two miles along the towpath and then turned about. The nearer I drew to the village, the more alive the surroundings seemed to become. It was as if something which had been dormant when I was in the wood were coming alive. I must have drifted into an exalted state. The moon, when I looked up at it, seemed to have become personalised

and observant, as if it were aware of my presence on the towpath. A sweet scent pervaded the air. Early shoots were breaking from the sticky buds of the balsam poplars which bordered the canal; their pleasant resinous odour conveyed good-will. The slowly moving waters of the canal, which was winding its unhurried way from the battlefields to the sea, acquired a 'numen' which endorsed the intimations of the burgeoning trees. The river conveyed that it had seen me before in other places and knew something about me. It was now concerned with my return to the village [...] A feeling that I was being absorbed into the living surroundings gained in intensity and was working up to a climax. Something was going to happen. Then it happened. The experience lasted, I should say, about thirty seconds and seemed to come out of the sky in which were resounding majestic harmonies. The thought, 'that is the music of the spheres' was immediately followed by a glimpse of luminous bodies – meteors or stars – circulating in predestined courses emitting both light and music.[12]

In the above experience a personal conversation is initiated between the experiencer and the river, the moon and the trees, who all take on relatable characteristics. It is not an experience of simple mystical oneness, but rather implies a world that consists of a plurality of non-human points of view. These many beings seem to contribute to the mounting intensity of the experience, culminating with a symphonic mystical harmonising of the diverse voices of nature into a whole conceived as 'the music of the spheres'. It is not so much a picture of oneness as a picture of profound multiplicity and deep interconnection. The study of sacred geography, then, is about listening to this music, and acknowledging the presence of the multiple harmonising voices of the non-human world.

Non-Human Animal Consciousness

Remarkably, it was not until 2012 that the consciousness of non-human animals was formally recognised by the scientific community. This recognition was marked by the publication of what has come to be called *The Cambridge Declaration on Consciousness*. The declaration summarises evidence for consciousness in a range of non-human animals – notably in African Grey Parrots, which are said to evidence 'near human-like levels of consciousness'. The paper concludes that:

> The absence of a neocortex does not appear to preclude an organism from experiencing affective states. Convergent evidence indicates

that non-human animals have the neuroanatomical, neurochemical, and neurophysiological substrates of conscious states along with the capacity to exhibit intentional behaviors. Consequently, the weight of evidence indicates that humans are not unique in possessing the neurological substrates that generate consciousness. Non-human animals, including all mammals and birds, and many other creatures, including octopuses, also possess these neurological substrates.[13]

In addition to consciousness in non-human animals, there have been a number of studies in recent years that also suggest the prevalence of *culture*, defined as socially learned behaviours, in a wide variety of non-human species – amongst primates and other mammals, as well as widely divergent species such as fish and cephalopods.[14] With this recognition of non-human cultures comes the realisation that the concept of 'folklore' might extend far beyond the anthrosphere. Writing in 1989, and drawing on his own experience of playing rule-based games with his pet dogs, the folklorist Jay Mechling sought to expand the boundaries of folkloristic research into the sphere of the non-human, explaining that out of 'all the criteria generally used by folklorists to decide if they are in the presence of communication worthy of being called "folklore," I see no persuasive reasons why non-human animals cannot be included in "the folk." It is only a fiat, by speciesism, that folklorists define folklore as a unique possession of human animals'.[15] Once these perspectives are taken into consideration, landscapes, and the rich biodiverse ecosystems that constitute them, clearly represent much more than just physical spaces, occupied by non-conscious objects – they are, in fact, vast, active, living intelligence systems, full of non-human cultural knowledge. Biodiversity, therefore, is also *psychodiversity*.

While it has taken mainstream western science until the twenty-first century to recognise and acknowledge the subjective cognitive worlds of non-human animals, many non-western and indigenous perspectives have incorporated non-human consciousness into their worldviews for thousands of years.

Indigenous Perspectives

Although it is difficult to speak of indigenous cultures in generalised terms, as there are so many diverse living traditions on every continent, there are nevertheless some characteristic cross-cultural hallmarks that give a sense of the differences in perspective between indigenous and western scientific worldviews. For example, in many indigenous worldviews the category of personhood is understood to extend far beyond the human, while in the dominant western view personhood applies only to human beings. In indigenous traditions, animals, plants, rocks, features of the landscape, or landscapes as a whole, may be acknowledged as living and active in ways that the dominant materialist-scientific worldview is yet to recognise.[16] In many indigenous traditions such non-humans may even be seen as the ancestors of human communities - as 'kin'.[17] Potowotomi biologist Robin Wall Kimmerer refers to this as the principle of 'animacy', denoting an indigenous understanding of the world as 'full of unseen energies that animate everything'.[18]

'Animism' is by now a popular and widely used term. It derives from the Latin word *anima*, meaning 'soul' and was first employed as a scholarly category by the founding anthropologist Edward Burnett Tylor (1832–1917). Tylor used it to refer to the widespread, cross-cultural 'belief in spiritual beings'. His analysis of the ethnographic literature of the time had led him to understand animism as the very earliest expression of religious thought, from which all later branches of religion have ultimately stemmed. Tylor further reasoned that animism was essentially erroneous, with origins in the misinterpretation of dreams and other altered states of consciousness. He reasoned that:

> When the sleeper awakens from a dream, he believes he has really somehow been away, or that other people have come to him. As it is well known by experience that men's bodies do not go on these excursions, the natural explanation is that every man's living self or soul is his phantom or image, which can go out of his body and see and be seen itself in dreams [...][19]

Influenced by Charles Darwin's (1809–1882) evolutionary model, Tylor's anthropology was closely wedded to a form of social evolutionism known as *developmentalism* that was particularly popular during the latter half of the nineteenth century.[20] This view saw animism as a 'primitive' mentality, superseded by scientific rationalism, which if found in the present day was said to be a 'survival' from a pre-rational past. Embedded in the early conceptualisation of animism, then, were a range of colonial and Euro-centric biases and assumptions, which were actively used as a point of differentiation between the European, rationalist colonial worldview and the many indigenous worldviews found in the colonised territories. Professor of African Studies Harry Olúdáre Garuba (1958–2020), explained that:

> [...] animist understandings of the natural and social world functioned within discourses of colonial modernity as the aberration, the past-in-the-present, to be disciplined so as to create civilised worlds and

subjects [...] In other words, animism has functioned as the metaphoric receptacle for everything that is a negation of the modern.[21]

Over the last two decades or so, however, animism as an etic category has been re-conceptualised in the academy as a feature of worldviews centred around notions of 'personhood', 'relationship' and 'reciprocity'. As already noted, Graham Harvey has influentially – and usefully – re-defined animists as 'people who recognise that the world is full of persons, only some of whom are human, and that life is always lived in relationship with others'.o He goes on to explain that:

> Animism is lived out in various ways that are all about learning to act respectfully (carefully and constructively) towards and among other persons. Persons are beings, rather than objects, who are animated and social towards others (even if they are not always sociable). Animism [...] is more accurately understood as being concerned with learning how to be a good person in respectful relationships with other persons [...][22]

Relationships – rather than notions of rationality, cultural survivals and 'primitive mentality' – are now understood as central components of animistic cosmologies, constituting what have come to be referred to as 'relational ontologies'.[23] As Robin Wall Kimmerer explains, in order to live sustainably from an indigenous perspective it is necessary to live in good relationships with the other-than-human persons that make up the ecosystems that sustain us:

> In such cultures, people have a responsibility not only to be grateful for the gifts provided by Mother Earth, they are also responsible for playing a positive and active role in the well-being of the land. They are called not to be passive consumers, but to sustain the land that sustains them.[24]

The founder of ecopsychology Theodore Roszak (1933–2011) has suggested that animism's emphasis on the formation of 'right relationships' with other-than-human and non-human persons might have 'a proven ecological utility', in that 'it disciplines the relationship of humans to their environment, imposing an ethical restraint upon exploitation and abuse'.[25] Animistic worldviews encourage us to participate in an 'intersubjective cosmos', in which we must take seriously the perspectives of other-than-human persons[26] Anthropologist

Eduardo Viveiros de Castro has highlighted another important element of animist relational ontologies, which he has labelled 'perspectivism'. He explains that in Amerindian cosmological models the world is often thought to be 'inhabited by different sorts of subjects or persons, human and non-human, which apprehend reality from distinct points of view'. He elaborates:

> Typically [...] humans see humans as humans, animals as animals and spirits (if they see them) as spirits; however animals (predators) and spirits see humans and animals (as prey) to the same extent that animals (as prey) see humans as spirits or as animals (predators) [...] By the same token animals and spirits see themselves as humans: they perceive themselves as (or become) anthropomorphic beings when they are in their own houses or villages and they experience their own habits and characteristics as a form of culture [...] they see their food as human food [...] they see their bodily attributes as body decorations or cultural instruments, they see their social system as organised in the same way as human institutions are [...][27]

From an animist, relational and perspectivist point-of-view, then, we are living in a world of many minds, in which it should come as little surprise that plants, animals, landscapes and other non-humans possess interior subjectivities.

Other-than-Human Persons and Ultraterrestrials

The concept of 'other-than-human personhood' was first employed in an academic sense by the anthropologist Alfred Irving Hallowell (1892–1974) in the context of his research into Ojibwa cosmology and ontology, where animacy and personhood – as in many other indigenous traditions around the world – are fundamental properties of the cosmos, extending far beyond the human sphere.[28] Kenneth Morrison explains that for the Ojibwa:

> [...] 'other-than-human persons' share with human beings powerful abilities, including intelligence, knowledge, wisdom, the ability to discern right from wrong, and also the ability to speak, and therefore to influence other persons. In Ojibwa thought, persons are not defined by human physical shape, and so the Ojibwa do not project anthropomorphic attributes onto the world.[29]

While the term non-human is frequently taken to include the biological lifeforms, geological processes, and other physical factors that constitute the living planet around us, the concept of the 'other-than-human' also expands out to consider what might be referred to as 'meta-empirical', 'spiritual', 'daimonic', or 'paranormal' forms of life and consciousness.[30] This would include spirits and modalities of mind beyond what we can easily categorise, but no less a part of the natural world than sparrows and blue whales.[31] This is the sense in which one of the founders of psychical research, the Cambridge classicist F.W.H. Myers (1843–1901), first coined the term 'supernormal' (which later mutated into 'paranormal'). Myers intended to shift the dialogue around 'psychical phenomena' into the realm of the natural. He explained how the 'word supernatural is open to grave objections' because 'it assumes that there is something outside nature. Now there is no reason to suppose that the psychical phenomena with which we deal are less a part of nature [...] they are above the norm [...] rather than outside [...] nature'.[32] Other-than-human persons, then, may be more paranormal than supernatural – that is, *part of the natural world*, rather than separate from it.

It is interesting to note that pioneering paranormal researchers such as Charles Fort (1874–1932) and John Keel (1930–2009) – who followed in Myers' footsteps by spending their lives and careers investigating the anomalous – eventually came to consider the possibility that there might be a greater intelligence underlying the many diverse manifestations of paranormal phenomena that they documented.[33] John Keel wrote, for example, that:

> It is quite possible – even probable – that the Earth is really a living organism, and that it in turn is a part of an even larger organism, that whole constellations are alive, transmitting and receiving energy to and from other celestial energy sources. Up and down the energy scale the whole macrocosm is functioning on levels of reality that will always be totally beyond our comprehension. We are a part of it all, just as the microbe swimming on the microscope slide is unknowingly a part of our dismal reality, and, like the microbe, we lack the perceptive equipment necessary to view the larger whole. Even if we could view it, we could not understand it.[34]

Keel's idea essentially represents a sort of paranormal Gaia-hypothesis, taking James Lovelock's (1919–2022) Gaia concept in directions he likely never imagined.[35] Keel also coined another useful concept for considering the psychodiversity of our living planet – the notion of the *ultraterrestrial*. The idea emerged in response to the dominant view in UFOlogy that UFOs/UAPs are *extra*-terrestrial in origin – coming from another planet in physical outer space.[36]

Keel pointed out that many of the stranger UFO encounters that he investigated did not seem to support this hypothesis, suggesting instead that UFOs and their occupants (along with other paranormal entities), actually originate from the earth – *ultra* rather than *extra*- terrestrial – and have likely been here much longer than human-kind, existing on different frequencies of the electromagnetic spectrum. Keel explains:

> At this moment you are surrounded by all kinds of energy, much of it manmade, vibrating on every frequency from the ultra high frequencies [to] the very low frequencies [...] There are other forms of energy tied in as well [forms of energy] on such high frequencies they cannot be detected with even the most sophisticated scientific instruments [...] If you could peer into this super spectrum, you would undoubtedly see some frightening things - strange shapes and eerie ghostlike forms moving through a sea of electrical energy like fish in some alien sea.[37]

These 'strange shapes and eerie ghostlike forms' are the *ultraterrestrials* – paranormal beings native to the Earth, existing on all manner of different frequencies, but no less indigenous or alien to the planet than human beings. For Keel, then, the cosmos was very much alive – overflowing with life, in fact. This is what Keel referred to as *Our Haunted Planet*.[38] There are resonances here with what agroecology researcher Julia Wright has called 'subtle ecologies', which she characterises as ecological models in which 'a non-material dimension [is understood to exist alongside materially based ecological] systems'.[39] Sensitivity to, and awareness of, these frequently invisible ecosystems is often deeply ingrained in indigenous cosmologies, and becoming aware of them in their natural habitats through participation is a primary objective of sacred geography research.[40]

Conclusions

As part of the pedagogical approach to sacred geography in the Sophia Centre we encourage students to enter into conversations with the external world of landscapes, places and their non-human inhabitants. Such experiences of interaction suggest that geographical landscapes, their features and places, are alive – filled to the brim with varied forms of life and mind, with whom it is possible to engage in meaningful and respectful communication. Nevertheless, these external landscapes – and the non-human minds that inhabit them – are still experienced through the body's sensory apparatus and cultural frames of reference which mould and influence the way we perceive the world around us. This represents the Durkheimian element of human social construction of the sacred. Crucially, however, the landscape, and indeed the world, cannot be reduced to these human perspectives – it is *very much more* than a projection – representative of Otto and Eliade's positions on the nature of the sacred. To this extent, the scholar of the environment Adrian Ivakhiv has suggested that 'orchestration' rather than 'construction' might provide a better metaphor for understanding this relationship, as it acknowledges 'an active, agential more-than-human world' that often resists the 'orchestral scores laid out and performed in their midst'.[41] Indigenous cosmologies have long recognised the personal nature of the world and the need to engage it in dialogue, and have established ceremonial and respectful modes of interaction between the human and non-human. As Paul Devereux explains, the view that the world is somehow 'alive, enchanted, sentient and capable of communicating with us' is the 'essence of all sacred geographies, regardless of specific cultural beliefs and differences'.[42] Anthony Thorley adds that 'Sacred Geography is part of the important post-enlightenment academic rediscovery of an animistic worldview relevant to Western Culture'.[43]

Notes

1 Émile Durkheim, *The Elementary Forms of the Religious Life* (Oxford: Oxford University Press, 2008).

2 Mircea Eliade, *The Sacred and the Profane: The Nature of Religion* (New York: Harcourt Inc., 1987), p. 21

3 Mircea Eliade, *Patterns in Comparative Religion* (Lincoln, NE: University of Nebraska Press, 1996).

4 Laura Béres, 'A Thin Place: Narratives of Space and Place, Celtic Spirituality and Meaning', *Journal of Religion and Spirituality in Social Work*, 31, no. 4 (2012): pp. 394–413.

5 Rudolf Otto, *The Idea of the Holy* (Oxford: Oxford University Press, 1958), p. 126.

6 Arne Naess, 'Intrinsic value: Will the defenders of nature please rise', in *Wisdom in the Open Air*, ed. P. Reed and D. Rothenberg (Minneapolis, MN: University of Minnesota Press, 1993), pp. 70–82.

7 David J. Hufford, *The Terror That Comes in the Night: An Experience-Centered Study of Supernatural Assault Traditions* (Philadelphia, PA: University of Pennsylvania Press, 1982).

8 Lauri Honko, 'Memorates and the Study of Belief Materials', *Journal of the Folklore Institute*, 1, no. 1/2 (1964): pp. 5–19.

9 Neil Dagnall, Ken G. Drinkwater, Ciaran O'Keeffe, Annalisa Ventola, Michael A. Jawer, Brandon Massullo, G. B. Caputo, and James Houran, 'Things that go bump in the literature: An environmental appraisal of "haunted houses"', *Frontiers in Psychology* (2020).

10 Walter T. Stace, *Mysticism and Philosophy* (London: Macmillan, 1960), p. 15.
11 Graham Harvey, *Animism: Respecting the Living World* (London: Hurst & Company, 2005), p. xi.
12 RERC Reference: 000035, Male, 1917.
13 Cambridge Declaration on Consciousness, 2012.
14 Robert M. Sapolsky, 'Social Culture among Nonhuman Primates', *Current Anthropology*, 47, no. 4 (2006): pp. 641–56; J. Mann and E. M. Patterson, 'Tool Use by Aquatic Animals', *Philosophical Transactions of the Royal Society - Biological Sciences*, 368, no. 1630 (2013): p. 1–11.
15 Jay Mechling, '"Banana Cannon" and Other Folk Traditions between Human and Nonhuman Animals'. *Western Folklore*, 48, no. 4 (1989): pp. 312–23.
16 Kelly D. Alley, 'River Goddesses, Personhood and Rights of Nature: Implications for Spiritual Ecology'. *Religions*, 10, no. 502 (2019): pp. 1–17.
17 Alfred I. Hallowell, 'Ojibwa Ontology, Behavior and World View', in G. Harvey, ed., *Readings in Indigenous Religions* (London: Continuum, 2002), pp. 17–50.
18 Robin Wall Kimmerer, *Braiding Sweetgrass: Indigenous Wisdom, Scientific Knowledge, and the Teachings of Plants* (Minneapolis, MN: Milkweed, 2013), p. 49.
19 Edward Burnett Tylor, *Anthropology: An Introduction to the Study of Man and Civilization* (London: C. A. Watts, 1930), p. 88.
20 George W. Stocking Jr,, *Race, Culture, and Evolution: Essays in the History of Anthropology* (Chicago, IL: University of Chicago Press, 1982).
21 Harry Olúdáre Garuba, 'On animism, modernity/colonialism and the African order of knowledge: Provisional reflections', in *Contested Ecologies: Dialogues in the South on Nature and Knowledge*, ed. L. Green (Cape Town: HSRC Press, 2013), p. 45.
22 Harvey, *Animism*, p. xi.
23 Wesley J. Wildman, 'An Introduction to Relational Ontology', in *The Trinity and an Entangled World: Relationality in Physical Science and Theology*, ed. John Polkinghorn (Michigan: Wm B. Eerdmans Publishing Co., 2010), p. 55.
24 Robin Wall Kimmerer, 'Restoration and Reciprocity: The Contributions of Traditional Ecological Knowledge" in *Human Dimensions of Ecological Restoration: Integrating Science, Nature and Culture*, ed. D. Egan, E.E. Hjerpe and J. Abrams (Washington, DC: Island Press, 2011), p. 257.
25 Theodore Roszak, *The Voice of the Earth: An Exploration of Ecopsychology* (New York: Bantam, 1993), p. 84.
26 Kenneth M. Morrison, 'The cosmos as intersubjective: Native American other-than-human Persons', in *Indigenous Religions: A Companion*, ed. Graham Harvey (New York: Cassell, 2000), p. 25.
27 Eduardo Viveiros de Castro, 'Cosmological Deixis and Amerindian Perspectivism', in *A Reader in the Anthropology of Religion*, ed. Michael Lambek (Oxford: Blackwell, 2006), pp. 307–08.
28 Hallowell, 'Ojibwa Ontology, Behaviour and Worldview'.
29 Morrison, 'The Cosmos as Intersubjective', p. 25.
30 Angela Voss and William Rowlandson, *Daimonic Imagination: Uncanny Intelligence* (Newcastle: Cambridge Scholars Press, 2013).
31 Jack Hunter, *Greening the Paranormal: Exploring the Ecology of Extraordinary Experience* (Hove: August Night Press, 2019).
32 Cited in Jeffrey J. Kripal, *Authors of the Impossible: The Paranormal and the Sacred* (Chicago, IL: University of Chicago Press, 2010), p. 67.
33 Charles Fort, *The Book of the Damned: The Collected Works of Charles Fort* (London: Tarcher Penguin, 2008).
34 John Keel, *The Eighth Tower: On Ultraterrestrials and the Superspectrum*

(Charlottesville, VA: Anomalist Books, 2013), p. 248.

35 Hunter, *Greening the Paranormal*.

36 Steven Mizrach, 'The Para-Anthropology of UFO Abductions: The Case for the Ultraterrestrial Hypothesis', in *Strange Dimensions: A Paranthropology Anthology*, ed. Jack Hunter (Llanrhaeadr-ym-Mochnant: Psychoid Books, 2015), pp. 299–336.

37 Keel, *The Eighth Tower*, p. 17.

38 John Keel, *Our Haunted Planet* (London: Neville Spearman, 1971).

39 Julia Wright, *Subtle Agroecologies: Farming With the Hidden Half of Nature* (Abingdon: CRC Press, 2021), p. xxix.

40 Lance Foster, 'The Invisible Landscape', in J. Hunter, ed., *Greening the Paranormal: Exploring the Ecology of Extraordinary Experience* (Hove: August Night Press, 2019).

41 Adrian Ivakhiv, 'Orchestrating Sacred Space: Beyond the 'Social Construction of Nature,' *Ecotheology*, 8, no. 1 (2003): 11.

42 Paul Devereux, *Sacred Geography: Deciphering Hidden Codes in the Landscape*, (London: Gaia, 2010): 152.

43 Anthony Thorley, 'Sacred Geography: a conceptual work in progress,' *SPICA: Postgraduate Journal for Cosmology in Culture*, 4, no. 2 (2016): 8.

I

SITTING WITH A DANDELION: PLANTS AS DOORWAYS TO THE SACRED

Amanda-Jane Page

This chapter discusses out-of-the-ordinary experiences that can be classed as having sacred elements and that involve plants directly or indirectly, through their settings in gardens and woodlands. Sacred here means something connected with God or a god and is considered to be holy – *god* is expanded here to mean goddess, the divine, source, deity, or whatever one would wish to call that which is holy or spiritual. Durkheim's scholarly definition relates to anything supernatural or extraordinary approached via ritual or rites: 'sacred, the characteristic of all that is religious; not characterized by its exalted position, but by its distinction from the profane'.[1] The chapter will also consider why such a strengthened relationship with nature might be important. It contextualises the meaning of extraordinary experience; looks at the main thinkers of the past century; holds up empirical research studies; and explores the brain/mind question in terms of these strange experiences.

Overall, the central question is what particular relationship is being formed between human and natural organisms and nature as a whole. Plants have been chosen, as humans have a long-established relationship with herbs, shrubs and trees in terms of *use* value: they provide our food, our medicine and fuel to keep us warm. Humans could not survive without them, yet Western culture (that is to say cultures that have historical ties to European countries) does not perceive, as do some other cultures, plants as being sacred. Could this have led to the current socio-ecological disaster we find ourselves in the midst of? What can we learn from the plants themselves to establish more balanced and reciprocal relations? Jack Hunter suggests that 'it is through interaction that non-human intelligences manifest', and this is what is discussed in the final section. Thus this chapter considers types of experiences that have been classified as religious or mystical. Examples will be provided from the archives of the Alister Hardy Religious Experience Research Centre (RERC), an archive that consists of over 6,000 accounts of first-hand reports of people from across the world who have had a spiritual or religious experience, and it compares these examples, recorded in and around 1969, with other historical and contemporary accounts, including my own experiences at an immersive herbal retreat that I attended in 2023, to show that these type of mystical experiences in nature are universal and do indeed have purpose.

What is an Extraordinary Experience and what kinds are there?

'Without experience... mankind would not be able to reason', said F.C. Happold, 'experience is, therefore, the primary thing'.[2] There is a particular kind of experience to discuss, here: it is the extraordinary kind. But what is extraordinary experience? For example, there are paranormal experiences that would fit the out of the ordinary brief – such as out-of-body, near death, or supernatural events – that do not always have a locus in or orientation towards the natural world. Therefore, for the purpose of clarity, this discussion will concentrate on moments that take place outdoors with plants, and those that capture a feeling of interconnectedness with the natural world. To further pin down the meaning, extraordinary experiences, as defined by Bhattacharjee and Mogilner, are 'uncommon' and 'infrequent' occurrences.[3] Their aim was to show not only what counts as extraordinary but also how moments such as these can have a lasting and influential effect on a person. Bhattacharjee and Mogilner's paper, published in the *Journal of Consumer Research*, builds on prior research to reveal that greater happiness comes from life experiences rather than from possessions. It looks at the difference between the two types of experiences and how each relate to a person's happiness. An individual travels through life collecting these experiences – or 'momentous events' such as graduation, marriage and the birth of children – these forming a collection of experiences that can have 'important consequences for self-definition, well-being, and life-satisfaction'.[4] Furthermore, extraordinary experiences can be life-changing for an individual.

Bhattacharjee and Mogilner conducted their study to see what kinds of experience were deemed important: Two hundred and twenty-two people were recruited to participate in the study and the results were split across twelve categories of experience such as social relationships, career, and nature. The study indicated a consensus on what counted as an ordinary and what counted as an extraordinary experience, representing an underlying, and one could say universal, understanding of the types of feelings associated with the two types of experience. Although the data did not describe what the experience entailed, according to the summary results, 0.9% or 2 people had experiences *in nature* that were categorised as extraordinary.[5] This research is crucial in understanding how human beings create meaning for their life through experiences. The writers further comment that these 'special' moments 'capture people's attention and endure in memories'.[6] All the experiences listed were about relationships: with other people, with work, or with the self. It is the experience that creates meaning for that relationship either in establishing it or building importance for the person. Nature, however, is the focus here. Jack Hunter argues that, following an extraordinary experience in nature, a person is left with 'an enhanced sense of connection to the environment'.[7] The next section explores different ideas about how this might happen.

Mystical And Religious Experience: A Short History

It is useful to look at the key academics of the last century on the subject of extraordinary experience. The lineage stretches from F.W.H. Myers to William James and his text *The Varieties of Religious Experience* in 1901-2, to Dr Rudolf Otto, who wrote *Das Heilige* (*The Idea of the Holy*) in 1917, through to F.C. Happold, who produced an anthology of writing on Mysticism in 1963, and Sir Alister Hardy and the publication of the Gifford Lectures of 1964-5 under the title *The Divine Flame,* published in 1966. William James proposed that one of the defining qualities of a religious experience is its capacity to change the outlook of an individual. James termed this the 'fruits' of religious experience.[8] For James, after a religious experience, 'a new life opens'. He suggested that various theologies agree that religious experiences exist: for some it is related to personal god/s and to others it is the 'eternal structure of the world' – but the experience of the 'union' differs just as every individual differs.[9] Happold writes on Mysticism – which is anything that is unexplainable, supernatural or magical – and describes it as 'a break through the world of time and history into one of eternity and timelessness'.[10] For Happold, mystical experiences have the 'quality of transiency': that return you to your senses but the experiences can increase in frequency.[11] The result is a 'feeling of passivity', a 'consciousness of the oneness of everything', and the experience of existence as a 'unity'.[12] In an attempt to make supernatural phenomenon more scientific, F.W.H. Myers started The Society for Psychical Research.[13] His work aimed to record mind-to-mind communication, which he termed *telepathy*, now referred to as psi phenomena in order to root the paranormal in empirical science. Otto coined the term, *numinous*, defining it as a 'sense of the divine presence and part of the reality and character of that presence'.[14] For Otto, it is the loveliness of nature which inspires in us a feeling of 'awefulness' (sic) – 'fear and beauty'.[15] Hardy believed that spiritual awareness was universal and used newspaper and radio advertisements to collect accounts of religious experiences from members of the general public in and around Oxford.[16]

As well as a deep interest in mystical and religious experience evident in these thinkers' writings, there is also a pattern emerging (unusual, awe-full and uncommon that leaves a person changed in some way) which can be directly mapped onto other events that create meaning and define a person's life. Specific examples will be discussed later, but for now it is worthwhile considering William James' suggestion that 'religious awe is the same organic thrill which we feel in a forest at twilight or in a mountain gorge'.[17] And vice versa. James saw a direct correlation between religious awe and sublime natural experiences.

For Stephen Harrod Buhner these mystical moments have 'accompanied our species through millennia'. They are an important part of what make us human and are not uncommon.[18] According to The Alister Hardy Trust website, research suggests that half the population of the UK has had a spiritual experience.[19] In the US, one third of people surveyed in recent years declare they have had a mystical experience.[20] Thomas and Cooper aimed to uncover what was 'mystical' about experience so they conducted a study of three hundred young adults, who responded to the question: 'Have you ever had the feeling of being close to a powerful spiritual force that seemed to lift you out of yourself?' Roughly one third of respondents answered *yes* (the same as the wider surveys). Of those 2% (six people) reported mystical experiences (categorized as type 2) which they described using expressions such as *awesome*, *ineffable* and *oneness*, indicating an underlying feeling that is both recognised and, also, that an equation between God and nature exists for people.[21] A further 12% reported psychic experiences (type 3), described as 'other-worldly' and associated with spirituality or religious in nature. However, in discussion, although 72% answered yes only 5% were deemed as having a mystical-type experience. So, this fits with the initial assertion that extraordinary experiences are uncommon. Thomas and Cooper go on to state that more research is needed as although this was a limited study, it reached similar results to prior studies by others in the field, indicating that empirical study is a possibility.[22]

Is this all in my head?

As well as looking at what experts in the field have said about extraordinary experience and how it can affect a person, it is also important to look at how humans process experience to see if it is possible to uncover any mechanism at play. Helminiak's description of extraordinary experiences includes 'seeing visions, hearing voices, sensing an overwhelming presence, perceiving realities with uncommon and "transcendent" vividness, experiencing ecstasy, and the like'.[23] His paper discusses neurological, neurochemical and psychological conclusions reached by scientists to explain these responses. For example, reductionist explanations put such experiences down to 'a misfunctioning' of the brain or a personality disorder.[24] Instead, Helminiak suggests that a mechanism similar to problem solving or the 'creative process' is at play when a person experiences phenomena where a solution forms and is presented in the moment and is then acted upon.[25] Much as with William James' notion of *fruits,* 'authenticity' is a key measure.[26] He claims that an extraordinary experience (regardless of form) moves a person 'further along a path of growth... of the human spiritual nature'.[27] This 'holistic conception of development' integrates and works 'harmoniously toward the unfolding of the highest potential of the individual'.[28] Helminiak's work describes the particular elements involved in extraordinary experiences as well as their results.

Paul Cunningham's work explores the split between mind and body – or rather consciousness/thinking and brain matter – with the hypothesis that 'the brain could be a filter, a conductor or... mechanism that conveys rather than contains or causes the religious experience'.[29] He suggests that:

> the brain... may not produce religious cognitions and emotions, but instead mediates them. The mediating function of the brain might be one of "straining, sifting, canalizing, limiting, and individualizing" that larger mental reality existing behind the scenes.[30]

Indeed, this idea, Cunningham claimed, would make sense of a variety of paranormal phenomena such as dreams, near death and out-of-body experiences.[31] That 'larger mental reality' is what we are grasping at here: the worlds glimpsed during moments of extraordinary experience.

What is the purpose?

Regardless of the exact mechanisms involved, or the ultimate formulation of the brain/mind relationship, extraordinary experiences seem to lead to a strengthening of regard for and awareness of the natural world. Jack Hunter argues that it is possible that there is a connection between abnormal and extraordinary experiences and 'the development of ecological consciousness'.[32] Indeed, William James posits that 'regenerative change' could happen when we communicate with the sacred.[33] Is this the purpose? Westerners have often seen themselves outside of nature rather than in it – and this may be related to the reductionist and dominant view of both religion and science. David Abram suggests that we have replaced our sense of loss of connection with the natural world with the idea of a 'supernatural heaven',[34] and it is this hierarchical ordering that has set humans 'above and apart from all others'.[35] In a chapter titled 'Reclaiming the Invisible', Buhner argued that our culture – and in particular Western schooling and education systems – has blocked a deeper perception of the environment and a sense of interrelationship with the world. Yet, one of the assertions Happold made is that the human, 'if prepared to make the necessary effort', can identify with their 'true self' connected with the Divine and 'nature'.[36]

Gardens, it can be suggested, are places where such relationships might start, with or without an extraordinary experience taking place, and have a long history in Western culture. Jeremy Naydler documents the history of gardens as places of worship and connection to the divine: from the temple gardens of Egypt to Islamic gardens with paradise symbolism to medieval walled gardens and on to Monet's sacred art garden of Giverny.[37] Naydler suggests that Monet's garden is a 'conclusion of things becoming manifest'.[38] Here, the garden is more than the sum of its plants, it is where the human and other-than-human commune together. Indeed, it could be said that one-ness is what is being 'manifested'.

Western versus Indigenous Relationships

Hunter argues that a culture that entertains 'the possibility of communion between human and non-human intelligence' will have better luck at producing such experiences than, say, a culture which does not believe in such a possibility.[39] Thus, Westerners need to find their own way – or remember a time when they lived in greater harmony with earth's cycles, for example. Yet, what seems extraordinary in the Western context may not be perceived in the same way by other cultures, in particular peoples who have lived on the same land for thousands of years and have developed complex relationships with the ecology of the place (otherwise known as indigenous people). Robin Wall Kimmerer argues that as people develop their own ways of 'becoming indigenous' by belonging and being integral to, and inseparable from, the ecosystems where they live they will reconnect to make reciprocal relationships with non-humans.[40]

Indeed, there are some historical examples where people in the UK have maintained a relationship with plants. Ronald Hutton started on an endeavour to link seasonal church rituals to pre-Christian pagan rituals.[41] In an exhaustive study, however, only two customs were found to have been performed by both Christian and pagan communities and just one involves plants. The two customs were the giving of presents at New Year and the decorating of sacred places with greenery and flowers throughout the year. John Stow describes the Feast of John the Baptist in 1540 thus: 'everyman's door being shaded with green birch, long fennel, St John's wort, orpin, white lilies... garlands of beautiful flowers'.[42] It is interesting to note that four of these plants – St John's wort flowers, fennel leaves and seeds, orpin or sedum roots and birch leaves – have long-standing medicinal uses. Moreover, church warden records show that the use of holly and ivy evergreens at Christmas was common practice and it is curious that both were traditionally used as herbal allies for winter ailments. In the UK, people still decorate sacred spaces, bring greenery indoors at Christmas, and keep houseplants for décor and to refine the air, and create living green spaces for reflection in their gardens. The connection to plants is there, just as the connection to food, medicine and fuel is long established. Given the environmental difficulties of the current period then what is required is a deeper relationship that has not been formed yet and extraordinary experience could prove to be the key to reaching that wider audience. Notwithstanding Western indigenous green roots, it is helpful to look at how non-Western indigenous peoples support a relationship with nature and the perceived role of extraordinary experience as a central part of that.

Robin Wall Kimmerer writes that 'paying deep attention' to nature allows 'an experience of connection and meaning making' to occur.[43] The Kogi of the Sierra Nevada are another indigenous people who pay deep attention to the Earth, speaking on its behalf from what they term *The Heart of the World*.[44] Amba J. Sepie writes that the Kogi reached out to the world, wanting to teach the Westerner (who the Kogi term 'younger brother') that all is connected and that the 'Earth and other beings are kin', in order to bring an end to ecological and environmental damage.[45] The Kogi Mámas (Elder Brothers) were not angry, as they said younger brother had forgotten the connection to other living things.[46] Therefore, they reached-out to documentary maker Alan Ereira, inviting him to document their message as both a reminder and a warning before 'Nature herself' put an end to humankind.[47] Ereira went to Columbia twice, as the first film and book did not persuade younger brother to change his destructive ways; the second film, titled *Aluna*, documents the Kogi's belief in the Law of cause and effect and that as humans are custodians of Earth they must protect this environmental balance.[48] But it seems that the Kogi's message is slow in getting across: is this because not enough people have established a deep enough connection to other living beings? Could extraordinary experience provide a starting point to access something like *The Heart of the World*? Sepie suggests that the Westerner *can* experience extraordinary moments in nature, but that they often seek 'consensus as to what interpretation is true'.[49] Just as every individual is different, these experiences cannot be reduced to a standardised list of thoughts or feelings to be ticked-off: relationships are complex things. This is new learning for Western culture, whereas indigenous people have had years of practice and ritual to allow this 'attuned communication'.[50] Sepie claimed that most Westerners have lost the thread of continued deep connection due to religious reasons or scientific ones (and far too many to explore here.)[51] The importance of 'attuned communication' in establishing and maintaining a relationship with nature is examined in the next section.

How to have a relationship with a plant

Well-documented historical accounts of shamanic rituals describe how plants and humans can communicate. Julio Glockner defines a shaman as 'someone capable of maintaining a permanent link with the spiritual dimension', and says that a shaman will commune with sacred plants in order to help generate this link, or relationship, with the spirit world.[52] Christian missionaries widely recorded the use of plants to produce manifestations and visions throughout the sixteenth and seventeenth centuries, and these rituals were continued 'disguised under the semblance of Catholic ceremonies'.[53] Antonella Fagetti details the use of these sacred plants as a healing modality. She describes a ritual, performed by the Mazatec (an indigenous people of the Sierra Mazateca region of Mexico), in which the deities of the plants speak directly to the person who has consumed them to resolve problems, 'profoundly transforming their own life' in doing so.[54] The plants are not being *used* as a substance, nor are they dominated – there is a reciprocal relationship. These plants are revered as sacred, and there is open communication between the plants and the person Indeed, Lilian Gonzalez states that 'the most important aspect is the plants' willingness to act – to cure, to predict, to protect, to appease, to restore, to facilitate, to reveal, to ward off – investing them with meaning'. For her, it makes sense that the creator gods of Mexico would offer 'humanity an entheogenic means to make contact with the divine'.[55]

Of interest here is Glocker's question of 'hallucination or sacred revelation'. Are these interactions real? In reductionist science, hallucinations arise 'in absence of any external reality,' whereas visions reached via shamanic trance are understood to be authentic in many indigenous traditions, so that 'one's perception is valid in and of itself'.[56] Shamans interpret messages as coming from the spirits of the plants themselves. Is it necessary to understand this? Not really: Western reasoning is 'not espoused by traditional societies' therefore it is not pertinent to oppose Western understanding and traditional ecological knowledge: something does not need to be scientifically proven for it to be real.[57] Glockner asserts that:

> these messages come from a divinity that is neither fantastical nor unreal. It is part of a spiritual "compresence" (the state of existing

together concurrently), of an infinite reality that is not tangible to the senses, but that exists in the present and that is necessary to life.[58]

The plant scientist Monica Gagliano puts such experiences of plant communication into a Western scientific context.[59] Through shamanic ritual, fasting and drinking plant medicine, she connected with the spirits of the plants, and they spoke to her, telling her what experiments she needed to conduct to demonstrate plant intelligence. A series of experiments were dictated to her by these encounters, such as a companion planting experiment proving that plants use pheromones to communicate with other plants, and the Mimosa experiment, which showed that plants can remember, learn and act individually. Ayahuma (Couroupita guianensis) told her to use a maze and pea plants to train them, thereby showing that plants are able to recognise signs and imagine food.[60] By shifting her perception through altered states of consciousness and opening a door to imagination, Gagliano communicated with the spirit of the plants to prove plant cognition. The plants showed her that 'the reality we perceive is a narrow set of familiar things and contexts we feel at home with'.[61]

In her editorial piece in *Sacred Plants*, De Orellana puts forward her argument that the indigenous relationship with psychoactive plants such as Turbina corymbosa (morning glory), Nicotiana rustica (tobacco), Nymphaea ampla (white water lily) and Theobroma cacao (cacau) is a correct one to have if one is to maintain a respectful and deep connection to the Earth rather than a purely exploitative one.[62] As De Orellana explains, 'taking a step toward this shift in perception, anthropologists employ the term "entheogen," derived from the Greek *en theos genor*, meaning "that which generates the divine within"'.[63] She argues that Westerners should look at the cultural relevance of these sacred Mexican plants and not see them merely as recreational drugs.[64] For example, Rios and Cubero detail the reverence the Otomi have for the Holy Rose (Cannabis sativa), offering prayers, performing rites and making ceremonial altars to her as they are 'permanently indebted' to the Earth for sustenance.[65] A perception shift is what is being called for: plants should be seen as beings with agency and a more balanced relationship between humans and other living things should be the outcome.

Comparing Accounts

The last part of this chapter compares texts of extraordinary experience to discern if the individuals have established a relationship with nature, and what the longer-term outcome of that may be. The archive of the RERC holds over six thousand records of people who answered the question: 'Have you been aware of or influenced by a presence or power whether you call it god or not, which is different from your everyday self?' Hundreds of records resulted from typing *nature* in the search bar. Here are two accounts written by women that took place in the countryside (there were many such accounts):

> 1) I was walking across a flowery field... when I had the most extraordinary feeling of joy, and seemed to be caught up in another dimension. It has illuminated my life.[66]
>
> 2) I feel that I saw the heart or heard the heart - or became one with the heart of Nature. For a moment the world changed, or disappeared, or I changed.[67]

An example similar to the many in the RERC archive is the record of Richard Jeffries in 1887 describing a walk in the hills: he writes, 'the inexpressible beauty filled me with a rapture, an ecstasy'.[68] These experiences can be said to contain what Happold calls nature-mysticism, which he defines as a 'sense of immanence of the one or God or soul in Nature'.[69] Again, there is the near equation of the divine with the natural, not just a similarity to or a likeness to the divine. These examples shine with the divine. But to what end? There is no way to discern what life-long changes have been established other than that they were important enough to each of these people to both remember the event and feel compelled to write into Alister Hardy to say that these experiences had changed them – and that should be taken at face value. Here, then, is the story of Aldo Leopold, which may prove useful to show the influence that such a moment can have in altering the course of a life. Leopold shot a she-wolf in the Apache National Forest, Arizona, in 1909. As she lay dying, he looked into the 'fierce green fire' dying in her eyes and this encounter, or moment, 'illuminated' his life as he pivoted from being a park ranger to an iconic conservationist.[70]

I cannot finish without presenting two recent extraordinary encounters I myself have experienced and witnessed. I was recently a participant in a year-long herbalism course based at an old spruce plantation in Pembrokeshire. Seven women meet each month around the time of the full moon to establish relationships with medicinal plants that are in season. At the beginning of December, I had a close encounter with Norway spruce. The tutor led us to a stand of trees and performed a ritual to connect us to the trees on a physical and spiritual level – we had to walk around the trees and meet them on a one-to-one basis, as you would a friend. This proved an intense experience. I was able to discern the different personalities of each tree – one was very loving, another stand-offish, one grabbed my scarf as I passed – and when the time came to find a quiet spot for alone reflection, I sat under a beautiful spruce tree. Ivy spread underneath the tree and I followed her as she (I felt this plant had strong feminine energy) grew up into the tree. The crisscross of the spruce branches mirrored the ivy on the ground and in an instant I felt included – I instinctively knew that I had been welcomed to that spot ,and was absorbed by it and into it, to become one with the living green plants.

I do not know if the MA reading has shifted my perception to see what has always been there, or if it is simply the reductionist explanation that my mind is misbehaving, but the fact is that I *experienced* these things and I am writing about them, now. On the same day, one of the other women was sharing her reflection experience. She had been having a difficult time with some members of her family and a robin came and sat by her. She cried as she said, she *knew* this robin was her dead grandfather. The robin had jumped onto her wellington boot and hopped up to sit on her knee as she cried. She described this experience as the most magical she had ever had in nature. It was strange and magical that I was there to witness it and it came in addition to the experience I have just recounted, as if another magical encounter was required. Thus, the cumulative effect of the experiences revealed to me that what Happold calls 'mystical consciousness' exists.[71] This consciousness results in 'an enlargement and refining of perception' that has a 'a noetic quality'[72] and rests on the convictions that a) 'humans possess an organ or faculty of discerning spiritual truth', and b) human beings 'must in essential nature be spiritual'.[73] To press the point further, I present this one last comparable account from the RERC archive: 'I know that God exists and does communicate with me, though on most occasions He uses mountains, seas, sunsets and forests as opposed to words'.[74] Yet another example of this ides is found in Thomas Traherne's text: he writes in 1674 that 'God teaches through the world, not through books'.[75] This teaching and communication is done via extraordinary experiences.

Conclusion

Everything is connected and extraordinary experiences with plants allow humans to be a part of that one-ness. In this chapter I have argued for the importance of extraordinary experience – it universally defines a person's life and could have an evolutionary function. If people searched for these experiences in nature, and they become as important to an individual as other defining moments, then cultural transformation could happen. I have argued that mystical experiences play a role in establishing a deep, sacred relationship with nature. Reclaiming ancestral knowledge of the land could prove useful to help human beings learn a new way of interacting and building a more ecological collaboration with plants and, by extension, the more-than-human world. By seeing everything as interconnected, everyone has a part to play and is important to the whole – from the tiniest fruit-fly to a forest ecosystem. If, like the Kogi, Westerners start appreciating living beings as kin, shifting their perception to allow friendship to flourish, then this could be the evolutionary purpose these experiences fulfil. Anyone can find a plant to form a relationship with, wherever they live: try sitting with a dandelion. Never has it been more important to get outside in the garden, or take a walk to the park or the woods to connect with the Spirits of Place. So there is hope – and there is history: how could herbalists have acquired knowledge of plant medicine without a form of communication? It is as Jack Hunter says, 'we have to look for signs and nurture conversation'.[76] And by really listening to what the Earth is saying we humans can form the sacred bond needed to save ourselves.

Notes

1 E. Durkheim, *The Elementary Forms of the Religious Life* (2012) Dover Publications [accessed: 31 March 2023].

2 F. C. Happold and others, *Mysticism: A Study And An Anthology* (Middlesex: Penguin Books Ltd, 1977), p. 25.

3 Amit Bhattacharjee and Cassie Mogilner, 'Happiness From Ordinary And Extraordinary Experiences', *Journal of Consumer Research*, 41.1 (2014), 1–17 (p. 2) [accessed 27 December 2022].

4 Bhattacharjee, 'Happiness From Ordinary And Extraordinary Experiences', p. 2.

5 Bhattacharjee, 'Happiness From Ordinary And Extraordinary Experiences', p. 5.

6 Bhattacharjee, 'Happiness From Ordinary And Extraordinary Experiences', p. 13.

7 Jack Hunter, 'Greening The Paranormal: Re-wilding And Re-enchantment', in *Greening The Paranormal*, ed. by Jack Hunter (USA and UK: August Night Press, 2019), pp. 1–42 (p. 21).

8 William James, *The Varieties Of Religious Experience* (London and Glasgow: Collins Clear-Type Press, 1975), p. 41.

9 James, The Varieties Of Religious Experience, p. 485; James, The Varieties Of Religious Experience, p. 485.

10 James, The Varieties Of Religious Experience, p. 18.

11 James, The Varieties Of Religious Experience, p. 45.

12 James, The Varieties Of Religious Experience, p 46.

13 F. W. H. Myers, *Human Personality And Its Survival Of Bodily Death* (Charlottesville: Hamptons Roads Publishing Company, Inc, 2001), p. 314.

14 Alister Hardy, *The Divine Flame: An Essay Towards A Natural History of Religion* (London: Collins, 1966), p. 107.

15 Hardy, *The Divine Flame*, p. 111.

16 The Alister Hardy Trust (2021) [accessed 15 December 2022].

17 James, *The Varieties Of Religious Experience*, p. 45.

18 Stephen Harrod Buhner, *Plant Intelligence And The Imaginal Realm: Beyond The Doors Of Perception Into The Dreaming Earth* (Rochester: Bear & Company, 2014), p. 18.

19   The Alister Hardy Trust (2021) [accessed 15 December 2022].
20   L. Eugene Thomas and Pamela E. Cooper, 'Measurement And Incidence of Mystical Experiences: An Exploratory Study', *Journal For The Scientific Study Of Religion*, 17.4 (1978), 433–437 (p. 433) [accessed 10 December 2022].
21   Thomas, 'Measurement And Incidence', p. 435.
22   Thomas, 'Measurement And Incidence', p. 436.
23   Daniel A. Helminiak, 'Neurology, Psychology, and Extraordinary Religious Experiences', *Journal Of Religion And Health*, 23.1 (1984), 33–46 (p. 33) [accessed 20 December 2022]
24   Helminiak, 'Neurology', p. 43.
25   Helminiak, 'Neurology', p. 37.
26   Helminiak, 'Neurology', p. 37.
27   Helminiak, 'Neurology', p. 38.
28   Helminiak, 'Neurology', p. 38.
29   Paul F. Cunningham, 'Are Religious Experiences Really Localized Within the Brain? The Promise, Challenges, And Prospects Of Neurotheology', *The Journal of Mind and Behavior*, 32.3 (2011), 223–249 (229) [accessed 27 December 2022]
30   Cunningham, Are Religious Experiences', p. 235.
31   Cunningham, Are Religious Experiences', p. 236.
32   Hunter, 'Greening The Paranormal', p. 21.
33   James, *The Varieties Of Religious Experience*, p. 491.
34   David Abram, *The Spell Of The Sensuous: Perception And Language In A More-Than-Human World*, (New York: Vintage Books, 2017), p. 10.
35   Abram, *The Spell Of The Sensuous*, p. 48.
36   Happold, *Mysticism,* p. 20.
37   Jeremy Naydler, Gardening As A Sacred Art, (Edinburgh: Floris Books, 2011)
38   Naydler, *Gardening As A Sacred Art*, p. 91.
39   Hunter, 'Greening The Paranormal', p. 22.
40   Robin Wall Kimmerer, 'Weaving Traditional Ecological Knowledge into Biological Education: A Call to Action', *BioScience*, Volume 52 Issue 5 (2002)
41   Ronald Hutton, The Rise and Fall of Merry England The Ritual Year 1400 – 1700, (New York: Oxford University Press, 1994)
42   Hutton, *The Rise and Fall of Merry England The Ritual Year 1400 – 1700*, p. 57.
43   Seabird McKeon and others, 'Human Dimensions', *Bulletin Of The Ecological Society Of America*, 101.1 (2020), 1–7 (p. 4) [accessed 18 December 2022].
44   Amba J. Sepie, 'Listening To The Elders: Earth Consciousness And Ecology', in Greening the Paranormal, ed. By Jack Hunter (USA and UK: August Night Press, 2019), pp. 59– (p. 60)
45   Sepie, 'Listening To The Elders', p. 64.
46   Sepie, 'Listening To The Elders', p. 61.
47   Sepie, 'Listening To The Elders', p. 60.
48   Sepie, 'Listening To The Elders', p. 61.
49   Sepie, 'Listening To The Elders', p. 65.
50   Sepie, 'Listening To The Elders', p. 65.
51   Sepie, 'Listening To The Elders', p. 65.
52   Julio Glockner, 'A Chronicle of Misunderstandings', *Artes de México*, 127, (2017), 64–80 (p. 66) [accessed 20 December 2022]
53   Glockner, A Chronicle of Misunderstandings', p. 66
54   Antonella Fagetti, 'Nocturnal Journeys: The Sacred Plants Of The Mazatec', *Artes de Méxic*, 127 (2017), 64–80 (p. 71) [accessed 20 December 2022].

55 Lilian Gonzalez, 'Tenexyetl: Tobacco in the Traditions of the Nahua of Guerrero', *Artes de México*, 127, (2017), 64–80 (p. 76) [accessed 20 December 2022].

56 Glockner, 'A Chronicle of Misunderstandings', p. 67.

57 Glockner, 'A Chronicle of Misunderstandings', p. 67.

58 Glockner, 'A Chronicle of Misunderstandings', p. 67.

59 Monica, Gagliano, *Thus Spoke the Plant: A Remarkable Journey Of Groundbreaking Scientific Discoveries And Personal Encounters With Plants* (Berkeley: North Atlantic Books, 2018)

60 Gagliano, *Thus Spoke the Plant*, p. 64.

61 Gagliano, *Thus Spoke The Plant*, p. 90.

62 Margarita, De Orellana, 'Visionary Nature', *Artes de México*, 127 (2017), 64–80 (p. 64) [accessed 20 December 2022].

63 De Orellana, 'Sacred Plants', p. 65.

64 De Orellana, 'Sacred Plants', p. 65.

65 Maria Rios and Maria Cubero, 'Santa Rosa: A Plant That Heals And Conveys Knowledge', *Artes de México*, 127 (2017), 64–80 (p. 78) [accessed 20 December 2022].

66 Alister Hardy Religious Experience Research Centre, 000114 [accessed 18 December 2022].

67 Alister Hardy Religious Experience Research Centre, 000136 [accessed 18 December 2022].

68 Happold, *Mysticism*, p. 387.

69 Happold, *Mysticism*, p. 43.

70 Karen Jones, 'Restor(y)ing The 'Fierce Green Fire': Animal Agency, Wolf Conservation And Environmental Memory In Yellowstone National Park', *BJHS Theme*, 2 (2017), 151–168 (p. 151)

71 Happold, *Mysticism*, p. 17.

72 Happold, *Mysticism*, p. 17.

73 Happold, *Mysticism*, p. 27.

74 Alister Hardy Religious Experience Research Centre, 000846, <https://alisterhardytrust.uwtsd.ac.uk/> [accessed 18 December 2022].

75 Happold, *Mysticism*, p. 368.

76 Hunter, 'Greening The Paranormal', p. 24.

2

THE LAPIS NIGER OF ANCIENT ROME: HIEROPHANY OR SOCIAL CONSTRUCT?

Sarah Bisby

My research aimed to explore the ancient cityscape of Rome with a view to considering the nature of sacred landscapes. As I began this journey my attention became focussed around the Lapis Niger (black stone), an ancient shrine in the heart of the Forum. Together with the Rostra, it is the only surviving parts of the Comitium, the open-air meeting space around which all Roman political, judicial and religious life was centred. It was linked to the Palatine and Capitoline Hills by the *Via Sacra*, and situated next to the *Umbilicus Urbis Romana*, the omphalos of Rome from which all measurements were made.[1] It therefore sat at the centre of the sacred landscape of the ancient city. The Lapis Niger itself is a black marble pavement, under which was found a sanctuary filled with sacrificial objects, including a *cippus* (engraved pedestal) with the oldest known Latin inscription (approx. 570 BCE) written on four sides.[2] However, the sanctuary itself was already ancient and considered sacred by this time, even though the reason for this sanctity was unknown. As part of the Comitium area, it retained its significance throughout the Roman period, and mythology and legend linked it with the foundation myth of Rome, the murder and burial of Romulus, and to the art of augury.[3] Yet today it is under canvas and blocked off, scarcely noticed by the thousands of visitors who pass through the Forum each year, leading me to pose the question – is sacredness a natural part of this place, or is it bestowed by an outside force that needs to be maintained through ritual?

The question was explored through field work undertaken in October 2022 in which I 'participated' in the topography and landscape of Ancient Rome. I took a phenomenological approach by making observations, videos and taking pictures and measurements, using myself as a reflexive tool. I used the philosophical framework of Aristotle and his notion of 'proper place' to 'interview' the site and the research of theorists such as Christopher Tilley and Belden C. Lane to define what makes a landscape sacred. The theological theorists Mircea Eliade and Emile Durkheim were referenced to suggest a definition of sacred space, and I drew on the mythology of ancient Roman writers and the archaeological record as primary sources to determine the sacred nature of the Lapis Niger.

The Lapis Niger and Comitium area

Ancient Rome could be described as a 'sacred', in the way Lane did when discussing the nature of a sacred landscape, as a 'constructed reality where myth/imagination and geography interact'.[4] The seven hills on which the city was founded comprise volcanic tuffs formed from pyroclastic flows from the Monti Sabatini volcanic fields dating back approximately 600,000 – 300,000 years, and this geology is what has provided the city with water and building material from the earliest of times.[5] The area that is called the Forum today lies in a valley between the Capitoline and Palatine Hills, and was boggy and marshy until it was intentionally filled in and a gravel pavement laid.[6]

At some point in geological time, there was a landslide of *cappellaccio* from the tuff of the Capitoline Hill forming a large volcanic outcrop in the west of the Forum. This resulted in a series of raised 'stepping stones' emerging from the swampy landscape that could have been used for ceremony. Indeed, according to Albert J. Ammerman, a geologist who mapped the site, this area was a 'locus of ceremonial significance'.[7] By 700 BCE the *cappellaccio* had been cut down to form a surface and, still consisting of a prominent knoll that rose by 5 – 6 m, it became known as the Comitium, the place in which the Lapis Niger is situated.[8] The Lapis Niger today comprises a trapezoid-shaped pavement of black marble measuring 12 feet by 13.5 feet, fenced in by a wall of white marble (travertine).[9] Giacomo Boni, the archaeologist who excavated the site in 1899, described it as a '*locus religiousos*' because the travertine frame had been carefully cut to accommodate its strange trapezoid shape.[10]

The black marble was probably laid during the time of Augustus to protect the even older structure underneath. Boni found nine successive layers of different material resting on the tuff base and a layer of arenose gravel from the Tiber on average 28 cm thick that had been carefully poured round pedestals. On the top there was a U-shaped shrine, two stelae, a *cippus* and numerous votive offerings of both pottery and bronze.[11] The shrine had been deliberately set on fire, probably during the Gaulish invasion of 390 BCE, and the pedestals and stelae vandalised. Boni described how layers of gravel were brought from the Tiber as a 'purifying medium' to lay on the old tuff flooring of the Comitium, which had been polluted by the 'sacrilegious Gaul'. This was overlaid with a 'sacrificial layer of the expiatory offering to the Gods' comprising animal bones, astragals, dice, votive bronzes, terracotta pots and ashes, all poured round the altar with what Boni described as 'scrupulous care'.[12]

The U-shaped shrine, known as the *sacellum*, is situated on the boundary line between the Forum and the Comitium and according to Christian Hülsen, a German archaeologist who excavated the Forum in 1904, was 'dedicated according to the rules of the auspicious discipline', so that the sides of the rectangle corresponded to the four cardinal points.[13] Later buildings such as the Curia (senate) and the Rostra (speaking platform) were orientated to the Lapis Niger.

Methodology

In October 2022, I visited Rome and walked the topography of the ancient city with a view to engaging with it as a possible sacred landscape. The Lapis Niger in the Forum area emerged as a site of interest and I then made this the focus of my studies. The qualitative methods I used included conducting several field trips to the site at various times of the day and night, and making observations from different perspectives. I used myself as a reflexive tool; as Maurice Merleau-Ponty argued, 'the human body provides the fundamental mediation point between thought and the world'.[14] I recorded observations in a notebook, and took videos and photos, and I also took some basic orientation measurements using Google Earth. Taking a phenomenological approach, I used my 'embodied experience of the landscape to see how the landscape presented itself to me'.[15] I also 'participated' in the landscape by 'moving through with intent and openness to dialogue', as described by Levy-Bruhl.[16] I interviewed the landscape using a series of questions based on Aristotle's notion of 'proper place', which I used to frame my discussion.[17] As I am taking a reflexive and epistemological approach, I need to demonstrate self-awareness in relation to my personal, social and cultural context, so my background is relevant.[18] I am a white, Celtic/Anglo-Saxon who is deeply emersed in European culture, and have chosen to engage culturally with this site as an Indo-European. I am also a middle-aged mother, wife and daughter with a strong connection to the chthonic feminine, which informs how I engage with landscapes. I used the writing of ancient Roman authors and combined this with information from the cultural and material record to draw together mythology, archaeology and iconography, as this is also another way in ascertaining how a site 'speaks'. In this way, as described by Jon Cannon, 'personal experience can be brought to bear on the phenomenology of landscape itself as a way of exploring the possible causes of a particular conversation...'.[19]

The religious theorists Mircea Eliade and Emile Durkheim offer an initial framework with which to explore that nature of the sacred, which both agree is somehow set apart from the everyday, the profane. Durkheim wrote that religious phenomena divided the world into two, the sacred and the profane, embracing all that exists but excluding one another. 'Sacred things differ from profane things in their very nature and... their essence is different'. [20] Eliade was deeply influenced by the work of Rudolf Otto, who described the experience of the sacred as 'numinous' and consisting of three components – the *mysterium tremendum et fascinans* (wholly other), the *mysterium tremendum* (evoking terror) and the *fascinans* (gracious).[21] Taking these ideas and applying an ontological approach, Eliade conceptualised a sacred space as one that constitutes a break in space itself through which the divine can literally 'irrupt' and is qualitatively different from homogeneous and neutral profane space.[22] Eliade used the term 'hierophany' to describe this irruption of the sacred out of the profane, allowing something 'of a wholly different order from 'natural' realities to occur'.[23] Eliade's platonic influence attributed agency to the sacred, so sacredness is allocated by place, not people, and the way humans deal with this is either 'archaic or modern'.[24]

The notion of 'agency' has a philosophical basis in the work of Aristotle, who wrote of the 'power of place'. In *Physics*, he argued that the motion of any body, which was composed of the natural elements of fire, earth, air, and water, 'show not only that place is something, but also that it exerts a certain influence'.[25] As Edward Casey elaborated, 'place is something with its own inherent powers, a premetric phenomena that holds its own quality independent of contents'.[26] When a body was drawn to the place by this 'influence', a form of gravity, Aristotle considered that it was in its 'proper place'.[27] According to Bernadette Brady, this is a 'form of phenomenological gravity, the force that draws an individual or indeed any form of life to where they feel whole, complete, and thus find stillness'.[28] Claude Levi-Strauss also confirms the notion of proper place by saying that 'all sacred things must have their place... they therefore contribute to the maintenance of order in the universe by occupying the places allocated to them'.[29] Thus, through the work of Aristotle, Eliade and Brady, agency can be ascribed to a place.

For Durkheim, on the other hand, the sacred was something eminently social and 'religious representations are collective representations which express collective realities'.[30] Religions are founded on and express the real, and sacred spaces are kept sacred by the actions of people, who set them apart through performing ritual, and indeed, they only remain sacred as long as this ritual is performed.[31] He stated 'the categories of understanding consist of essential spatial and temporal contexts that enable the mind to understand experience'.[32] These categories are constructed by the 'collective consciousness', which is transcendental social intelligence.[33] For Durkheim, therefore, the human mind attributes the sacred, so sacred places are a function of the collective consciousness. A phenomenological approach also places the human at the centre of the experience of place, because as stated by Tilley, it, 'examines the activity of living, being, and experiencing from a fully physical and human perspective'.[34]

Belden C. Lane, however, suggested that ' a sacred space is not chosen, it chooses', implying that the identification of a site as sacred 'is never one of communal recognition, it demands its own freedom to choose'.[35] Lane's second 'axiom of the sacred' suggests that 'a sacred place can be trod upon without being entered', so just moving into a sacred place does not necessarily make one present to it.[36] However, once having 'chosen', the place – which could have been an ordinary place – is 'ritually made extraordinary'. The *Topos* (what Aristotle described as the inert container) can be turned to *Chora* (according to Plato, place as something with its own energy) by carrying out deliberate ritual activity.[37] Seen through this lens, a sacred site 'participates in its own becoming' and a third perspective emerges, one that sees the sacred and profane as 'overlapping dimensions of human experience'.[38] So sacred places could be reframed as an emergence between life forms and the environment in which both are participating.

Evidence for this 'third way' is seen in the work of Jon Cannon, who described certain landscapes as being 'set apart', possessing a 'strong character that evokes feelings to which human beings respond' – though maybe this definition should be expanded to include the other-than-human.[39] Once the landscape has drawn in a life-force, humans will engage with the landscape through ritual or myth, often making sacred places 'storied places'. When they are named, they then become what Tilley described as 'encultured landscapes', and attract more mythology.[40] Taking a slightly different approach, Tim Ingold envisaged this process of cultural influence as 'threads that produce meaning through intersection'.[41] As more 'nodes' arise through mutual exchange, more mythology, even archetypal beings, are then attracted to the original landscape, giving rise to what Henry Corbin called the *Mundus Imaginalis* , a world that he claims 'is ontologically as real as the world of the senses and that of the intellect'.[42]

Finally, according to Eliade, there is also a spatial and temporal dimension to a sacred site. His conceptualisation of a hierophany as an irruption of the sacred though non-homogeneous space led him to identify this place as a centre, 'an axis mundi or central axis for all future orientation... where the deepest meanings of sacred space are revealed, making passage from one cosmic region to another possible'.⁴³ Orientation is empowered or anchored by an encounter with an hierophany, so time as well as space is made sacred at this place. However, Jonathan Z. Smith questioned whether the notion of 'centre' has become too narrow and literal, and suggested that the periphery deserves equal attention.⁴⁴ For Durkheim, too, the sacred was not specific to the centre but was inherent in anything and everywhere.⁴⁵ Lane bought these different views together in one of his 'four axioms', which he used to define the features of a sacred space by saying 'the impulse of a sacred place is both centripetal and centrifugal, local and universal'.⁴⁶ The work of these theorists therefore suggests that a hierophany can manifest as both an axis mundi in both space and time and also as a liminal or threshold place.

Field Work Results and Discussion

I carried out a field trip to Rome in October 2022 to 'participate' in the sacred landscape with the hope of starting up a mutual conversation. I had been to Rome several times before and knew I should focus on the area round the Palatine and Capitoline Hills where the most ancient sites are situated. After walking round the topography of the hills, I descended into the Forum area (see Figure 1 for an overview).

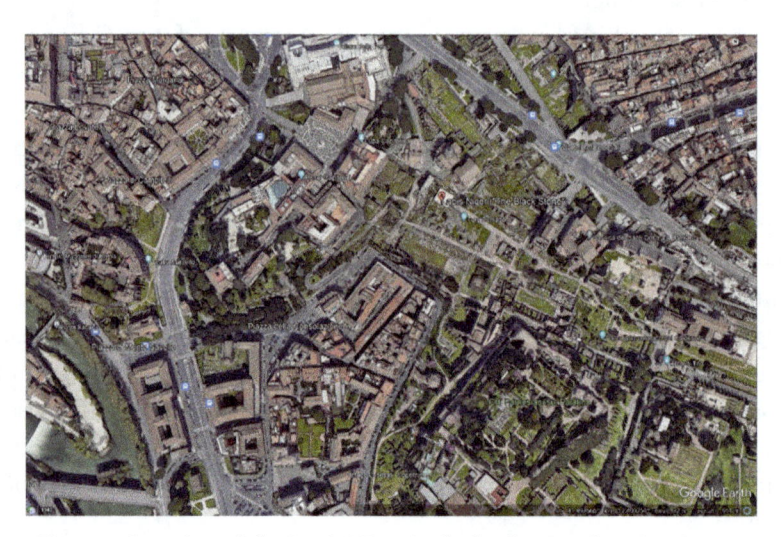

Figure 1: Location of the Lapis Niger in the landscape of ancient Rome. Note the Tiber on the far left, the Palatine Hill bottom right and the Capitoline Hill top left. Image: Google Earth Pro (October 2022). Roman Forum, lat. 41.892694 degrees, lon. 12.484985 degrees, elev. 0 m [Online] Available at https://earth.google.com [Accessed 31.10.22].

I walked the *Via Sacra* and headed towards the Capitoline Hill, walking straight past the Lapis Niger, not even noticing the blocked off area under tarpaulin by the Arch of Severus. It was my son, determined to find the ruins of the ancient Rostra, who saw it first, and his sense of excitement rooted me to the spot, allowing the site to emerge for me. As Lane wrote, 'a sacred place can be trod upon without being entered'.[47] The Lapis Niger was certainly veiled, hiding in plain sight from the majority of visitors to the Forum, including myself (see Figure 2). It also seemed neglected and forgotten – it wasn't even mentioned in my guide book – and as I made observations over the next few days, I noticed most people passed it by, scarcely even glancing at the blocked off area. According to Lane, a sacred site is not chosen, it chooses, and I had to delve further to find the mechanisms to gain entry.[48]

Figure 2: The veiled Lapis Niger.
Image: S. Bisby, October 2022.

The archaeologists who surveyed the site described it as a *locus religiousos*, yet neither Boni (1899) or Romanelli (1950s) completed publication of their findings.[49] It remained unexplored for years, then in 2008, rain washed away the wooden covering protecting it, revealing it briefly, before 'restoration projects' barred entry for another decade. This was a site that did not reveal itself easily, and it also felt raw, somehow elemental. According to Boni, it had been sanctified by the water of the Tiber, both defiled and purified by fire, and in recent times, 'revealed' by flooding. Aristotle wrote how the elements (earth, air, fire, water) move in accordance with their own nature, to where they want to be, giving a place potency.[50] It was as though this place had 'command' over the elements, attracting them to shape a story that it alone controlled, possibly contributing to its wholeness. I was also aware that taking a phenomenological approach such as this has been heavily critiqued, not least because, as Tilley himself said, there can be no methodology that provides a clear guide to empirical research arising from this approach.[51] However, it can be justified in that it attempts to understand the land from its own standpoint, through what Ingold described as, 'a way of being in the landscape'.[52] Using this approach, I could try and discern what land had drawn into it, in Lane's words, to ask 'what perspective would allow me to enter it anew?'[53]

Axis Mundi

I turned to mythology and to the *Mundus Imaginalis* for further insights, and found the Lapis Niger was intertwined with the foundation myth of Rome by Romulus himself. According to both legend and history, the valley of the Forum became incorporated into the city of Rome with the conquest of the Etruscan/Sabine tribe of the Quirinal. Mythologically, this event related to the 'rape of the Sabines' by Romulus's men, resulting in further battle, but when the adversaries were reconciled through the intervention of the Sabine women, the two kings made peace at the 'meeting place' (Comitium) under the Capitoline Hill.[54] Plutarch describes the consecration of the site according to sacred principles learnt from the Etruscans:

> digging a circular trench around what is now the Comitium in which were deposited first fruits of all things the use of which was sanctioned by custom as good and by nature as necessary... men brought a small portion of the soil of his native land and these were cast in with the first fruits and mingled with them....they called this trench as they do the heavens by the name of mundus, then taking this as the centre, they marked out the city in a circle round it.[55]

The Lapis Niger, in the centre of the Comitium area, can then be defined as a place of origin, as per Eliade, an axis mundi, or central locus that defined space.[56] As I surveyed the sacred landscape from the perspective of the Lapis Niger, I began to perceive how this axis mundi had drawn into it not just religious sanctity, but also laws that defined and regulated politics and economics of everyday Roman life. It demanded respect, ritual and oratory. Some of Rome's greatest temples stood nearby, for example, the Temple of Saturn, and both the Curia and Rostra were orientated to it. Further surveying revealed that it was also metres away from a tiny plaque marking the *Umbilicus Urbis Romana*, the point that was used to measure all distances in the Empire.[57] This axis mundi literally stood at the physical centre of the Roman world.

The Lapis Niger and Comitium area was also associated with the measurement of time. Boni stated that the pavement was aligned NE/SW in his archaeological survey, and with reference to the work of Roman writers, described how the consuls announced *meridies est* when the sun was seen between the Rostra and Grecostasis, suggesting an astronomical meridian.[58] I used a compass whilst at the site to check the general orientation of the Lapis Niger with the Via Sacra/Capitoline Hill, then compared them to azimuth measurements in Google Earth. Both gave an azimuth of approximately 119° which is comparable to the SE/NW axis.

Though this is just a rough indication of the orientation of the Lapis Niger, it does correspond with Boni's theory that the monuments of the Comitium were deliberately aligned to the movement of the sun. For Rome, the summer solstice sunrise is at an azimuth of 54° with a sunset azimuth of 304° and for the winter solstice the sunrise is at an azimuth of 124° with a sunset azimuth of 234°. Thus the orientation of the Lapis Niger is towards the winter solstice sunrise. It is five degrees wide of this, but still significant as a general orientation given the constraints of landscape topography. So, as well as measuring profane time, the axis could also have been a reflection of a mythical time, re-enacted by the movement of the sun and embodied in the structures of the Comitium, as Eliade said, 'enabling the passage between one cosmic medium and another'.[59] More research would be needed to confirm this.

It was self-evidenced that a hierophany had occurred here, but did it 'irrupt' from the landscape itself? The position of the Lapis Niger in the valley between the hills enables the topography to naturally draw the human in, attracting as it did the people who first saw the distinctive mounds of the *cappellaccio* rock emerging from the swamp. In this way, the landscape 'spoke' to them and as the geologist who surveyed the site remarked, 'In this case, it is fair to say then that Roman religious practice had deep roots both in time and in the landscape itself'.[60] Therefore it is possible to view this landscape as having agency, drawing sacredness to itself independent of human conscious action.

The Lapis Niger in legend and myth

Legends of sacred birth and sacrificial death were also associated with this site, making it a 'storied place', and from a phenomenological perspective, another way in which it appeared to draw the human into a form of mutual conversation. Plutarch described how a sacred fig tree once stood on this site, 'where the casket of Romulus and Remus came to rest after it was set adrift on the Tiber'.[61] According to Pompeius Festus it was also associated with death:

The black stone in the Comitium marks an unlucky spot: according to some it was intended to serve as the grave of Romulus, but this intention was not carried out, and in the place of Romulus his foster-father Faustulus was buried.[62]

Dionysius of Halicarnassus referred to a stone lion, 'the noblest place in the Roman Forum, close by the Rostra', that marked the place where Faustulus was buried after falling in battle.[63] He also quotes Varro, who said Romulus was buried close to the Rostra, and Livy named the Vulcanal as the site of the murder of Romulus, an early shrine also once located in the Comitium.[64] As Tilley wrote, 'storied landscapes can become humanised and encultured by saturation with place names, mythology'.[65] Throughout its history, the Comitium area was indeed 'saturated' with Roman culture, attracting oratory, laws and politics, and housing statues of celebrated augurs and great figures of the time, but it was also used as an execution and punishment site, demanding both sacrifice and expiation. After it was vandalised by the Gauls in 390 BCE, Boni commented on the extreme care with which the 'sacrificial layer' was put down to cleanse and purify the altar of the *sacellum*.[66] Later, in 44 BCE, when Julius Caesar tried to relocate the sacred area of the Comitium he was ritually murdered then cremated within a few metres of the site.[67] Were these some of the ways that made this site 'whole'? At its inception the site was associated with peace, not blood-shed, yet over time both were repeated, forming layers of sacredness maintained by ritual so that both peace and bloodshed became an integral part of Roman culture.

The cippus and augury: liminality

The *cippus* found beneath the Lapis Niger confirms that human activity kept this landscape sacred for hundreds of years, and therefore it could be deemed a social construct, as per Durkheim. An inscription written in an early form of Latin resembling Greek/Phoenician or Etruscan used a style called 'boustrophedon', lines alternately written to the left and right, thought to resemble the movement of an ox driving a plough.[68] The meaning of the inscription is disputed, but Georges Dumézil used the work of Cicero to make links with the ancient art of augury. He pieced together the words '*rex*', his '*calator*' (public servant), 'animals under the yoke' and '*iugues auspicium*' as references to laws associated with the rituals of inaugurating archaic kings.[69] Valens Varro also described how the inaugurating augurs, probably the king, processed from the arx (citadel) on the Capitoline Hill along the *Via Sacra* and had to avoid, at all costs, meeting an *iugues auscpicium*.[70] According to Michael Grant, the *iugues auspicium* was an inauspicious omen that would occur if 'two yoked draught cattle should happen while passing by to drop excrement simultaneously'.[71] Other writers regard the text as a chthonic curse, making the Lapis Niger, where the cippus was found, a m*ysterium tremendem*, a sacred place that inspires terror and awe, though Dumézil does not agree with Grant's translation.[72]

The inaugurating *rex* and his procession along the *Via Sacra* was 'essential' for the health of the Republic so ritual did play its part in maintaining the sacredness of this place.[73] Yet the Durkheimian definition of a sacred space as only a human construct maintained by ritual does not fully suffice. The rituals are no longer carried out, yet it is still capable of pulling elements into it, and 'talking back'. There was an agency inherent in the landscape that that seemed to speak, emphasising that its position at the threshold between the Capitoline Hill and the *Via Sacra*, was of primary importance, a key aspect by which it 'participated in its own becoming'.

As a liminal place, it could no longer, by definition, be defined solely as an axis mundi. As I observed the Lapis Niger from different perspectives over a series of days, my perspective began to change. too. Seen from the localised perspective on top of both the Palatine and Capitoline Hills (see Figure 3), it was a liminal zone, a threshold space deemed so sacred it had to be protected from inauspicious auguries with curses. From a broader perspective it was an axis mundi, an omphalos from which all measurements were made. So, depending on perspective, in the words of Lane, it was both centripetal and centrifugal, local and universal.[74] It was also humbling to know that the deep sacredness of this site, its status as *mysterium tremendum,* was rooted in the mysteries of defecating oxen. This fitted Lane's definition of a 'Chora', an ordinary place that once having chosen, is ritually made extraordinary.[75]

Figure 3: The Lapis Niger from the top of the Capitoline Hill. Image: S. Bisby, October 2022.

Reflexive considerations

What does the landscape want to say through me? What am I bringing to it? From a reflexive perspective, this place stirred in me that-which-had-been-veiled, the part of the story not given much prominence by the early writers, though the landscape itself had drawn it in. Stories of the Vestal Virgin Rhea Silva who had birthed the twins Romulus and Remus after a rape and later threw herself into the Tiber, and Tarpeia, another Vestal killed by the Sabines after she allowed them into the city. Her memorialisation through the naming of the Tarpeian rock used to execute criminals spoke to a degrading of the Feminine, the imprint of which seemed to be held in this chthonic site, the only site on the Forum with an underground aspect, as shown in Figure 4. These were the voices of the *Mundus Imaginalis* and, using myself as a participating tool, I could hear them. Otto describes how all experiences of the numinous seem to originate in something 'other', and Lane that sacred place 'was more than a construction of the human imagination alone'.[76] Possibly, in the words of Ingold, I was 'not so much calling up an internal image, stored in the mind, as engaging perceptually with an environment that is itself pregnant with the past'.[77] Was this place 'talking back' through the uncovering of its history, mythology and archaeology? Taking a reflexive approach was both a strength and a weakness in my methodology, and this approach has been criticised because, as noted by Ingold, 'interpretation is not always matched by evidence and ambiguity that can lead to multiple meanings'.[78] Yet the more I delved, the more I was drawn into a deeper sense of personal wholeness through a mutual participation in a shared story. As Lane says, this place allowed me to 'renew my sense of being in mystery, possibly contributing in the process to the greater wholeness of the place'.[79] According to Levi-Bruhl's law of participation, 'If you believe something and act upon it, it becomes real... This relationship need not be justified, there is a causality, a mystical relationship'.[80]

Finally, this was a place that had been named, becoming what Tilly described as an 'encultured landscape', and upon reflection I could see that it was the partly the name 'Lapis Niger' that drew me in. I did not have access to the site, and could not properly see it as it was under tarpaulin, but in my imagination I always saw a black stone. Yet, when it was 'unveiled' there is no 'black stone', only a dark mottled marble pavement, and neither was the *cippus* black. Boni speculated that a black stone could have once sat on the altar in the *sacellum* and indeed it was he who made the link between the Black Stone of Festus and the site that he excavated in 1899. Naming this place had certainly empowered it by, as Tilley said, 'intermingling topography, human intentionality and mythology'.[81] But is this a function of the human imagination or does it come

Figure 4: The underground access to the sacellum beneath the Lapis Niger. Image: S. Bisby, October 2022

from the land itself? When perceived through the lens of the *Mundus Imaginalis*, the two become intertwined.[82] When the land is given agency, its voice speaks through myth and metaphor, so maybe it was the black volcanic landscape that demanded this name be given to its most central and sacred site? In the words of Lane, 'It demanded its own integrity, its own participation in what it "becomes," its own voice'.[83] And though this voice is no longer maintained by ritual or human agency, it can be heard emanating from the landscape itself – if it so chooses.

Conclusion

This chapter set out to explore the question: can the Lapis Niger of Ancient Rome be described as a hierophany or a social construct? A field trip to the site revealed that the sacred nature of this place operated on many levels. Using Durkheim's definition of the sacred it was seen that humans have been attracted to and maintained this site through ritual for many centuries, without fully understanding why. Eliade's definition of a hierophany showed that it is both an axis mundi, providing orientation in both space and time, yet also a liminal and threshold site, an emanation of the numinous as *mysterium tremendum*. Iconography, mythology and the legends recorded by Plutarch and Festus provide evidence. From a phenomenological perspective, it is a site that chooses, and is not chosen, and that can be trodden without being seen, as my initial experience demonstrated. It is also an encultured landscape through being named, and it is a landscape where topography is primary, as evidenced through geological surveys.

Using Aristotle's notion of proper place and 'interviewing' the site revealed that it also 'functioned' on an elemental level, drawing in through its chthonic powers all the institutions, both religious and political, that once gave rise to, and drove, the Roman Empire. It is a place that demands ritual, expiation and sacrifice, yet also veils itself. It inspires awe and terror, peace and bloodshed, yet in its origins it was wholly mundane. Evidence for these observations was found in the archaeological, geological and iconographical record. From a reflexive perspective, it is a storied landscape that attracted foundation myths and legends of sacred birth and sacrificial death, all of which can be accessed through the *Mundis Imaginalis*, where it 'talks back'. Based on this evidence I conclude that the Lapis Niger's sacredness is both a hierophany and a human construct, and could be described as an empowered and storied landscape, with a voice born from its volcanic topography that draws in the elements and speaks in a way that humans have interpreted through the myths and legends of the *Mundus Imaginalis* in a mutual exchange of 'becoming'.

Notes

1   Christian Hülsen, *The Roman Forum, Its History and Its Monuments* (Rome: Loescher and Co., 1906), p. 80.
2   Giacomo Boni, 'The Niger Lapis In The Comitium At Rome', prefaced and translated by St. Claie Baddeley, Esq, 1900, pp. 183–184.
3   Michael Grant, *Roman Forum* (London, 1974) p. 50.
4   Belden C. Lane, *Landscapes Of The Sacred: Geography And Narrative In American Spirituality* (Baltimore: The Johns Hopkins University Press, 2002), p. 36.
5   Albert J. Ammerman, 'The Comitium in Rome from the Beginning', *American Journal of Archaeology*, Vol. 100, No. 1 (Jan., 1996), pp. 121–136, (p. 124) [Accessed 31.10.22].
6   Hülsen, *The Roman Forum*, p. 3.
7   Ammerman, 'The Comitium In Rome From The Beginning', p. 135.
8   Ammerman, p. 135.
9   Hülsen, p. 103.
10   Giacomo Boni, 'The Niger Lapis In The Comitium At Rome', p. 176.
11   Boni, p. 177.
12   Boni, p. 178.
13   Hülsen, *The Roman Forum*, p. 6.
14   Christopher Tilley quoting Maurice Merleau-Ponty, in *A Phenomenology of Landscape* (Oxford: Berg, 1994), p. 14.
15   Christopher Tilley, *A Phenomenology of Landscape* (Oxford: Berg, 1994,) p. 26.
16   Lucien Levy-Bruhl, *How Natives Think*, (Washing Square Press, 1966), p. 14.
17   Aristotle, 'On the Heavens', in *The Complete Works of Aristotle*, Volume 1, ed. Jonathan Barnes, trans. J. L. Stocks (Princeton, NJ: Princeton University Press, 1984), 447–511: IV 3, 310a, at 35.
18   Liz Henty, 'Skyscape Archaeology: an emerging interdiscipline for archaeoastronomers and archaeologists', *Journal Of Physics: Conference Series*, 385 (2016) pp.

19   Jon Cannon, 'Time And Place At Brentor: Exploring An Encounter With A 'Sacred Mountain', in *Space, Place And Religious Landscapes : Living Mountains*, edited by Darrelyn Gunzburg, Bernadette Brady (London: Bloomsbury Publishing, 2022), p. 74-75.
20   Emile Durkheim, *The Elementary Forms Of The Religious Life*, 2nd edn (New York: Dover Publications Inc, 1995), p. 118.
21   Rudolf Otto, *The Idea of the Holy*, trans. John Harvey, 2nd edn (Oxford: Oxford University Press, 1958 [1923]),
22   Eliade, *The Sacred And The Profane*, p. 20-21.
23   Eliade, p. 10.
24   Eilade cited in Barth, 'In Illo Tempore, At The Center Of The World', p. 61.
25   Aristotle, 'Physics', in *The Complete Works of Aristotle*, Volume 1, ed. Jonathan Barnes, trans. R. P. Hardie and R. K. Gaye (Princeton, NJ: Princeton University Press, 1984), 315-446: 4.2, 208b11.
26   Edward S. Casey, *The Fate of Place, a Philosophical History* (Berkeley, CA: University of California Press, 1998), p. 70-71.
27   Aristotle, 'On the Heavens', in *The Complete Works of Aristotle*, Volume 1, ed. Jonathan Barnes, trans. J. L. Stocks (Princeton, NJ: Princeton University Press, 1984), 447-511: IV 3, 310a, at 35.
28   Bernadette Brady, 'Mountains Talk Of Kings And Dragons, The Brecon Beacons', in *Space, Place And Religious Landscapes : Living Mountains* ed. by Darrelyn Gunzburg and Bernadette Brady (London: Bloomsbury Publishing, 2022), pp. 183-190.
29   Claude Levi-Strauss, *The Savage Mind*, in Belden C. Lane, *Landscapes Of The Sacred: Geography And Narrative In American Spirituality* (Baltimore: The Johns Hopkins University Press, 2002), p. 36.
30   Durkheim, *The Elementary Forms Of The Religious Life*, p.9.
31   Karen Field, *Translator's Introduction*, in Durkheim, *The Elementary Forms Of Religious Life*, p. xiv.
32   Durkheim, *The Elementary Forms Of The Religious Life*, p.9.
33   Durkheim, p. 10.
34   Tilley, *Phenomenology of Landscape,* p. 29-31
35   Lane, *Landscapes Of The Sacred* p. 20.
36   Lane, P. 19.
37   Lane, p. 39.
38   Lane, p. 43.
39   Cannon, 'Time And Place at Brentor', p. 72.
40   Tilley, *Phenomenology of Landscape*, p. 33.
41   Tim Ingold, *Lines: A Brief History* (London: Routledge, 2007).
42   Henry Corbin, 'Mundus Imaginalis or the Imaginary and the Imaginal' (Spring, 1972), p. 5.
43   Ibid p. 37.
44   Jonathan Z. Smith, 'The Wobbling Pivot', *The Journal of Religion*, Vol. 52, No. 2 (Apr., 1972), pp. 134-149 (p. 145).
45   Durkheim, *The Elementary Forms Of The Religious Life*, p. 10.
46   Lane, *Landscapes Of The Sacred*, p. 19.
47   Lane, *Landscapes Of The Sacred*, p. 30.
48   Ibid, p. 30.
49   Ammerman, 'The Comitium in Rome from the Beginning', p. 125-126.
50   Aristotle, 'On the Heavens', in The Complete Works of Aristotle, Volume 1, ed. Jonathan Barnes, trans. J. L. Stocks (Princeton, NJ: Princeton University Press, 1984), 447-511: IV 3, 310a, at 35.

51 Christopher Tilley cited in Vicki Cummings, Andrew Jones and Aaron Watson, 'Divided Places: Phenomenology And Asymmetry In The Monuments Of The Black Mountains, Southeast Wales', *Cambridge Archaeological Journal*, 12:1,(2002) pp. 57–70, (p.58).

52 Tim Ingold, *The Perception of the Environment: Essays in livelihood, dwelling and skill* (London: Routledge, 2000), p. 191.

53 Lane, *Landscapes Of The Sacred*, p. 30.

54 Hülsen, *The Roman Forum, Its History and Its Monuments*, p.5.

55 Plutarch, *Lives. Romulus*: Bernadotte Perrin (trs.) Loeb Classical Library (Cambridge MA: Harvard University Press, 1914), XI, pp. 118–119.

56 Eliade, *The Sacred And The Profane*, p. 21.

57 Hülsen, p. 80.

58 Boni, 'The Niger Lapis In The Comitium At Rome, p. 182.

59 Eliade, *The Sacred And The Profane*, p. 47.

60 Ammerman, 'The Comitium in Rome from the Beginning', p. 136.

61 Plutarch, *Lives. Romulus*, XI, pp. 118–119.

62 Sextus Pompeius Festus, *The Lexicone of Festus*, p. 177.

63 Festus, *Lexicone*, p. 177.

64 Livy, *The History Of Rome*, Book 1, Rev. Cannon Roberts, Ed. (New York: E. P. Dutton and Co., 1912) XVI, [4]

65 Tilley, *Phenomenology Of Landscape*, p. 24.

66 Boni, 'The Niger Lapis In The Comitium At Rome', p. 178.

67 Gaius Suetonius Tranquillus, *Lives Of The Twelve Caesars* ('Caesar' 84 – 85), (Livius.org).

68 Hülsen, p. 108.

69 Georges Dumézil , 'A propos de l'inscription du Lapis Niger', *Latomus*, T. 29, Fasc. 4 (Octobre - Decembre, 1970), pp. 1038–1045 https://www.jstor.org/stable/41526825 [Accessed 1.11.22].

70 M. Terentius Varro *De Lingua Latina*, R.G. Kent (trans.,) (Loeb Classical Library, Cambridge, MA: Harvard University Press), Vol.47.

71 Michael Grant, *Roman Forum* (London, 1974) p. 50.

72 Robert E. A. Palmer, *The King and the Comitium. A Study of Rome's Oldest Public Document* (Wiesbaden 1959), p.51 ff.= Historia. Einzelschriften 11 1969.

73 Wayne Tucker, 'Cicero, Augur, De Iure Augurali', *The Classical World* Vol. 70, No. 3 (Nov., 1976), pp. 171–177 Published by The Johns Hopkins University Press on behalf of the Classical Association of the Atlantic States <https://www.jstor.org/stable/4348603> [Accessed 30.11.22].

74 Lane, *Landscapes Of The Sacred*, p. 19.

75 Ibid, p. 139.

76 Lane, *Landscapes Of The Sacred*, p. 4.

77 Tim Ingold, 'The Temporality of the Landscape', World Archaeology, 25.2, 1993, p.152-153.

78 Fleming cited in Johnson, 'Phenomenological Approaches In Landscape Archaeology', p. 277

79 Lane, *Landscapes Of The Sacred*, p. 45.

80 Levi-Bruhl, *How Natives Think*, p. 14.

81 Tilly, *A Phenomenology of Landscape*, p. 83.

82 Henry Corbin, 'Mundus Imaginalis or the Imaginary and the Imaginal', p. 5.

83 Lane, *Landscapes Of The Sacred*, p. 12.

3

A CAVE OF STORIES: FINDING SACRED SPACE AT WAYLAND'S SMITHY LONG BARROW

Amy R. Mercy

The aim of my research was to investigate the process by which a variety of human activities in a particular place over a long period of time can create stories that emerge and enmesh to establish sacred space. My study focused specifically on the Neolithic tomb known as Wayland's Smithy, combining an experiential examination of the site with archaeological, historical, and folklore research. I looked at how the site has been conceived in the past in order to reframe it as an example of *heterotopia* (or 'other-place'), formed by the sheer diversity of layered significances. My case study was based on field notes, sound recordings, and photographs collected on six different visits to Wayland's Smithy in November and December 2022. The evidence is considered through a theoretical framework that integrates Émile Durkheim's model of the fundamentally social origin of sacredness, Michel Foucault's concept of the *heterotopia*, and Barbara Bender's work on the contested nature of space resulting from divergent modern uses of ancient places. Tim Ingold's landscape theories of 'dwelling' and lines, and Christopher Tilley's phenomenological principles inform my methodology.

Wayland's Smithy is a well-known Neolithic chambered tomb of the Cotswold-Severn type nestled within a ring of tall beech trees and located adjacent to the ancient track of the Ridgeway near Ashbury, Oxfordshire. The surrounding landscape is rich in tumuli and ancient monuments, and the chalk hill figure of the Uffington White Horse lies a mile away to the north-east. From the time the site was first chosen as a burial place in the early thirty-sixth century BCE, it has been rebuilt, reused, and re-interpreted over and again throughout the ages.[1] With use of the site continuing up to the present day, it presents a fascinating palimpsest of meaning.

Scholarship relating to the site of Wayland's Smithy represents a number of fields of study. The work done by Alasdair Whittle and his team on carbon-dating the archaeological remains informs much of what is known about the phases of use at the site.[2] There is a growing body of research devoted to interpreting the use of ancient sites by people in the past, exemplified in relation to Wayland's

Smithy by the work of Chris Gosden and Gary Lock, who coined the term 'prehistoric histories', and Ronald Hutton's examination of Romano-British activity at the site.[3] These scholars attempted to go beyond simply showing that past peoples were interested in their own histories, in order to understand 'different constructions of the past' over time.[4] Modern ritual activity at the site is considered both as pagan practice and as contemporary ritual behaviour, with the controversial term 'ritual litter' coined by Wallis and Blain proving to be something of a shibboleth, dividing scholars into opposing camps – either condoning or disapproving of modern depositional activities – once again highlighting the contested nature of the site.[5]

Primary sources for the folklore of Wayland include the Viking song of *Völundarkviða* and the Old English poem *Deor*, which elucidate the character of the legendary figure, and perhaps hint at the origins of the site's nomenclature.[6] Including folklore in this study allows a consideration of the way that a storied site can itself generate stories. The main primary source is of course Wayland's Smithy itself, experiential analysis of which is discussed below and which informed much of this study's interpretation of sacredness within the modern site.

My examination attempts to balance the factors that work together to inform human perception of Wayland's Smithy, including its origins, changing historical usage, its name and associated folklore, its appearance, and the lived experience of being in the space. Today it is a place that attracts walkers, cyclists, tourists, families, neo-Nazis, vandals, pilgrims, pagans, and spiritual seekers, who each create their own memories and meanings.[7] It is an ideal site through which to explore the complex and contested layering of sacredness that can stem from diverse human interaction with a specific place over time.

Émile Durkheim (1858–1917) was an early proponent of sociology whose seminal book *The Elementary Forms of Religious Life* (hereafter '*Forms*') was one of the earliest works to qualitatively categorise space as sacred or profane.[8] Durkheim proposed that sacredness has an entirely human foundation, stating that 'society is the soul of religion'.[9] Lynn Badia's reappraisal of *Forms*, one hundred years later, pulled focus away from the problematic ontological binary of sacred/profane.[10] She suggested that the engine behind Durkheim's sociology was in fact an 'energetic epistemology', where human cognition invests energy 'in the form of continually enacted and evolving material practice, thought, and attention' which accumulates in objects and spaces to suffuse them with meaning and engender sacredness.[11] Thus the individual perceives the reality of sacredness due to the 'work of attention and focus (in essence, the energy) contributed by many minds to the sacred objects'.[12] As twenty-first century scholars begin to push back against 'the old Durkheimian folklore of sacred-profane' in the search for a more practice-based theoretical framework, Badia's re-reading has helped to animate Durkheim's model, re-introducing the human element into theories of sacrality.[13]

Durkheim's depiction of sacred space as 'a special world entirely different from the ordinary' was reflected in the work of philosopher Michel Foucault (1926–1984).[14] Foucault also proposed that humans exist in 'heterogeneous space', and characterised that transformed 'special world' as an existential *heterotopia* or 'other-place'.[15] Contestation is at the heart of the *heterotopia*, as Foucault suggested it is 'capable of juxtaposing in a single real place several spaces, several sites that are in themselves incompatible'.[16] Barbara Bender's work on contested space at Stonehenge investigated the co-existence of several such incompatible layers of significance that affected different interpretations by different groups.[17] Each of these theorists recognised that the sacredness of space arises from human action and belief, and placed the manifold complexities of such space at the centre of their work. This study, in examining such a storied monument as Wayland's Smithy, engages with these complexities both in analysing the history of the site and through experiential research; it attempts to bridge the gap between these two methodologies in a manner inspired by the landscape research of Nicola Whyte, aiming to harmonise archival research with phenomenology.[18]

To understand the complex landscape, Christopher Tilley and Kate Cameron-Daum advocated a phenomenological approach, undertaking 'material experience' of the space.[19] They cited Bender in their assertion that all landscapes are inevitably contested, and proposed that this contestation arises from landscapes being historically contingent, subjectively experienced, and co-created along with those inhabiting them.[20] In their belief that 'persons and things are mutually constitutive', they concurred with Tim Ingold's synthesis of the temporality of the landscape with the human action that structures it.[21] Ingold theorised that the landscape does not simply exist in chronological time, but in 'social time', requiring an agent to perceive it.[22] This could be extended to sacred space, embodied and maintained by social actions, perpetuated by the accumulating significance of actions over time rather than, as Ingold argued that Durkheim would have it, simply measured by those actions.[23] To Ingold, 'the inhabited world is a reticulate meshwork' of constantly rewoven trails, demonstrated by the re-treading of paths in the landscape.[24] Both Ingold and Tilley endorsed an active process of subjective – but not personal – engagement with the research subject as a sort of 'auto-ethnography' in order to develop what Ingold referred to as a 'dwelling perspective'.[25]

METHODOLOGY AND PERSONAL REFLECTION

This study's methodology combined participative and historical research to encourage Ingold's 'dwelling perspective', reconciling humanity with the landscape by considering them together as an ever-unfolding story.[26] This approach was inspired by Whyte's suggestion that phenomenology 'opens up creative space for thinking through the documentary evidence', invoking Tilley's credo that 'knowledge of the past in the present is only to be satisfactorily gained through the direct medium of the sensual and sensing body'.[27]

My experiential research of the site took place over six visits in November and December 2022, during which I took field notes, photographs, sound recordings, and observations on the layout and lived experience of the space as a sacred site, including the way that other visitors interacted with the monument. Conducting the study in winter proved a limitation of the research due to reduced footfall of visitors, but the coincidence of the study with the Winter Solstice allowed an exploration of the ritual offerings and objects left at the site. The extensive graffiti on the surrounding beech trees was investigated, in order to consider how the act of marking engages with themes of memorialisation and place-making, reinforcing the sacred or special value of the site, and contributing visually and symbolically to the ongoing story of Wayland's Smithy. I have taken care in my methodology to consider myself as a research instrument. I have had to reflect on whether my presence in the space affected the activities of other visitors, despite my attempts to be unobtrusive, contributing to what Whyte termed 'cognitive boundaries' that serve to 'constrain movement and shape experience'.[28]

The site is well known to me - I was born and have lived most of my life within Oxfordshire and the bordering counties, and I feel a strong connection to the spaces and stories of this landscape. I live close to Wayland's Smithy, and frequently spend time on the surrounding chalk downs. I invariably encounter this landscape in the company of others, which has led me to experience it in an active, companionable way as we walk and talk together. By contrast, undertaking observations at Wayland's Smithy by myself – a diminutive middle-aged woman alone at a remote location often engulfed in dense freezing fog – produced surprising sensations of vulnerability and trepidation that may have influenced the earliest part of my research.

My field notes recorded how the poor visibility, the constant rustling of the tree canopy, the erratic shrieks of crows and pheasants, and distant gunshots in the valley made me uneasy and hypervigilant: I felt unexpectedly aware of being isolated in a wide and inscrutable environment. During my second visit I started to feel more confident being alone, and was more able to focus in an immersive way on the sonic experience of the site, to view myself as an integral element of the landscape, and to inhabit the full layout of the space more assertively. Moving around the site was a means to sensorially engage with Ingold's 'dwelling perspective', and to incorporate his phenomenological concept of a 'total system of body orientation', with knowledge of the surroundings 'forged in the very course of... moving through them'.[29] Perhaps my increasing familiarity with the place also allowed me to engage in my own process of story-creation, bearing out Tilley's assertion that 'spatial knowledge requires the coupling of an accumulated time of memory to overcome an initially hostile and alienating encounter with a new place'.[30]

HISTORY AND FOLKLORE

Complementing the phenomenological research, an outline of Wayland's Smithy's long and varied history formed an important part of this study. Although its history is only one factor shaping the lived experience of the site today, its original function strongly informs modern heritage interpretation and visitor expectations. Considering Wayland's Smithy as a *heterotopia* also required consideration of how it embodies what Foucault called 'slices in time'.[31] Foucault termed this quality *heterochrony*, the temporal aspect of the spatial *heterotopia*, a sort of other-time where time exists in complex multiplicity – for example, in the way that a grave can simultaneously signify both the end of life and everlasting rest.[32] Wayland's Smithy has not just one story but many, remembered or lost, which are interwoven and superimposed through time. Bender stressed this recognition of temporal complexity when she stated that 'one can only understand the contestations and appropriations of a landscape by careful historical contextualisation'.[33] As well as its ancient funerary and ritual functions, its changing significance to the local community over the millennia, and its modern status as a heritage destination, Wayland's Smithy has undergone archaeological excavation at least twice. It is from the 1962-3 excavations that much of the data is derived concerning its construction and early use.[34]

Excavations have shown that there was prior occupation of the site before the first Neolithic monument was built sometime between 3610 and 3550 BCE, but they revealed nothing about why the location was chosen for a burial monument.[35] The ceremony of death and memorialisation set the place apart, however, and, according to Whittle's interpretation, a shrine incorporating wooden posts and a long wooden mortuary box was constructed to house the remains of the deceased (see Fig. 1). Fourteen individuals were buried here, some of whose bodies may have been exposed prior to interment, perhaps in front of the grave itself.[36] Among these were two men who may have been exposed

Figure 1: Reconstruction drawing of the first Neolithic phase of Wayland's Smithy, c.3610-3550 BCE, according to Whittle et al (2007). Copyright Jennie Anderson Archaeological Illustration, www.jennieanderson.co.uk

to the elements for some time before they were placed into the lidded wooden box, the fragments of the flint arrowheads that likely killed them still lodged in their skeletons.[37] In contrast to the tranquil, bucolic space experienced by today's visitors, the sights and smells of Wayland's Smithy in the early thirty-sixth century BCE may have been visceral and grisly, and those visiting may have been mourners haunted by the sudden deaths of loved ones in conflict. The bodies were laid to rest in the mortuary box over a single generation, and eventually a mound was raised over it, sealing it off.[38]

The grave was left untouched and became overgrown for another generation before a stone-lined chambered tomb was created over it between 3460 and 3400 BCE, reiterating the earlier tomb's SSE/NNW alignment and incorporating a 55m long mound fronted by an impressive megalithic stone façade – similar to the reconstructed monument visible today.[39] Little is known about the dead of this second phase of burial, as much physical evidence was destroyed during slipshod excavations in 1919-20, although it has been possible to deduce that the tomb's second inhabitants were also buried over a very few generations.[40] The style of this second Neolithic monument was already old-fashioned when it was constructed. Whittle *et al.* interpreted its design as being deliberately archaic, suggesting a community 'consciously harking back to ideas and practices already old' and exploiting a 'sense of history' to lay claim to the land.[41] This seems not so very far removed from the modern role of heritage sites. When considering the temporal aspect of sacrality at Wayland's Smithy, it is striking that even though the 'ancient' site seems timeless today, its early years of repeated burials and rebuilding were as dynamic and contested as modern uses of the very same space.

There were echoes of these historicising resonances nearly four thousand years later in the re-use of the monuments surrounding the Uffington White Horse. Archaeological evidence suggests that the Romano-British turned the Iron Age hillfort of Uffington Castle into a 'ritual space', where they conducted ceremonies inside the enclosure, regularly scoured the Bronze Age White Horse chalk figure, and buried a hundred of their dead on the hilltop.[42] Ritual offerings of coins and food were left in barrow mounds, perhaps to appease the spirits of the place, or, as Hutton suggested, to satisfy 'a greater need to relate to past human activity' following the socio-political and ideological upheaval of the Roman conquest.[43] Wayland's Smithy itself is exceptional among local monuments in having escaped this ritual treatment, as its human bones were removed and its barrow mound encroached on by cultivation. Hutton warned against ascribing a purely disrespectful motive to these acts, however, and it may be that a Roman-period ditch dug across the façade and filled with sarsen boulders and human bone may have represented ritual practice or reverent reburial.[44] Whatever the values invested in this landscape by the local Romano-British inhabitants, it clearly remained for them a site of numinous significance associated with their enigmatic ancestors, and a powerful locus for the mythical past.[45]

The early medieval period saw continued burial and ritual use of the site and the surrounding landscape, and it may be then that it was first associated with the Saxon legend of Wayland, the name appearing in a land charter of King Eadred in 955 CE.[46] Whyte suggested that in non-literate communities in the past, the naming of places acted to bound the spaces, enabling navigation through the landscape both physically and in communication.[47] In considering the role of movement in establishing oral memory, she highlighted the importance of local place names remembered and passed down in a society where 'identification of the traces of the past in the landscape was essential to the circulation of knowledge and practice'.[48]

Wayland's Smithy takes its name from the Norse god and 'prince of elves' Völund, an expert metalworker, whose tragic tale of lost love, exile, enslavement, and forced labour as a smith, followed by his dark deeds of revenge, rape, and murder, feature in the Viking saga of *Völundarkviða*.[49] The legend may predate the Danish incursion across the chalk downs in 870 CE, as Wayland's story travelled with the mobile societies of the Early Middle Ages.[50] He also appeared in the tenth century CE in the Old English poem *Deor*, where his endurance of mutilation and incarceration, and his subsequent vengeance, were celebrated.[51] It is not difficult to see why such a being, capable of superhuman feats of engineering and exiled in a remote location, might inspire the naming of a mysterious, cavernous megalithic ruin on a remote hilltop. Tilley wrote that 'through an act of naming and through the development of human and mythological associations such places become invested with meaning and significance'.[52] The fearsome Völund had, by the nineteenth century, been reduced to the legend of 'an invisible smith' who would shoe a traveller's horse in return for a coin left on the stones of his cave.[53] Nonetheless his story endured, reworked by countless tellers, anchored in the stones and shadows of his legendary workshop.

The forging of sacred space at Wayland's Smithy is tied powerfully to its name and attendant folklore. In an evolution from the funerary context of the earlier monument, the place became charged with enchantment as its mythologisation by the community arose from their lived experience of the site. Tilley's phenomenological work addressed the way that narrative can accentuate perception, and he maintained that 'to understand a landscape truly it must be felt, but to convey some of this feeling to others it has to be talked about, recounted, or written and depicted'.[54] My research presented here aims to combine both of these elements, with a phenomenological enquiry – the next part of this study – attempting not just to understand the landscape, but to explore how human actions continue to imbue it with sacredness.

SPACE, BOUNDARIES, AND *HETEROTOPIA*

The instantiation of sacredness at Wayland's Smithy has both temporal and spatial components, as the juxtaposed histories and stories jostle up against the symbolic boundaries of the space. Tilley distinguished physical and conceptual 'forms of space', even as he recognised that the 'sedimented meanings' of places make such typologies inherently fluid.[55] In my own phenomenological research I identified several physical and non-physical boundaries that combined to delineate the experience of sacred space from the surrounding landscape: the visual and auditory envelopment of the fog, the ring of kerb-stones around the mound, the grove of trees encircling the site, and the barbed-wire fence separating the heritage site from the surrounding farmland.

On three of my six research visits Wayland's Smithy was shrouded in dense freezing fog, cutting the site off from the nearby Ridgeway and the

Figure 2: Left: freezing fog on the Ridgeway 0.5 miles SW of Wayland's Smithy, 11 December 2022. Right: the passageway and central chamber of Wayland's Smithy, with trees visible in fog beyond, 29 November 2022. Copyright Amy Mercy, 2022

wider landscape. Sounds from the valley beyond were muffled, and the site felt powerfully atmospheric (see Fig. 2). With temperatures as cold as -4°C it was noticeable how visitors, swathed in layers of warm clothing, kept their voices low as though inhabiting a more restricted, controlled space. On milder days some visitors still maintained a reverent hush, particularly around the entrance to the tomb, but others felt free to shout, play, and call to each other across the mound. The elemental drama of the fog seemed to experientially change the physicality of the space, shaping the visitors' lived experience of the site's numinous qualities. Perhaps it also acted to enhance perception of Wayland's Smithy as a *heterotopia,* where one could more readily envisage history, myth, and sacrality coexisting to create an other-place, what Foucault described as a 'simultaneously mythic and real contestation of the space in which we live'.[56]

The barrow mound itself is outlined with a ring of sarsen kerb-stones that materially echo the megaliths dominating the entrance to the barrow and lining the passageway of the tomb. They mark out the margins of the Neolithic funerary area, and stand witness to fifty-six centuries of ever-changing story played out in this space. Their significance seems to transcend time, and the majority of visitors to Wayland's Smithy instinctively reached out to touch the stones, making a haptic connection with the storied past. However, aside from several instances of ritual activity (discussed below), it was noted that few visitors were tempted inside the chambers of the barrow. Even in inclement weather the cramped cells seem to attract mainly small children and dogs, with adults perhaps uncomfortable at the sinister thought of crawling into a grave. These moral boundaries seem to reveal an ongoing reverence for the sacredness of the tomb, even as it co-exists as a heritage site and tourist destination.

Setting the mound apart in the landscape is a physical perimeter formed by a ring of tall beech trees. Their form echoes the very earliest upright wooden poles erected around the first burials (see Fig. 1), but today their significance is rooted in the sensory effect they have on visitors. Their great height gives the site a sense of monumental presence in the landscape even as they isolate it from its surroundings. In winter, when this study was conducted, the bronze leaves still cling to the branches, blocking the heat and light of the sun, casting shadow, and acting as a windbreak and rain shelter. The constant whispering of the canopy and creaking branches form the soundtrack to the sensory experience of the space. In foggy weather they draw an acoustic veil around the site, creating a sonic curtain of persistent dripping as the thick mist condenses on their leaves, punctuated only by birds fluttering in and out of the space like messengers. Whether the visitor recognises it or not, the trees act on the senses to reinforce the boundary of the sacred space, making of it what Ingold would define as not simply space, but a place: 'the union of a symbolic meaning with a delimited block of the earth's surface'.[57]

Just beyond the trees is a barbed wire fence, presumably installed by land managers at the National Trust. The line of the fence describes the cultural, legal, and political boundary of the heritage site, but the ground itself is visibly similar on both sides of the fence. This boundary is as much ideological as it is physical, and yet visitors do not stray beyond it: it is the symbolic perimeter of the sacred site today. In a similar way, the site is bounded and controlled by copious signage. Bender, writing about the enclosure of Stonehenge, railed against contemporary heritage bodies promoting 'a socially empty view of the past in line with modern conservative sensibilities'.[58] An assessment of the seemingly arbitrary demarcation and manipulation of the space at Wayland's Smithy, although on a different scale to Stonehenge, allows it to be similarly defined as contested space, its complex ownership and interpretation a 'proprietorial palimpsest'.[59]

PEOPLE AT WAYLAND'S SMITHY

Navigating the space

The shape of the site invites perambulation of the mound, which observations revealed nearly all visitors do by going clockwise. This produces an unintentionally ceremonial quality, but is likely due to the manipulation of access into and around the site by its heritage managers. In order to explore the most impressive area, the megalithic forecourt, visitors must head west from the site entrance to cross to the tomb opening (see Fig. 2), from where a woodchip path encourages continuation clockwise around the mound. Applying *a posteriori* Badia's Durkheimian model of sacralising social behaviours, the question arises as to whether this non-sacred processional activity inadvertently forms a sense of repeated, sacralising action in the minds of visitors as they re-tread the paths forged by others, and perhaps by themselves on past visits. Ingold explored this theme with his theory of lines in the landscape, stating that 'it is along paths… that people grow into a knowledge of the world around them, and describe this world in the stories they tell'.[60]

Navigation of the space is therefore contingent on its layout, the uninviting exclusivity of the cramped tomb chambers, and the way the huge megaliths control visibility of the rest of the site. These are modern limitations imposed by ancient builders (although re-iterated in the tomb's reconstruction after the 1962-3 excavations). Tilley observed that this sort of mediation may have been a conscious attempt to 'freeze perspective' of the landscape 'through the architectural lens of the monuments themselves', establishing control over both the topography and the individual's 'possibilities for interpreting the world'.[61]

Dogs, however, are not subject to such mediation and do not respect culturally-defined heritage boundaries. The few visitors who did not navigate the mound clockwise were all dog-walkers following animals that had preceded them into the space. The atmosphere of the place may nevertheless affect animals: a sound recording made at the Winter Solstice reveals two women discussing how their dog has been 'affected by the energy' as he – apparently uncharacteristically – tumbles enthusiastically around the mound's forecourt.[62] Whether the tomb truly has a spiritual energy capable of stimulating animals in this way, or whether the women were simply ventriloquising their own beliefs, the visitors evidently perceived Wayland's Smithy as emanating a numinous significance.

Ritual activity

It is perhaps then not surprising that evidence of ritual activities was observed in and around the tomb. Peaking at the Winter Solstice, these seem to represent pagan offerings, with evidence of burnt incense and sage scattered around the entrance, perhaps used to purify the space. Candles and wax were left in the central chamber (see Fig. 3), and although a grave seems an incongruous place to celebrate a seasonal festival, Wallis and Blain suggested that 'much pagan use takes place with little knowledge of either archaeological interpretation, or what practices are detrimental or problematic for other users'.[63] Practising Heathens

Figure 3: Ritual offerings at Wayland's Smithy, 20-22 December 2022. Clockwise from top left: paraffin candle wax spilled inside the central chamber, with burnt ends of incense sticks visible behind; a deposit of rosehips, beech nuts, and a stone placed into a hollow in the easternmost megalith of the façade of Wayland's Smithy; a square-headed horseshoe nail temporarily removed for recording from its deposition spot in a hollow of the megalith west of the tomb's passageway entrance; a small green leatherette pouch with ritual items deposited among the roots of a tree at the western edge of the site. Copyright Amy Mercy, 2022.

themselves, Wallis and Blain nevertheless condemned the lighting of fires and the leaving of what they called 'ritual litter' by pagans at archaeological monuments deemed to be sacred sites.[64]

Deposition of objects outside the tomb also occurred, perhaps connected more with superstition, folklore, or play than ceremony. Opportunistic deposits were most prevalent, perhaps resulting from a spontaneous need for ritual expression: rosehips, beech nuts, stones, and ivy, probably taken from the site or the adjoining Ridgeway and slipped into natural hollows in the megaliths (see Fig. 3). Several children were observed handling these, while their parents, perhaps more cognisant of the sacred reputation of the site, told them to put them back where they had found them.[65] Symbolic objects were also brought to the site and tucked into the roots of trees: a large blue marble, and a sealed green leatherette pouch containing a coin-shaped object and what may have been stones or crystals (see Fig. 3). These objects were placed not in the grave but at the site's perimeter, illustrating the way that the whole space is deemed sacred. Placed into a megalithic nook was a sprig of rosemary accompanying a square-headed horseshoe nail (see Fig. 3), possibly an allusion to the smith-god Wayland as a *genius loci*. Deviating from the legend of a coin exchanged for a reshod horse, Wallis and Blain considered that such acts might signify a pagan 're-enchanting' the place 'in line with how their paganisms understand people, deities and places'.[66] Given the legend noted earlier, the wider absence of coins – other than perhaps the object in the green pouch – was surprising, but research by Houlbrook confirmed that this story was deliberately removed from interpretation boards at Wayland's Smithy to discourage coin deposition that was becoming troublesome.[67] Even as stories wax and wane in this place, it continues to attract ritual behaviour; in Wallis and Blain's words, 'sacredness is made evident in stories' which express the complexity and contestation of sacred spaces.[68]

Figure 4: Tree graffiti at Wayland's Smithy, 20 December 2022. Clockwise from top left: a carved message commemorating a gathering at the site in 1995; graffito depicting a swastika (now partially defaced) at top, carved during 2019's neo-Nazi ceremony at Wayland's Smithy; graffito depicting a large heart, with the initials SS and GC carved inside; the anarchy 'A' symbol cut into a beech tree at Wayland's Smithy, with ivy climbing across the carving. Copyright Amy Mercy, 2022.

Graffiti: place-making and memorialisation

The surrounding beech trees are thickly inscribed with carved initials, symbols, and messages (see Fig. 4). Framing the graffiti as simple acts of vandalism is problematic, however, and Wallis and Blain denounced the behaviour, but also argued that 'inappropriate' actions contradicting the Protestant 'folklore of the preservation ethic' may still constitute ritual which need be neither sombre nor passive.[69] The graffiti might instead be interpreted as visitors seeking consciously or unconsciously to engage with the sacred nature of the site in an act of memorialisation. Such mark-making, however frivolous, forges a connection between the carver and the forces that motivated the initial place-making of the barrow site as a memorial space, giving tangible form to the place's ritual significance.[70] As a *heterotopia*, the multifarious stories symbolised by each carving simultaneously occupy and contest the site. They epitomise the sacralising power of Badia's Durkheimian 'many minds':[71] generations of carvers have written and overwritten their stories, interleaving their narratives with those of Wayland's Smithy, and by leaving their marks they inspire others to do the same.

Not all of the graffiti are benign, however, and a neo-Nazi gathering in 2019 resulted in the carving of swastikas and other hate symbols into the trees (see Fig. 4).[72] Their motives may be objectionable, but the neo-Nazis evidently hold Wayland's Smithy to be a place of power, sacred to them in their own way. Wayland's Smithy may not be as contentious a site as Stonehenge, but as an unofficial forum for ideological expression it offers another example of what Bender considered appropriation of a contested landscape.[73] The graffiti serve to inscribe the contestation into the fabric of the place itself, despite the endeavours of the site's legal guardians, who have contributed their own narratives through conspicuous but ineffectual signage requesting that visitors desist from leaving their mark. It is also, following the theories of Durkheim, another example of 'moral remaking', or the action of a community to 'sustain and reaffirm the collective feelings and ideas that constitute its unity and its personality'.[74] Expressions of love happily abound too (see Fig. 4), as the purposes of the graffiti are as diverse as their creators. The space is sacralised through re-performance of ritual acts, even those that are sentimental or politically offensive, and myth and history are renegotiated as new stories play out within the bounds of Wayland's Smithy.

CONCLUSION

This study has investigated the establishment of sacred space generated by the diversity of functions, meanings, and activities of its users over time. With its layers of varied history and contested significance, Wayland's Smithy typifies this process, and an investigation bridging the gap between documentary evidence and experiential insight has allowed each to inform a better understanding of how such sites can act as instances of complex alterity. The themes that emerged to structure the study were rooted in the site's temporal context: its stories were overlaid and interwoven through time, evidenced by the way that people have employed the place's history as a point of connection with the landscape and its ancestral inhabitants. Sacredness has been recurrently conferred onto the site through the ritual significance of its burials, its reuse by ancient people to connect with their mythological past, and the way that folklore maintains its otherworldly status, as reflected in the modern name for the place.

Examining the site's spatial context through phenomenological investigation produced themes of boundary, spatial navigation, ritual activity, and memorialisation. Exploring both the physical and conceptual boundaries of the space elucidated its qualitative 'otherness', allowing it to be framed as a Foucauldian *heterotopia*, where space and time exist differently. Mobility around the site is equally contingent on individuals and the form and layout of the monument itself. Its spatial limitations retain the fingerprints not just of modern heritage managers but the tomb's Neolithic designers, connecting distant times within the same physical space. Gosden and Lock described such places as 'engines for the creation of time, through the repetition at them of ritual acts'.[75] Accordingly, at Wayland's Smithy ritual activity can still be observed, tapping into the social foundation of the site's enduring sacredness. Examining tree graffiti reveals that even contentious use of the space serves to reinforce the contestation and complexity of meaning capable of co-existing in a qualitatively sacred space.

It can be concluded that perception of sacred space depends on the interplay of activity, history, and the materiality of a place itself. This spatio-temporal framework allows narratives to develop that ebb, flow, and adapt, supporting a multitude of contested meanings. With social cognition and action at its core, the experience of sacred space is as much sensory as ideological. It enables a site like Wayland's Smithy to exist as an anthology of ever-changing stories, anchored in the landscape but set apart, embodying time while remaining timeless.

Notes

1   Alasdair Whittle, Alex Bayliss and Michael Wysocki, 'Once in a Lifetime: the Date of the Wayland's Smithy Long Barrow', *Cambridge Archaeological Journal,* 17:1 (2007), pp.103–21.

2   Whittle et al., 'Once in a Lifetime', pp.113–17.

3   Chris Gosden and Gary Lock, 'Prehistoric Histories', *World Archaeology,* 30:1 (1998), 2–12; Ronald Hutton, 'Romano-British Reuse of Prehistoric Ritual Sites', *Britannia,* 42 (2011), pp.1–22.

4   Gosden and Lock, 'Prehistoric Histories', p.11.

5   Wallis and Blain, 'Sites, Sacredness, and Stories', 307; Ceri Houlbrook, 'The Penny's Dropped: Renegotiating the Contemporary Coin Deposit', *Journal of Material Culture,* 20:2 (2015), pp.173–89.

6   *The Elder Edda, Völundarkviða,* trans. by Andy Orchard (London: Penguin Books, 2013), 101–8; *The Exeter Book, Deor,* eds. Alex Fairbanks-Ukropen and Martin Foys, *Old English Poetry in Facsimile,* Center for the History of Print and Digital Culture, University of Wisconsin-Madison (2023), https://oepoetryfacsimile.org [accessed 4 May 2023].

7   BBC News, *Wayland's Smithy 'neo-Nazi ritual' reports spark more patrols* (2019), https://www.bbc.co.uk/news/uk-england-oxfordshire-49313179 [accessed 19 November 2022]; The British Pilgrimage Trust, *The Ridgeway* (2022), https://britishpilgrimage.org/portfolio/the-ridgeway/ [accessed 20 November 2022].

8   Émile Durkheim, *The Elementary Forms of Religious Life,* trans. by Carol Cosman (Oxford: Oxford University Press, 2001[1912]).

9   Durkheim, *Forms,* p.314.

10   Lynn Badia, 'Theorizing the Social: Émile Durkheim's Theory of Force and Energy', *Cultural Studies,* 30:6 (2016), 969–1000.

11   Badia, 'Theorizing the Social', pp.982–6.

12   Badia, 'Theorizing the Social', p.982.

13   Robert J. Wallis and Jenny Blain, 'Sites, Sacredness, and Stories: Interactions of Archaeology and Contemporary Paganism', *Folklore,* 114:3 (2003), 307–21(p.318).

14   Durkheim, *Forms,* p.164.

15   Foucault, 'Of Other Spaces', *Diacritics,* 16:1 (1986), pp.22–27 (p.23).

16   Foucault, 'Of Other Spaces', p.25.

17   Barbara Bender, *Stonehenge: Making Space* (Oxford/New York: Berg, 1998).

18   Nicola Whyte, 'Senses of Place, Senses of Time: Landscape History from a British Perspective', *Landscape Research,* 40:8 (2015), pp.925–38.

19   Christopher Tilley and Kate Cameron-Daum, *An Anthropology of Landscape: The Extraordinary in the Ordinary,* (London: UCL Press, 2017), p.5.

20   Tilley and Cameron-Daum, *An Anthropology of Landscape,* pp.7–10.

21   Tilley and Cameron-Daum, *An Anthropology of Landscape,* p.5.

22   Tim Ingold, 'The Temporality of the Landscape', *World Archaeology,* 25:2 (1993), 152–74 (pp.158–59).

23   Ingold, 'The Temporality of the Landscape', p.159.

24   Tim Ingold, *Lines: A Brief History,* (London/New York: Routledge, 2007), p.85.

25   Tilley and Cameron-Daum, 'An Anthropology of Landscape', p. viii; Ingold, 'The Temporality of the Landscape', p.152.

26   Ingold, 'The Temporality of the Landscape', p.152.

27   Whyte, 'Senses of Place, Senses of Time', p.936; Christopher Tilley, *Landscape in the Longue Duree: A History and Theory of Pebbles in a Pebbled Heathland Landscape,* (London: UCL Press, 2017), p.7.

28 Whyte, 'Senses of Place, Senses of Time', p.927.
29 Ingold, *Lines*, p.91.
30 Tilley, *A Phenomenology of Landscape*, p.28.
31 Foucault, 'Of Other Spaces', p.26.
32 Foucault, 'Of Other Spaces', p.26.
33 Bender, *Stonehenge*, p.100.
34 English Heritage, 'Research and Sources for Wayland's Smithy', https://www.english-heritage.org.uk/visit/places/waylands-smithy/history/research-and-sources/ [accessed 2 January 2023].
35 Whittle et al,. 'Once in a Lifetime', pp.104, 117.
36 Whittle et al., 'Once in a Lifetime', p.104.
37 Whittle et al., 'Once in a Lifetime', p.107.
38 Whittle et al., 'Once in a Lifetime', p.114.
39 Whittle et al., 'Once in a Lifetime', pp.104, 114.
40 Whittle et al., 'Once in a Lifetime', pp.108, 115.
41 Whittle et al., 'Once in a Lifetime', p.119.
42 Hutton, 'Romano-British Reuse of Prehistoric Ritual Sites', 13–15; Gosden and Lock, 'Prehistoric Histories', p.9.
43 Hutton, 'Romano-British Reuse of Prehistoric Ritual Sites', p.16.
44 Hutton, 'Romano-British Reuse of Prehistoric Ritual Sites', pp.10–11; Ann Woodward, *Shrines & Sacrifice*, (London: B.T. Batsford/English Heritage, 1992), p.28.
45 Hutton, 'Romano-British Reuse of Prehistoric Ritual Sites', p.16; Gosden and Lock, 'Prehistoric Histories', p.6.
46 Joshua Pollard, 'The Uffington White Horse Geo-glyph as Sun-horse', *Antiquity*, 91:356 (2017), 406–20 (p.418); British Library, *Cotton Claudius B. VI*, ff.40v-41r (Sawyer S564), https://esawyer.lib.cam.ac.uk/charter/564.html [accessed 3 January 2023].
47 Whyte, 'Senses of Place, Senses of Time', p.931.
48 Whyte, 'Senses of Place, Senses of Time', p.931.
49 *Völundarkviða*, pp.101–8.
50 L.V. Grinsell, 'Wayland the Smith and his Relatives: A Legend and Its Topography', *Folklore*, 102:2 (1991), pp.235–36 (p.235).
51 *Deor*, https://oepoetryfacsimile.org.
52 Tilley, 'A Phenomenology of Landscape', p.18.
53 Thomas Wright, 'On the Legend of Weland the Smith', *Archaeologia*, 32:2 (1847), pp.315–24 (p.324).
54 Tilley, 'A Phenomenology of Landscape', p.31.
55 Tilley, 'A Phenomenology of Landscape', p.15.
56 Foucault, 'Of Other Spaces', p.24.
57 Ingold, 'The Temporality of the Landscape', p.155.
58 Bender, *Stonehenge*, p.131.
59 Bender, *Stonehenge*, p.98.
60 Ingold, *Lines*, p.3.
61 Tilley, *A Phenomenology of Landscape*, p.204.
62 From sound recording made by the author at Wayland's Smithy, 21 December 2022.
63 Wallis and Blain, 'Sites, Sacredness, and Stories', p.310.
64 Wallis and Blain, 'Sites, Sacredness, and Stories', pp.308, 310.
65 From sound recording made by the author at Wayland's Smithy, 21 December 2022.
66 Wallis and Blain, 'Sites, Sacredness, and Stories', p.310.
67 Houlbrook, 'The Penny's Dropped', p.178.

68 Wallis and Blain, 'Sites, Sacredness, and Stories', p.318.
69 Wallis and Blain, 'Sites, Sacredness, and Stories', pp.310, 316.
70 Tilley, *A Phenomenology of Landscape*, p.204.
71 Badia, 'Theorizing the Social', p.982.
72 Hayley Dixon, 'Neo-Nazis use National Trust sites to launch 'English resistance' - Far-Right fanatics perform masked torchlit rituals and carve swastikas on trees to 'take back' ancient land', *The Telegraph*, 10 August 2019, p.7.
73 Bender, *Stonehenge*, p.98.
74 Durkheim, *Forms*, p.322.
75 Gosden and Lock, 'Prehistoric Histories', p.6.

4

AN UNEXPECTED PILGRIMAGE TO SEOUL'S NAMSAN MOUNTAIN

Holly McNiven

The aim of this chapter is to consider whether sacred space is a human construct or a natural phenomenon in the specific context of a personal ethnographic account of one of South Korea's most famous mountains– Namsan. From 2019 to 2020 I lived in Seoul and during my time living there I had an unexpected experience with Namsan ('Southern Mountain') – one of the most central peaks in the city, marked by the iconic Namsan Tower. On 8 March 2020 I had set out from my house and went for a stroll which unintentionally turned into a full day 'pilgrimage' through the city and up to the top of Namsan. My interpretation of 'pilgrimage' here reflects Justine Digance's modern definition of pilgrimage as 'undertaking a journey that is redolent with meaning'.[1] I kept a diary and took photographs to record my experience which I used as primary sources in this chapter. Drawing from contrasting theories on sacred space, from Émile Durkheim's socio-culturally constructed idea of sacred places to Mircea Eliade's spontaneous 'hierophanies', which had the sacred existing outside human consciousness, I will retrospectively analyse my experience with the mountain to consider to what extent my encounter with the 'sacred' was humanly constructed or naturally occurring.[2] Additionally, theories in phenomenology as considered by Tim Ingold and Christopher Tilley will be investigated in the context of my experience. I will first explore the journey to Namsan and how this impacted any feelings I had of 'sacredness'; secondly, I will discuss the idea of centredness and Namsan as an *axis mundi*; and finally, I will investigate my experience as an example of a 'hierophany'.

One of the core conundrums in the field of sacred geography is on the nature of 'sacredness' itself. Do human beings create sacred spaces or are we mere witnesses to a natural phenomenon that would exist with or without us? French sociologist Émile Durkheim argued for the former as he believed that societies and cultures were the fundamental creators of sacred places.[3] Sacred space for him was inherently impermanent and could only maintain its 'sacredness' as long as people continued to participate in the holiness of the place, separating and distinguishing it from 'profane' (unholy) space.[4] Durkheim theorised that this distinction between what was considered sacred and profane formed part of the 'collective consciousness', where people developed their understanding of the world through the collective effervescence of religious beliefs and cultural norms.[5] For Durkheim, the holiness of a given place was directly subject to human action and belief.[6] There would be no extraordinary places without humanity creating and maintaining them. Belden C. Lane agreed with this theory, stating that 'Sacred place is ordinary place, ritually made extraordinary'.[7]

In contrast, historian of religion Mircea Eliade believed the nature of sacred space went deeper than just human belief and societal norms. He developed his theory of sacred space around the concept of 'hierophany' (a manifestation of the sacred), whereby people encounter the sacredness of a given location through a 'revelation of an absolute reality, opposed to the nonreality of the vast surrounding expanse'.[8] Utilising the Durkheimian sacred-profane dichotomy (although Eliade never referenced Durkheim), Eliade observed that, for the spiritual participant, sacred space 'allows the world to be constituted, because it reveals the fixed point, the central axis for all future orientation'.[9] Thus, Eliadean sacred space provided a central point around which people and cultures could orientate and structure themselves. Eliade built his theory of hierophany around Rudolf Otto's earlier notion of the 'numinous'– experiences of the divine that could invoke terror, awe, or serenity.[10] Sites of hierophany were not person dependent for Eliade as he suggested that the emotional and/or physical response that a sacred place could provoke was evidence of a permanent underlying reality of sacredness.[11] Lane noted another adage that more accurately portrays the Eliadean view of sacred space, 'Sacred place is not chosen, it chooses'.[12] Here, sites of sacredness are seen as autonomous or even beings in their own right with their own agency. Paul Devereux stated '"otherworlds" of spirit and mind meet' at holy places, purporting a more Eliadean interpretation of sacred geography.[13] Often some of the most notable of these revered sites are places situated in high places, particularly mountains.

Christopher Tilley wrote about the subjectivity of experiencing high places, noting that mountains in particular are 'always in motion'.[14] No two people will experience a mountain in the same way, for as Tilley pointed out, 'mountains will always be different according to how we approach them… and the impact that directionality and the process of ascent… have on us'.[15] Scholar of sacred mountains Edwin Bernbaum has pointed out that mountains often are associated with the liminal and spiritual dimensions of human life as, among other reasons, they are places of great height that reach up into the heavens (both symbolically and physically), providing dramatic sites of inspiration and revelation.[16] They can be subject to sacralisation as centres of religious reflection, aesthetic beauty and places of pilgrimage and travel.[17] Tim Ingold theorised that all life is lived through lines and movement through the landscape, writing that 'the knowledge we have of our surroundings is forged in the very course of our moving through them, in the passage from place to place'.[18] With this in mind, I will consider in my research how my movement through the landscape of Seoul and Namsan contributed to any feelings I had of 'sacredness' and whether the sacredness of a place changes by the travel required. Additionally, I will explore Durkheimian themes of the sacred as socio-culturally driven, in addition to more Eliadean concepts of sacred places as hierophanies.

Methodology

The primary source for my research was my diary entries for that day and pictures I took during my journey, thus helping me to place my experience in the wider context of Durkheimian socially-derived sacred places and Eliadean hierophanies. Monique Hennink, Inge Hutter and Ajay Bailey pointed out that qualitative research is undertaken to 'understand behaviour, beliefs, opinions and emotions' from the unique viewpoint of the person who experienced the phenomena being studied.[19] Furthermore, David Abram stressed the value of phenomenological research in understanding the connection between humanity and the environment, as qualitative research can counter 'the modern assumption of a single, wholly determinable, objective reality'.[20] As I am the subject of this qualitative inquiry, I approached my primary sources as critically as possible as to avoid biasing the ethnographic data. By taking a qualitative phenomenological approach to the question of whether sacred space is a social construct or a natural phenomenon, I was able to use my experience as a case study and investigate more critically the meaning that I attributed to the journey and the mountain, considering both the socio-cultural and more spiritual dimensions of the study of sacred geography.

I am currently twenty-six years old, but at the time of my experience with Namsan I was twenty-four and I had been living in Korea for about eight months. I was working as an English teacher there and was under a lot of pressure from my job at the time. I am from Edinburgh in Scotland, but I have a family connection to Korea through my grandad who fought in the war there in the 1950s. He used to tell me stories about Korea when I was a little girl, and I was always fascinated by the place through my connection to him.

Findings and Discussion

Before I discuss my personal experience with Namsan, it is worth noting that the mountain has a long history of sacred associations. Shamanic artifacts and megalithic monuments have been found from the first century BCE and the mountain was considered sacred by the ancient Silla people and early Buddhists who adopted the site in the sixth century CE.[21] In 2000 Namsan was designated a UNESCO World Heritage Site with its forests protected under the National Park Law.[22] It is so integral to Korean history, identity and culture that the mountain is even mentioned by name in the national anthem 'Aegukga'.[23] However, this was not information that I knew when I set out for a walk one day and found myself climbing the mountain. Indeed, I was aware of the popularity of the site as a tourist destination and the iconic imagery of Namsan Tower used in almost all 'Visit Korea' posters and advertisements, but as a foreigner in Korea the mountain did not hold the same sense of national pride and identity for me as it may do for the Korean people. Nevertheless, my experience with Namsan had a profound impact on me and my own sense of belonging. The very journey itself was transformative and therapeutic in a time of my life that I had found very difficult and stressful.

The Journey

On Sunday 8 March 2020, I had woken up in the morning and decided I was going to go on a walk, stating in my diary that 'I felt like today was a good day for getting lost'.[24] I had been inundated with work and stress from school at the time and I wanted a day to myself where I did not have to think about anything. I had no destination in mind when I left my house that morning and, as I wrote, 'I was leaving it all up to fate and I was just along for the journey'.[25] I headed east and walked down whatever path presented itself to me as I passed through new areas of the city. Claudio Aporta investigated this kind of wayfaring, where movement through the landscape is not destination-oriented but rather 'the wayfarer has to sustain himself, both perceptually and materially, through an active engagement with the country that opens up along his path'.[26] Ingold described this path of the wayfarer as a journey that has 'no beginning or end' and that 'while on the trail the wayfarer is always somewhere, yet every "somewhere" is on the way to somewhere else'.[27] As I found myself in new areas of Seoul that I had never been to before, I noted that 'I didn't feel lost, even though I didn't know where I was or where I was going to'.[28] I was 'somewhere', but I was on my way to somewhere else, I just did not know where that 'somewhere' might be.

Analysing my diary for this chapter, I have retrospectively attributed my journey through Seoul that day as a form of pilgrimage. Justine Digance offered a contemporary definition of pilgrimage as 'a journey redolent with meaning',[29] while Paul Devereux noted that pilgrimage offers the opportunity for self-realisation 'through preparations for and expectations of the journey, the mental and physical rigours and experiences of the travelling itself, and the liberation from normal everyday life'.[30] My journey through Seoul was certainly 'redolent with meaning' for me and the act of freedom in having no plans and no destination in mind felt extremely liberating as this state of mind was so far removed from my hectic everyday work life. As I was walking through the city, I noticed Namsan and its tower starting to appear in-between the buildings and skyscrapers (Fig. 1). I noted that 'I felt a tug pulling me' towards the mountain, so I decided in that moment to head in that direction.[31] I had to weave in and around buildings and side streets, but I eventually found myself at the National Korean War Memorial. This was the part of the journey for me that started to imbue my once casual stroll with 'meaning' and feelings of 'sacredness' as my grandad was a Korean war veteran and I felt in that moment a deep ancestral connection to the landscape. I wrote that 'I longed in that moment to bring him to that place' and that 'there was connection here to my family and my family history that I suddenly felt quite moved by'.[32] Here I was, alone on the other side of the world, yet I had found my grandad and I had found the thread that tied me to the landscape around me. It was in this moment of self-discovery that I saw Namsan peering down at me from above and I recounted that 'I was going to go up there and find out what she wanted from me' (Fig. 2).[33]

The journey up to Namsan took me through the busy district of Itaewon and up a steep forest path that threaded through the trees of the mountain. Tilley considered the propensity of mountains to be utilised as places for 'pilgrimage, religious contemplation, and aesthetic appreciation'.[34] He wrote that these could evoke 'emotional responses such as a feeling of being purified as one ascends, or notions of a heightened ascetic or religious insight'.[35] As I ascended the mountain I was captivated by the beautiful green of the forest and how Namsan Tower would occasionally appear through the leaves like a beacon calling out for me to follow (Fig. 3). By the time I had reached the peak, night had fallen and the path was lit up with lights leading me directly towards the tower. I felt exhausted and I wrote in my diary that 'I was sweaty', 'my feet were hurting', and that 'my lungs felt clogged and heavy with pollution'.[36] I did not feel a physical 'purification', rather the opposite – I felt quite unclean from the effort, but I had a deep sense of accomplishment and, through my connection to my grandad, a sense of belonging to the landscape.

Figure 1: Namsan mountain and Namsan Tower in the distance. 8th March 2020, Seoul, South Korea. Photo: Holly McNiven

Figure 2: Namsan mountain and Namsan Tower looking over National Korean War Memorial Museum. 8th March 2020, Seoul, South Korea. Photo: Holly McNiven

Figure 3: The view of Namsan Tower through the trees. 8th March 2020, Seoul, South Korea. Photo: Holly McNiven

Tilley noted that 'the visceral agency and power of the mountain itself' is 'mediated through an embodied kinesthetics in which it directly exerts its influence impinging on the muscles and sinews, the lungs and the heart'.[37] As evidenced in my diary, the physical strain of climbing Namsan certainly took both a physical and emotional toll on me. Frank Prendergast has commented on the emotional impact of ascending high places, stating that the experience is 'sharpened by the indefinable but conscious state of passing through metaphysical thresholds created in the mind'.[38] As I was ascending the mountain, I felt a sense of determination as well as a feeling of being unstoppable. I was going to reach the top of the mountain no matter what. Buddhist scholar Lama Govinda has commented on the magnetic power that the Himalayas hold for those attracted to climb the mountains there, stating that 'people are drawn to them from near and far… and… will undergo untold hardships and privations in their inexplicable urge to approach'.[39] My 'urge to approach' Namsan that day is something that has puzzled me since it happened, and the purpose of this chapter is to analyse as critically as possible whether I was drawn to Namsan by some sort of hierophanic call of sacredness or whether I was participating in a socio-cultural human-made sacredness.

Centredness

Tilley noted that 'mountains like other places *gather*', doing so in 'dramatic... ways because they are visible from afar, punctuate the skyline, and connect the earth to the heavens, acting as an *axis mundi* in relation to which people understand themselves'.[40] The concept of *axis mundi* ('world axis') was introduced by Eliade in the twentieth century and relates to what he described as the 'connection between Heaven and Earth'.[41] He wrote that 'every inhabited region, has a Centre... a place that is sacred above all'.[42] As discussed previously, Namsan certainly has historical evidence to support its status as an *axis mundi*, but also in the context of my modern day experience it was as if the roads and the infrastructure of the city itself had been designed to lead me to the mountain. I was fascinated by my own sense of space and time during my wayfaring, a feeling I described as being 'outside of time'.[43] I must have walked for hours and hours on end without stopping, yet it felt like I had been walking for both a short time and a long time. This paradoxical sense of timelessness was mentioned by J. Anna Estaroth in her fieldwork at Clava Cairns, where she noted feeling a 'temporal distortion... or time-lived-differently' when walking through the landscape.[44] Ingold echoed this sentiment, stating that the wayfarer 'moves with time'.[45] My movement through the city took me to Seoul's physical and cultural centre, punctuated by the eye-catching and iconic Namsan Tower.

Jon Cannon noted that there may be 'an important cross-fertilization between mountains and religious buildings', considering that both are 'architectonic forms, powerful, eye-catching, and high'.[46] While Namsan Tower itself is not an official religious monument or place of worship, people from far and wide flock to the site and uphold the tower as both a symbol for the city as well as a central pivot around which the city seems to grow.[47] Thomas Tweed referred to these kinds of places that are set apart or considered more special as 'differentiated spaces'.[48] Durkheim would consider this distinction between 'differentiated' and 'undifferentiated' space through the lens of what is socio-culturally deemed 'sacred' and 'profane'.[49] From this perspective, would I still have been drawn to Namsan if the tower had not been built there, earmarking the land as a 'differentiated' space separate from the 'profane' land around it? Durkheim would argue that the 'sacredness' of Namsan is upheld by the 'collective consciousness' of the society that ritually maintains the sanctity of the mountain.[50] By definition I was an outsider to Korea, but even as a foreigner I was aware of the mountain and Namsan Tower's symbolic significance to the country, in the same way the Statue of Liberty could be considered a cultural emblem of the USA. Lane considered sacred place to be 'storied place' where 'places become valued in proportion to the number and power of stories that are attached to them'.[51] I knew no stories or folklore of Namsan specifically when I lived in Seoul, but as a member of Korean society (if only temporary and as a foreigner) I would argue that I was participating in the sacredness of the mountain. As Lane pointed out, 'to experience a place as sacred is to participate'.[52] This aspect of my experience with Namsan implies a more Durkheimian understanding of sacred space as Lane reiterated with the proverb 'Sacred place is ordinary place, ritually made extraordinary'.[53] With this mindset, the tower was constructed on Namsan to pinpoint a sacred centre from which local people could orientate and structure their lives, cultures and societies.

The concept of symbolic world centres was discussed by Devereux, who noted that the world-centre idea has been so widespread throughout the world and throughout history because it is 'essentially the projection of human physiology and neuropsychology outwards onto the land'.[54] The human being is thus seen as an axis with 'four bodily directions... extended outwardly in the world-centre scheme'.[55] In the context of my encounter with Namsan, I wrote that the pull towards the mountain felt like 'I was going home'.[56] There was an inexplicable sense that I would be safe and find some sort of peace by reaching the top. It was not an overwhelming feeling but rather a pre-cognisant knowledge that this would be the case. Aristotle (384–322 BCE) theorised that place 'exerts a certain influence' (or a 'potency', as Peter Machamer translated) and that all organic and inorganic matter is drawn towards its 'proper place'.[57] Here, the 'potency' of place is seen to draw matter alike in its inherent nature towards its centre.[58] Once in its natural place, the body can rest and form a sense of unity and completeness; as Aristotle stated, 'the movement of each body to its own place is motion towards its own form'.[59] Edward Casey commented on this Aristotelian understanding of place, acknowledging that place is a 'unique and nonreducible feature of the physical world' and that place has 'its own inherent powers'.[60] This outlook on sacred space suggests that sacredness is immanent to the earth rather than humanly-constructed as Durkheim might argue. Namsan certainly had a 'potency' for me as I wrote how I felt drawn to the mountain and how I achieved a sense of calm from reaching the summit, despite the physical effort it took to walk such a long distance. If the sacredness of Namsan is innate to the place itself, this is suggestive that my experience could be described as an Eliadean 'hierophany'.

Hierophany

By the time I had reached the top of Namsan, night had fallen and as I approached Namsan Tower I came to realise how busy the place was. I saw a path descending down the mountain where there were much less people, so

I decided to walk in that direction. I wrote in my diary that I was 'skipping and singing to myself', feeling 'absolutely giddy' even though 'I didn't really know why'.[61] I contemplated that maybe 'it was the sense of freedom' or the 'achievement of walking for hours without a break' that was contributing to my overall sense of elation. Walking alone and away from the crowds I came across Namsan Park Southern Observatory that overlooks the city. It was here that I would argue I experienced what Rudolf Otto described as the 'numinous'– feelings provoked by the revelation of a divine essence,[62] a theory that Eliade utilised in the formulation of his concept of 'hierophany'.[63] I noted how I looked up at the night sky in that moment and found 'Venus looking lonely' in a 'polluted haze' (Fig. 4).[64] As an avid stargazer I should have felt disappointed by the absolute lack of stars, but I wrote contrarily that I was 'profoundly moved by it somehow'.[65] Bernbaum stated that 'the sacred does not simply present itself to our gaze: it reaches out to seize us in its searing grasp'.[66] Likewise, I felt 'seized' simultaneously by my place high up on the mountain and by the sudden realisation of my own existence in the wider universe. I wrote in my diary:

> It was that lonely point of light that called to me somehow and I felt completely imbedded in that precise moment in space and time. It was like 'Wow, I actually exist'. It felt like the stars had all been pulled down from their places in the heavens and were now below me. Or maybe I had climbed so high that I was above them now. I had an incredible sense of perspective... and I felt connected to the land and the sky and everything for a moment.[67]

If I consider this experience of the numinous to be a hierophany as per Eliadean thinking, this is suggestive, as per the axiom presented by Lane, that Namsan was not a sacred place *chosen* by myself, but rather that Namsan *chose* me.[68]

Echoing Eliade, Lane also stated that 'sacred place is necessarily more than a construction of the human imagination alone', suggesting that sacredness is not just a human creation as Durkheim claimed.[69] That being said, Lane acknowledged that the human imagination has a 'tendency to exaggerate or hyperbolize the wonder... of a given site', noting that 'the ordinary is projected beyond first appearances so as to be seen as the extraordinary'.[70] Durkheim discussed a similar phenomenon where people reach a state of effervescence – 'vital energies become overstimulated, passions more powerful, sensations stronger' – and that in those moments 'man does not recognize himself; he feels he is transformed, and so he transforms his surroundings'.[71] Durkheim said that when this experience of the sacred occurs the spiritual participant 'endows' the

Figure 4: The view of Venus from the Namsan Park Southern Observatory. 8th March 2020- Seoul, South Korea. Photo: Holly McNiven

place or the object 'with properties that they do not have, exceptional powers, virtues that the objects of ordinary experience do not possess'.[72] Thus, was my spiritual experience with Namsan solely a projection of my own imagination and will?

Ingold noted, 'the knowledge we have of our surroundings is forged in the very course of our moving through them', stating that wayfaring in particular is 'neither placeless nor place-bound but place-making'.[73] When I found myself in that moment on Namsan looking over the city I felt like I had found my place (or rather that I had forged a place for myself). I even wrote about how I was 'infatuated with the idea of planting myself there' and never leaving the moment of hierophany.[74] I felt connected and grounded to the world around me in a way I had not experienced as a foreigner in Korea before. Simone Weil wrote that 'to be rooted is perhaps the most important and least recognized need of the human soul'.[75] There is no doubt that I had been struggling to find my place in Seoul at the time and I often felt alienated from Korean culture by virtue of not only being a foreigner but being labelled as a foreigner wherever I went. Durkheim saw sacredness as something inherently social and shared by the collective mind of society.[76] By my own admission, I had felt disconnected from society prior to my 'pilgrimage' and the hierophany I experienced at Namsan, which would suggest a more Durkheimian socio-cultural connection between feelings of 'sacredness' and feelings of oneness with the social order and society.

Final Thoughts

Following the analysis of my encounter with Namsan, the question remains: Is sacred space a human construct or a natural phenomenon? Durkheim would suggest the former, as evidenced by Namsan's symbolic significance as part of the cultural identity and religious history of Korea.[77] The whole city itself appears to have been structured around the mountain as a place set apart from the surrounding 'profane' space, suggesting that Namsan has a socially-constructed sacredness by virtue of its symbolic and geographical centredness around which society has oriented and structured itself. From the analysis of my own ethnographic account of Namsan, I found evidence of a more Durkheimian relationship between my personal feelings of sacredness with Namsan and my social connection to the landscape and to Korea itself. My experience of finding an ancestral connection on my journey through my grandad and the Korean War Memorial, as well as the sense of belonging that connection invoked, arguably contributed significantly to my feelings of Namsan as a sacred space. Additionally, as I had travelled on foot, the physical and psychological effort to reach the summit, I have argued, factored into my sense of accomplishment and sacredness. As Tilley pointed out, 'high places' are 'frequently accredited with spiritual power, simply because they are often set apart from the routines of everyday life'.[78]

That being said, to reduce the sacredness of Namsan down to a mere social construction or figment of the human imagination feels disrespectful and dishonest even to myself, based on my own personal encounter with the mountain. Barry Lopez wrote that 'we will always be rewarded if we give the land credit for more than we imagine'.[79] Whether an Aristotelian pull to find my 'proper place' or a manifestation of some kind of divine power through Eliadean 'hierophany', I was drawn through the city and up towards Namsan by a force that I felt noteworthy enough to document in writing and with pictures (which is not normal behaviour for me). I attempted in my own words to recount my feelings of the experience at the time, and I struggled when writing my diary to articulate accurately the nature of the 'numinous', as it is something to be experienced in the moment rather than described retrospectively. Tilley remarked on the French artist Paul Cézanne's work in trying to capture the mountain Sainte-Victoire in painting, noting that Cézanne's attempts to represent the mountain on canvas brought about the realisation for him that 'representations whether they be in the form of images or words... are always partial, ambiguous, changing, perspectival, undertaken from a point of view, shaped, and being shaped'.[80] This is a realisation that I have come to accept when conducting and writing this chapter, as the primary sources I have drawn from are flat and two-dimensional in comparison to the reality of experiencing the hierophany for oneself.

Conclusion

The aim of this chapter was to consider whether sacred space is humanly-constructed or a natural phenomenon within the specific context of a personal ethnographic account of Namsan mountain in Seoul, South Korea. Using my diary entry and photographs I recorded at the time of my encounter with Namsan on 8 March 2020, I have critically analysed my phenomenological data through the lens of Émile Durkheim's idea of socially-derived sacred spaces and Mircea Eliade's concept of naturally-occurring sacred spaces. Furthermore, I have drawn from theorists such as Christopher Tilley and Tim Ingold to help place my experience within a phenomenological framework, particularly their work with mountains and wayfaring, respectively. In this chapter I have considered three main themes: first, my physical journey or 'pilgrimage' through Seoul and Namsan; secondly, the idea of Namsan as an *axis mundi* or world centre; and thirdly, my encounter with Namsan as a hierophany. My journey wayfaring through Seoul brought me inadvertently to the Korean War Memorial and up to the peak of Namsan where I had a numinous experience, being alone with the mountain and the surrounding land and skyscape. The physical and psychological effort it took to climb the mountain certainly had an impact on my feelings of accomplishment and the sacredness I felt towards the mountain. Additionally, I noted how finding the ancestral connection to my veteran grandad through the Memorial contributed to my overall sense of belonging and connection to the land and to Korean society as a whole. Durkheim would suggest that this is evidence that sacredness and society are synonymous, as human beings create the sacred through the 'collective consciousness' of their socio-cultural and religious frameworks. Namsan has a long history as a sacred mountain, as evidenced by megalithic monuments and artifacts found at the site, and it seems like Seoul has been built around the peak, using Namsan as an *axis mundi* around which the city has been structured and orientated. My path through the city led me directly to this central point and the Eliadean perspective would suggest that the inherent sacredness of the mountain itself was the autonomous force that pulled me towards itself. On the other hand, Durkheim might point out that the city was structured by human beings to maintain the sacredness of Namsan as separate from the surrounding profane space. Ultimately, whether it was my own imagination creating the sacredness of the mountain (as Durkheim might argue), evidence of an immanent sacred reality at Namsan (as Eliade might claim) or a combination of the two (as I have argued), my experience with the mountain that day was profoundly meaningful to me and provided me with a sense of belonging during a time when I needed it most. Whether the sacrality of Namsan was forged by human consciousness or merely detected by it, I would like to thank Namsan for providing me personally with a sacred space from which to find my place in the world.

Notes

1 Justine Digance, 'Religious and Secular Pilgrimage: Journeys Redolent with Meaning', in *Tourism, Religion and Spiritual Journeys*, ed. by D.J. Timothy and D.H. Olsen (London: Routledge, 2006), pp. 36-48 (p. 36).
2 Émile Durkheim, *The Elementary Forms of Religious Life*, trans. by Carol Cosman (Oxford: Oxford University Press, 2001), p. 11.; Mircea Eliade, *The Sacred and the Profane: The Nature of Religion*, trans. by Willard R. Trask (Orlando, FL: Harcourt, Inc., 1987), p. 21.
3 Karen E. Fields, 'Translator's Introduction: Religion as an Eminently Social Thing', in *The Elementary Forms of Religious Life*, ed. by Émile Durkheim, trans. by Karen E. Fields (New York: Free Press, 1995), pp. xvii-lxxiii (p. xlvi).
4 Durkheim, *Forms*, pp. 36-37.
5 Kenneth Smith, 'Durkheim's Other Writings on the Concept of the Collective Consciousness', in *Émile Durkheim and the Collective Consciousness of Society: A Study in Criminology*, ed. by Kenneth Smith (London and New York, NY: Anthem Press, 2014), pp. 30-35 (p. 34).
6 Durkheim, *Forms*, p. 11.
7 Belden C. Lane, *Landscapes of the Sacred: Geography and Narrative in American Spirituality*, Expanded Edition (Baltimore, MD: Johns Hopkins University Press, 2002), p. 19.
8 Eliade, *Sacred and Profane*, p. 21.
9 Eliade, *Sacred and Profane*, p. 21.
10 Eliade, *Sacred and Profane*, pp. 8-10.
11 Lane, *Landscapes*, p. 20.
12 Lane, *Landscapes*, p. 19.
13 Paul Devereux, *Sacred Geography: Deciphering Hidden Codes in the Landscape* (London: Gaia, 2010), p. 6.
14 Christopher Tilley, 'Foreword', in *Space, Place and Religious Landscapes: Living Mountains*, ed. by Darrelyn Gunzburg and Bernadette Brady (London: Bloomsbury Academic, 2020), pp. xiv-xviii (p. xv).
15 Tilley, p. xv.
16 Edwin Bernbaum, *Sacred Mountains of the World*, 2nd edn (Cambridge: Cambridge University Press, 2022), pp. 289-90.
17 Tilley, p. xviii.
18 Tim Ingold, *Lines: A Brief History* (London: Routledge, 2016), pp. 3, 91.
19 Monique Hennink, Inge Hutter and Ajay Bailey, *Qualitative Research Methods*, 2nd edn (London: SAGE Publications Ltd, 2020), pp. 10-11.

20   David Abram, *The Spell of the Sensuous: Perception and Language in the More-Than-Human World* (New York: Vintage Books, 1996), p. 31.
21   Gina Barnes, 'Buddhist Landscapes of East Asia', in *Archaeologies of Landscape: Contemporary Perspectives*, ed. by Wendy Ashmore and A. Bernard Knapp (Oxford: Blackwell Publishers Ltd, 1999), pp. 101-123 (pp. 109, 112); Robert Oppenheim, 'Kyŏngju Namsan: Heterotopia, Place-Agency, and Historiographic Leverage' in *Sitings: Critical Approaches to Korean Geography*, ed. by Timothy R. Tangherlini and Sallie Yea (Honolulu: University of Hawai'i Press, 2008), pp. 141-56 (pp. 141-43).
22   UNESCO World Heritage Convention, *Gyeongju Historic Areas* (2022) <https://whc.unesco.org/en/list/976/> [accessed 28 December 2022].
23   Rosie Pentreath, *What is South Korea's National Anthem, and What are the Lyrics?* <https://www.classicfm.com/discover-music/periods-genres/national-anthems/south-korea-aegukga-lyrics-english-translation/> [accessed 28 December 2022].
24   Holly McNiven, *Diary Entry*, 8th March 2020.
25   McNiven, *Diary*, 8th March 2020.
26   C. Aporta, 'Routes, Trials and Tracks: Trail Breaking Among the Inuit of Igloolik', *Études/Inuit/Studies*, 28.2 (2004), pp. 9-38 (p. 13).
27   Ingold, *Lines*, p. 85.
28   McNiven, *Diary*, 8th March 2020.
29   Digance, 'Religious and Secular Pilgrimage', p. 36.
30   Devereux, *Sacred Geography*, p. 52.
31   McNiven, *Diary*, 8th March 2020.
32   McNiven, *Diary*, 8th March 2020.
33   McNiven, *Diary*, 8th March 2020.
34   Tilley, p. xviii.
35   Tilley, p. xviii.
36   McNiven, *Diary*, 8th March 2020.
37   Tilley, p. xviii.
38   Frank Prendergast, 'The Archaeology of Height – Cultural Meaning in the Relativity of Irish Megalithic Tomb Siting', in *Space, Place and Religious Landscapes: Living Mountains*, ed. by Darrelyn Gunzburg and Bernadette Brady (London: Bloomsbury Academic, 2020), pp. 13-42 (p. 26).
39   Lama Anagarika Govinda, *The Way of the White Clouds*, 40th Anniversary Edition (London: Rider, 2006), p. 197.
40   Tilley, p. xviii.
41   Mircea Eliade, *Images and Symbols: Studies in Religious Symbolism*, trans. by Philip Mairet (Princeton: Princeton University Press, 1991), pp. 48-51.
42   Eliade, *Images and Symbols*, p. 39.
43   McNiven, *Diary*, 8th March 2020.
44   J. Anna Estaroth, 'How the Shadow of the Mountains Created Sacred Spaces in Early Bronze Age Scotland', in *Space, Place and Religious Landscapes: Living Mountains*, ed. by Darrelyn Gunzburg and Bernadette Brady (London: Bloomsbury Academic, 2020), pp. 43-67 (p. 54).
45   Ingold, *Lines*, p. 105.
46   Jon Cannon, 'Time and Place at Brentor: Exploring an Encounter with a 'Sacred Mountain"', in *Space, Place and Religious Landscapes: Living Mountains*, ed. by Darrelyn Gunzburg and Bernadette Brady (London: Bloomsbury Academic, 2020), pp. 71-98 (p. 74).
47   N Seoul Tower, *Overview* <http://www.nseoultower.co.kr/eng/global/intro.asp> [accessed 28 December 2022].

48 Thomas A. Tweed, 'Space', in *Key Terms in Material Religion*, ed. S. Brent Plate (London: Bloomsbury Academic, 2015), pp. 223-30 (p. 225).

49 Daniel L. Pals, 'Society as Sacred, Émile Durkheim', in *Eight Theories of Religion*, 2nd edn, ed. by Daniel L. Pals (New York, NY: Oxford University Press, 2006), pp. 85-117 (pp. 95-100, 112-13).

50 Fields, p. xliv, xlvi.

51 Lane, *Landscapes*, p. 15.

52 Lane, *Landscapes*, pp. 3-4.

53 Lane, *Landscapes*, p. 19.

54 Devereux, *Sacred Geography*, pp. 42, 48.

55 Devereux, *Sacred Geography*, p. 48.

56 McNiven, *Diary*, 8th March 2020.

57 R. P. Hardie and R. K. Gaye, 'Physics', in *Complete Works of Aristotle, Volume 1: The Revised Oxford Translation*, ed. by Jonathan Barnes (Princeton: Princeton University Press, 1984), pp. 315-446 (p. 355).

58 Peter K. Machamer, 'Aristotle on Natural Place and Natural Motion', *Isis*, 69.3 (1978), 377-87 (p. 378).

59 J. L. Stocks, 'On the Heavens', in *Complete Works of Aristotle, Volume 1: The Revised Oxford Translation*, ed. by Jonathan Barnes (Princeton: Princeton University Press, 1984), pp. 447-511 (p. 506).

60 Edward S. Casey, *The Fate of Place: A Philosophical History* (Berkeley, CA: University of California Press, 1998), pp. 70-71.

61 McNiven, *Diary*, 8th March 2020.

62 Rudolf Otto, *The Idea of the Holy: An Inquiry into the Non-Rational Factor in the Idea of the Divine and its Relation to the Rational*, trans. by John W. Harvey (London: Oxford University Press, 1958), pp. 5-7.

63 Eliade, *Sacred and Profane*, pp. 8-10.

64 McNiven, *Diary*, 8th March 2020.

65 McNiven, *Diary*, 8th March 2020.

66 Bernbaum, *Sacred Mountain*, p. 5.

67 McNiven, *Diary*, 8th March 2020.

68 Lane, *Landscapes*, p. 19.

69 Lane, *Landscapes*, p. 4.

70 Lane, *Landscapes*, p. 26.

71 Durkheim, *Forms*, p. 317.

72 Durkheim, *Forms*, p. 317.

73 Ingold, *Lines*, pp. 91, 104.

74 McNiven, *Diary*, 8th March 2020.

75 Simone Weil, *The Need for Roots: Prelude to a Declaration of Duties towards Mankind*, trans. by Arthur Wills (Taylor & Francis e-Library: Routledge, 2005), p. 40.

76 Fields, p. xliv.

77 Oppenheim, pp. 141-48.

78 Tilley, p. xviii.

79 Barry Lopez, *The Rediscovery of North America* (London: Vintage, 1990), cited in Devereux, *Sacred Geography*, p. 152.

80 Tilley, p. xvi.

5

WINDY BANK: A JOURNEY INTO A SECLUDED WOODLAND

Karen Hanson

The purpose of my research was to explore the concept of place attachment and how this leads to ideas of sacred places, and additionally, to determine if this this attachment was a human construct or a natural phenomenon of place. Jennifer Cross suggested that a number of people can attest to having an attachment to place and developing affectionate bonds to their surroundings; this will be explored through personal field work.[1] An area within a mature, deciduous Woodland Trust walk named Windy Bank in Culcheth, situated in the north-west of England, has provided a prime location to examine why attachment to place occurs. As well as considering work from key theorists regarding place attachment, my research is founded on my own frequent, phenomenological interaction with a specific section of woodland within Windy Bank that is located outside the established path and is often overlooked through being overgrown.

Previous research, such as that by Scannell and Gifford, has examined cultural and sociological models for place attachment using experimental evidence to investigate the relationship between causal experience and emotional bonds.[2] While their results – which suggest that place attachment does contribute to positive thinking and behaviour – were comparable to my personal experience, this methodology of experiential evidence did not, as Kuo and Margalit posit, represent 'deep-rooted attachments'.[3] In addition, Hernandez, Hidalgo, and Ruiz have asserted that 'the study of bonds between human and places has not been accompanied enough by advances in the theoretical and empirical aspects'.[4] Therefore, I will be exploring how my own intimate experience and behavioural patterns within what I deemed to be a sacred space, have resulted in a deep attachment to the place.

Methodology

The research paradigm for this chapter has drawn upon Tilley's phenomenological approach, which 'involves the understanding and description of things as they are experienced by a subject', albeit a 'subject' who interprets through the dichotomous states of 'Being and Being-in-the-world'.[5] Tilley believes that to 'understand a landscape truly it must be felt but to convey some of this feeling to others it has to be talked about, recounted, or written and depicted'.[6] By keeping a field journal and taking photographs, my research will be positioned within a self-narrative inquiry paradigm, postulated by Trahar to enable insight into the meanings that are ascribed to personal experiences; to examine the thoughts and emotions that told the story of my experience.[7]

According to Lane, 'sacred places, are, first of all, "storied" places' and by inquiring narratively into my lived experience in the secluded woodland, I was able to examine the human and social constructs that are embedded within my perceptions; what Kushner refers to 'as the tension between individualism and collectivism.'[8] Lane contends that adopting either a phenomenological or social view would omit the significance of the multi-faceted dimensions of place and therefore a 'multidimensional understanding' is required.[9] Subsequently, the interweaving phenomenological, cultural and ontological considerations that come from personal experience will be used to determine if attachment to place is a human construct, a human experience, or a construct that can be experienced.

As I will be using my own lived experience as a qualitative source of information within my research, it is relevant to give a brief outline that describes my values, beliefs and understanding of the world. I am a white, British woman, aged forty-seven. I have a twelve-year-old child and a background in teaching. Considering that this phenomenological research is based upon self-reflective and, consequently, subjective field notes, this has presented several obstacles concerning reflexive bias. Clandinin and Murphy believe that since field notes are by nature fluid, changing, partial and to do with the 'for now' nature of experience, they are consequently a relational phenomenon and are validated only by the participant for whom the lived experience is documented and explored.[10] To attempt overcoming the ontological limitations of lived experience, I adopted Husserl's notion of 'bracketing' my cognitive biases, which allowed me to step outside of my subjective interpretation of the experience and to suspend judgement.[11] This allowed me to perceive the landscape not only as a mental image but moreover as a fluid, constantly changing and alive experience.

Topography

Encounters that invoke an emotional response through the physical features of a landscape often result in an intimate attachment between person and place. According to Lane, the inward mood of the person and the external landscape are not antithetical states, being 'enmeshed within webs of environmental relations'.[12] This informs an understanding of the emotional connection with the perceived topography through a subjective discernment and interaction which influences the bodily response. In the same manner, Shepherd suggested that the physical topography of the mountain as perceived by sight becomes mere shadows, in the recognition that there is an attachment derived through a merging of the self and a recounting of the lived experience.[13] To elucidate this crossover between self and place, Gunzburg and Brady termed these 'moments of crossings' as 'conversations' and questioned whether this attachment to the mountain 'is constructed by people, intrinsic to the mountain... or a mutual endeavour.'[14] An embodied emotional response when interacting with the topography present can therefore engender a sacred lived experience through a connection of the inner self with the perceived physical landscape.

Contrary to an individual, emotional experience of place, a collective attachment to place ensures an inclusive connection within the social group. Durkheim understood that, while it was the social collective and need for social belonging that formed place attachment, it was the provoked emotional response that transferred the sentiment from mind to physical place or object, though still within the collective group.[15] Comparably, Mooney concluded that the physical, social, and emotional aspects of topography are entwined within the concept of place attachment and are needed to sustain further connection.[16] A sentimental response to place as a social construct can be questioned through an understanding that personal experiences are individual, internal responses rather than a collective interpretation. This emotional solidarity regarding place attachment was contested by Eliade, for whom sacred place – being the outward manifestation of the divine – is a hierophany, and exists apart from the need to be known and experienced.[17] Conversely, Tuan asserts that 'deeply loved places are not necessarily visible' and a connection only results from meeting the needs, aspirations, and functional patterns of the individual and collective.[18] This would suggest that an attachment to place and active engagement with the topographical features is derived not only from the individual level but also at the collective level.

Tuan termed the notion of 'topophilia' as a neologism to describe affectionate ties with the material environment, extending beyond a physical and spontaneous attachment to place by being rooted in the deeper responses of belonging and emotional reactions.[19] Literally meaning love of place, topophilia can be used when describing any place that brings joy, wonder and a positive mood. Brown, Altman, and Werner asserted that 'topophilia involves affective bonds from fleeting to enduring', thereby creating concrete, lasting and substantial bonds between person and place.[20] Likewise, Cross stresses the importance of sensory interaction with the physical landscape to form attachments.[21] Nonetheless, it can be considered that the social structure impacts how the individual perceives the physical world around them, how they interact with the topography, and how they value this interaction. Woldoff's research on neighbourhood place attachment suggests evidence to the contrary of Cross, that it is not the physical landscape that the person becomes attached to but rather the sense of community that is derived from the place on a social level.[22] In accordance with these findings, Cuba, and Hummon found in their research that while topography was undoubtedly a factor, place attachment was also influenced by the individuals' bonds and ties with their social group[23]. This suggests that the social group influences not only how and why the attachment is formed but, moreover, the outward expression of the connection.

When the physical topography presents in such a manner that anthropomorphic features can be perceived and worshipped, then deep attachment to place can be formed and experienced. When looking at the Hindu worship of 'the face of the goddess on the tree', Haberman noted how the simulacrum of eyes and face on the neem tree allowed for a deep, intimate connection.[24] Likewise, regarding simulacra, Devereux argued that 'by coming to see the landscape as it was to the ancestors, full of mythic imagery, spirits, and powers', the dormant consciousness can be expanded.[25] This expanding of consciousness can be perceived individually but also experienced and worshipped within the collective group. Comparably, in examining the role of stones as a topographical feature of place attachment, Janowski considered how animistic ontologies allow humans to interact with the landscape as another 'sentient mind'.[26] Levy-Bruhl terms this interaction with inanimate objects such as stones as 'participation', a mystic perception that perceives a conscious reality to collective representations of material culture.[27] Just as the anthropomorphic features within the landscape can embody mythical ancestors and spirits, a stone arrangement or distinct stone can manifest a mystical being with powers and qualities beyond the dense, physical rock.

Within certain indigenous and tribal groups, Knobloch found that the practice of breaking open pottery offerings on certain points of the landscape, 'represent a ritual activity that ended with the smashing and burying of ceremonial vessels'.[28] By choosing where to release the offering inside the smashed vessel, the ritual could therefore demonstrate the sacred quality that the native groups bestowed upon the landscape and topographical features. Budka proposed that, in Egypt, the smashing of pots in a landscape constituted votive offerings. These pots were broken on sacred ground which had been set apart by the group.[29] This Egyptian practice of pot breaking was also widespread in other cultures.

Knobloch observed that the Wari people of Brazil considered their ceremonial pots as 'too sacred to be ever used again' and were buried as offerings on chosen sites.[30] It was through the ritualistic practice of isolating certain places on the land to perform this Wari tradition that the physical ground was able to take on sacred qualities from the meaning and intention infused upon it. Korpisaari and Pärssinen further linked smashed vessels to Shamanic ceremonies and noted how the placing of the fragments upon the landscape would mark the place they were 'killed'.[31] The topographical landscape is thus ritually shaped by the interaction and intention of the people and through their offerings of material culture on chosen, sacred ground and this then creates a strong connection between the land and the group.

Ownership

A personal or social connection to place can give rise to issues around ownership and a possessive attachment to a particular space. Lane considered the nefarious attributes of 'possession of place as an end in itself' and recognised the need to 'question our cultural considerations' and the ecological implications of laying physical claim to the land of which we are attached.[32] Through needing to physically own and control a place, there can be a tendency to recognise only the needs of the individual or cultural group over the intrinsic needs of the land. In addition, Sundarum explored how connecting with the sense of place within a 'servicescape', a setting in which customer and seller interact based on user needs, such as a coffee shop, hotel, or educational setting.[33] Sundarum suggested that by connecting with the sense of place within a servicescape, this allowed respondents to exercise 'ownership of spaces and construct their own meanings and experiences'.[34] A personal interpretation of place through ownership that allows a subjective experience for the service user is comparable with Ackerman's conclusion that the visitors at Walden exhibited a 'possessive attachment' to the place, asserting that 'possession of sacred property can empower the owner'.[35] Though possessive bonding to a place can be felt individually or collectively, it is empowering for the perceiver to return to the site to ensure continued loyalty and attachment.

Evidence suggests that sacredness manifests in a chosen physical space, from a religious church to a pagan henge. Through an outward expression and designation of their sacred space, Tuan noted how the Navaho had 'a strong sense of the limits of their own ground – one that is bounded by the four sacred mountains'.[36] For the Navaho, the sense of the sacred defines the boundaries of their land ownership, thereby allowing the collective group to experience the divine within their chosen place. Tilley found that physiographic features within a landscape such as rock art and being near to water was fundamental in a clan claiming territory on a sacred site.[37] The significance of ancestral activities and myths permeate the landscape with a numinous quality, and this brings about an awareness of the demarcated boundaries that segregate the sacred place. Eliade believed that sacred space implied an 'irruption of the sacred that results in detaching a territory from the surrounding milieu', and by therefore secluding land through boundaries, the resulting place attachment ensures a bond and strong sense of ownership with the chosen, consecrated land.[38] Establishing territory on a sacred site, set apart from other land, would appear to fulfil psychological and physical needs regarding ownership and place attachment.

An enduring attachment to place that results in the qualities of ownership and possession often comes about through initial feelings of pleasure, connection, and sacred devotion. Ujang and Zakariya attributed a powerful sense of commitment, pride, sentiment, loyalty, and love of place 'in developing the sense of "ownership" and "territoriality" reflecting the self and group identity'.[39] Such commitment and pride can lead to environmentally responsible behaviour and a desire to maintain and improve the physical surroundings, whether human made or natural. This is supported by Altman and Low's understanding that self-identity is tied to place attachment, 'where an expression of our unique identity is made manifest in the material world'.[40] This may suggest that place identity can occur on account of place attachment and, consequently, the sentiments of possession and ownership would then ensue.

Attachment to place is not axiomatically limited to a permanent location, or to experiencing the social constructs of ownership and possession when interacting with the land. For Tuan, the sense of 'rootedness' that occurs with ownership is not necessarily tied to a permanent place; he noted how nomadic hunters and gatherers often displayed the strongest sentiment and attachment for place.[41] Comparably, Scannell and Gifford found that place attachment is 'not necessarily territorial although the two may overlap' and a connection to place 'can be expressed without an underlying purpose of control'.[42] Looking at behavioural traits associated with attachment and ownership of a favoured place, the use of possessive language as well as visual markers to physically claim a land are evident as indicators of psychological ownership. When considering the psychological reasoning behind place attachment and ownership, Kuo et al. found that 'tourists regard tourist destinations as "theirs" and even experience a psychological state of possessiveness towards their destination'.[43] Comparably, in terms of marking territory to demonstrate ownership and place attachment, Davis noted how the Moai placement on the island of Rapa Nui could be used to determine 'land right ownership' and ' to "visually" control limited resources'.[44]

The framework of ownership is therefore not necessarily tied to a territorial possession of a constant place as the nomadic hunters as well as modern day tourists, experienced ownership within a temporary setting. Physical markers, however, can define possession of a permanent location.

Contrary to the attribute of ownership when considering place attachment, a strong connection to the land can occur without a need to possess, change, or control. Regarding the Ojibwe, an indigenous people of North America and Canada, Hallowell observed that the Ojibwa ontology did not pertain to a sense of ownership. Rather, the Ojibwa language opened up the possibility of a cooperative and respectful relationship with the earth in which interaction was structured 'as if they were dealing with persons'.[45] The Ojibwa are animists, understanding that they shared their space with the interconnected landscape and seeing no distinction between the physical and spiritual world. This belief system is comparable to Ingold's findings regarding the Koyukon Indians of Alaska who must 'move *with* the forces of their surroundings, not attempting to control, master or fundamentally alter them'.[46] Consequently, a strong bond between the individual or collective group to the land does not always pertain to the societal construct of ownership or the need to visually mark the landscape.

Frequent Visits

Repeat visits to a particular place can allow bonding to occur which can help sustain personal and social satisfaction. Tilley's concept of a powerful, emotional attachment to place results only 'after making many visits to the same locales'.[47] Tilley further asserted that there is a strong need to return often and dwell within a place to fully experience the connection, to 'sense the feel and character of the land' and interact with the topography through 'personal spatial experiences'.[48] Only by personally interacting with the landscape and forming a deep connection can a desired intention to return be established and a profound sense of place attachment take place. By collecting data on the frequency of visits to the Pebblebed heathlands in East Devon, Tilley and Cameron-Daum found in their survey of fifty visitors, that 'sixty percent visit on a very regular basis indeed', suggesting that the personal, embodied experience might be a factor in their return.[49] Place bonding appears more common when visitors return often to connect and interact with a chosen site, suggesting that familiarity might be a contributing factor to place attachment.

By making repeated visits, a particular place can be set apart from profane places to become a meaningful social and personal space through the consequential intention bestowed upon it. In this way, Durkheim's understanding of sacred space as a human construct demonstrates how repeated visits can bring about deeper levels of engagement and feelings of ownership with a place through the collective meaning imbued upon the landscape.[50] Frequent visits also allow the enchantment and wisdom of a place to develop over time and, correspondingly, Lane noted the importance of frequenting a place regularly to view anew and discern more than previously seen.[51] When time is invested within a favourite place, this also helps to develop the bond between person and place. Hashemnezhad, Heidari and Hoseini found that if an individual spent a substantial amount of time in a specific place, their emotional feeling towards that place increases too (and) in that case, place attachment is created.[52] The act of setting apart a place through an emotional connection and the ritual of returning and interacting with the land imbue the space with sacred meaning which can manifest at an individual or collective level.

Place attachment also can be significantly affected by the intention to revisit after dark due to diurnal changes transforming previous memories and dismantling the familiar topography. Chevrier considered how the experience of the numinous is diminished once the nocturnal spaces are flooded with light.[53] Equally, Moyes asserted that, regarding the dark space within a sacred cave, it was the darkest and deepest recess that was regularly visited for ritual purposes.[54] Recognising the need for nocturnal places that preserve the darkness of the night from artificial light as well as respecting the profound silence of the late hour can bring about the need for frequents visits to experience the numinous quality of the dark, shadowy space.

Findings and Discussion

Within a secluded area at Windy Bank Woodland Trust in Culcheth, I was able to consider the research question which examines place attachment as a human construct or human experience. The findings from my field work, recorded in my field journal (and the extracts below, indicated three emerging themes through which I can discuss this subject: topography, a sense of ownership, and making frequent visits to the site.

Topography

> Field journal excerpt: 'Stepping over the interwoven trees creates this liminality. I am going from the dark, overgrown expanse of trees and shrubbery to the lighter expanse, from the populated to the unpopulated, the known to the unknown that is innate but seldom aware. Like the stepping over into other realms through a portal in which everyday life is suspended'.

Figure 1: The liminal threshold of two trees entwined (left) and the all-seeing Aspen tree (right). Photos Karent Hanson.

When Lane contended that 'sacred place can be tred upon without being entered', it opened up the possibility that, like Levy-Bruhl's assertion that participation is first felt before it is thought, there is a striking dichotomy between a participation which is innately experienced and one that manifests only in the mind.[55] The sense of a distinct, numinous quality was apparent upon entering this place and seemed to invite my participation with the physical topography present. The physical sight of entwined tree roots (Fig. 1) provided in my mind what Brady and Gunzburg term, a 'material metaphor of liminal space... from one realm to another'.[56] For Eliade, this threshold separates the sacred space from the profane, the numinous from the ordinary – which was what I experienced as two distinct states between the physical border of the crossed roots (Fig. 1).[57] Yet I must question whether it was the juxtaposition of the light and darkness or the exclusion of most walkers to this secluded area that caused me to differentiate the spaces between my perceived physical threshold.

As Durkheim posits, once over the threshold, 'the profane life must cease', and therefore, by isolating this secluded place, am I attaching a higher value to what is seen and felt there?[58] A social construction within that needs a separate experience without. Tilley considers that not all space is the same but shaped by 'differential densities of human experience, attachment, and involvement', and this was my experience that, once over the threshold, a numinous quality was perceived.[59] I cannot say, however, that my subjective and ontological bias was excluded.

> Field journal excerpt: *'We call this tree, the "all-seeing eye." The Aspen is a familiar face within this numinous place. To interact implies eye contact and approaching the tree encourages discourse. I can f e e l the eyes upon me whenever I enter, a wise and calm presence'*.

The concept of a tree having a personality and especially eyes, Haberman argued, is vital in Hindu worship and this was certainly true of my experience with the Aspen tree (Fig. 1).[60] I do not know why I ascribe the attributes of wisdom and emotion to the tree or why I can converse with tree beyond words, but I do feel that my behaviour towards the tree is natural and without the constraints of memory or society. This is my darshan with the tree and, as Haberman observes within his research, anthropomorphic features such as eyes make the connection easier.[61] My findings are comparable with Hallowell's research on the Ojibwan ontology that opens up the possibility that a person is not necessarily human and Haberman's understanding that sacred trees within the Hindu culture are living, sentient and animate beings with feelings and consciousness.[62] This personification of the tree enabled me to make sense of the intimate connection I felt as I identified qualities within the conscious tree that were also seen within myself. As Haberman contends, 'the human-nonhuman boundary is ontologically fluid'. [63]

Devereux asked that when one looks at the simulacrum of a face in a rock, is one merely seeing a rock? Devereux asked these questions to loosen the bonds of culturally trained perceptions and when I initially discern an eye within the Aspen (Fig. 1), I perceive through the lens of contemporary culture and my 'mythic filter is active'.[64] I cannot say for certain where the one perception ends and the other begins; to fully emerge within the raw experience, as Devereux suggested, I do not approach as a person. Dreaming also removes the filters.[65]

> Field journal excerpt: *'I dreamt of the tree last night. Not just this Aspen but hundreds of Aspens and hundreds of eyes, some were open, but most were shut. The carved-out tree was also in the dream and by entering, I entered into the soul of the tree - another world'*.

The meeting of topography and the dreamworld has been examined by Devereux, suggesting 'that dreamtime perception was particularly evident in the use of simulacra'.[66] It is interesting to note that my dream world did not exactly match the physical topography of the woodland, rather, as Devereux suggested, 'cultural set and setting have to be temporarily transcended'.[67] By dreaming of entering the tree (Fig. 2) as a portal, my dream mind was able to

Figure 2: The carved-out tree (left), the lines more visible in winter (centre) and less visible in summer (right). Photos: Karen Hanson

penetrate through the clouded filters of societal norms and constructs to see the potentiality 'with eyes wide open'.[68]

Devereux viewed this as 'reaching back to deep springs of consciousness' and whilst in mundane life, one tree is seen, the mythic filters are dormant in dream state, and I can decipher the true presence of the landscape.[69] Nan Shepherd additionally found that whilst waking out of outdoor sleep in a trance like state on the mountain, 'the eye sees what it didn't see before, or sees in a new way what it had already seen'.[70] Perhaps, so tainted and engrossed with social constructs and ideologies, my eyes only see, as Shepherd asserts, 'a pallid simulacrum of their reality'.[71]

> Field journal excerpt: *'There are lines, more visible in winter, that lead to this place. They seem to link the physical paths to the lineal doorway of another world. They present as mundane tracks through the landscape, barely noticeable, picked up more on intuition than the physical foot. Often, they are walked only by myself, my dog, and the deer. The lines are more noticeable in the beginning then quickly descend into a disordered jumble of brambles and row upon row of Himalayan Balsam before reaching the threshold'.*

When considering the Kenyan Gabbra camel herders taking their ritual pilgrimages at the holy mountain sites, Tilley observed that this was only undertaken using ascribed routes and approaching the mountain in the right way, hence why certain paths became overgrown through lack of use.[72] I noted in my field work that if I kept to the ascribed route, I am following in the footsteps of others, sharing their constructs, and understanding that this path is the correct and acceptable route to follow. To follow the overgrown path (Fig. 2) is to experience the unknown, the uncertain and the intuitive internal compass that guides the way. Tilley understood paths as concerned with 'establishing and maintaining social linkages and relationships between individuals (and) groups' and I found that only by leaving the familiar, tarmacked route to follow barely visible lines (Fig. 2) could I interact, experience, and explore a landscape that was intensely alive and fresh.[73] Only by this initial, solitary wandering could I experience the sacred within this area of woodland and, just as Lane encountered the divine after taking 'a less-travelled path', I also travelled beyond the profane reality experienced on the tarmacked path.[74]

To sum up this theme, Scannell and Gifford argued that 'attachment, obviously can also rest on the physical features of the place'[75] This was certainly my experience. In this way, place attraction appears as a human construct through my observation of the physical topography. It was my interaction with the physical features present, such as the entwined roots, the Aspen and the walking lines that allowed an experience of the sacred. By being aware of and moreover by removing my 'mythic filter' as Devereux suggested, I could look beyond the physical materiality of the topography and sense the presence of an intuitive, natural phenomena of the immanent landscape.[76]

Ownership

> Field journal excerpt: *'I feel very protective towards this place. I tidy up any litter that the wind has carelessly brought in. I notice new stone sculptures left or any re-arrangement of existing ones as well as the ceramic pots laid out as votive offerings at the roots of estimable trees. The landscape is not merely the background as I walk around, it is part of my story and therefore, part of me.*

Within their research, Kuo *et al.* found that the possessive pronouns used by tourists when describing a favourite holiday destination was indicative of a sense of ownership concerning 'their own exclusive and personal base' and the language used within my field journal is certainly indicative of this.[77] Like the visitors at Walden, as Ackerman found, who demonstrated a 'possessive attachment to 'their place', I also experienced this sense of ownership and possessiveness to this area of woodland.[78] Tuan refers to this state as 'rootedness', an identification 'with a particular locality,' and I can attest that the memory and strong impression that this place imbued within me developed into an identification with the place and protective behaviour. This in turn, developed into a sense of ownership.[79]

Scannell and Gifford, when discussing a tripartite system of place attachment, comment that a connection to place is 'not necessarily territorial, although the two may overlap' and 'can be expressed without an underlying purpose of control'.[80] This might assume that my sense of ownership regarding the place is beyond a natural, spontaneous experience and rather the manifestation of psychological and social attributes that are demonstrated in a need, as Lane suggested, of laying physical claim to the land.[81] My need to continually experience this place has resulted in the human constructs of possession and ownership, though these qualities brought out in me could, however, also signify the sacredness of the place.

> Field journal excerpt: *'The stones are not boundless lumps of inanimate material. They have contributed to how they are arranged, inviting the person to participate with them. The sacred space is demarcated by these mystic stones. They mark the territory. Set apart for a higher purpose'*.

Figure 3: Stone formation on a branch and broken ceramic pots at the base of a tree.
Photos: Karen Hanson

Though rocks may appear as inanimate objects to the Western perspective, to Ojibwan ontology, as Hallowell observed, rocks are 'capable of social relations' with humans.[82] Levy-Bruhl further considered how certain rocks seem to invite our participation in 'mystic union with the visible and invisible beings who have revealed their presence there'.[83] By adopting Levy-Bruhl's model of participatory consciousness, I could therefore ask if the stones presented themselves in such a way as to consciously engage with their formation. Just like when I rub an obsidian stone within my pocket to connect with its power to protect and ground, the stone formations I observe (Fig. 3) are alive, animate, and capable of forming relationships, but only to those who are open to the possibility. As Ingold stated, 'to individuals who belong to different intentional worlds, the same objects in the same physical surroundings may mean quite different things'.[84] Ingold further postulated that, 'culture furnishes the forms, nature the materials' in the superimposition of the one upon the other, and the perceptual lens of culture and psychology that I perceive the stone formations through, appear to signify the traits of ownership and possession.[85] As Janowski suggested, 'stone is a lens through which we can view and question our own ontologies'.[86]

Hallowell asserted that the Ojibwa language does not relate to ownership of the land, yet my possessive pronouns as noted by Kuo *et al.* are indicative of owning this area of woodland.[87] Lane, as well as Scannell and Gifford, examined the need to mark the land as a territorial behaviour and I noticed several stone formations (Fig. 3) when I first entered this sacred space that seemed to mark this area.[88] Just as Davis expressed the possibility that the Moai placement was located to visually represent land ownership, this would fit in with my perception that the stone formations mark the land as social constructs as well as being outward expressions of participating with the sacred space.[89] In addition, Levy-Bruhl observed how the indigenous people of New Zealand, 'often leaves his property in exposed places... to show that it is private'; therefore, this participation with the stone formations (Fig. 3) that I observed could indicate a marking of territory, just as boundary stones define the space within.[90] Yet my experience of the numinous, according to Eliade, would not pertain to the societal constructs of ownership – after all ,the sacred stone is not adored as a stone but as a 'symbol' that allows the individual to awaken, experience ,and transmute it into a spiritual act.[91] Through removing my 'mythic filter', as suggested by Devereux, I can move beyond the human constructs of possession and need for marking territory to realise, as Levy-Bruhl observed, that 'since the property is thus made "sacred" there is no need to defend it by external means'.[92]

Field journal excerpt: *'The pots are smashed, obviously not meant to be used again. Broken and cracked, they are moved and placed under different trees in a circular pattern, almost like a ritual'.*

Just as Lane asserts that a sacred place is ritually made extraordinary, I considered the ritual element of placing broken pots under certain trees (Fig. 3) and, consequently, the symbolic understanding that through being smashed, they cannot be used again.[93] I also found that Knobloch's understanding that the 'beautiful' Wari pots were smashed intentionally offered significant insight when I considered if the ornate pots I came across, no longer able to be used for their original intention, had been carried purposefully to this secluded woodland as a ritual.[94] Within ancient Egypt, Budka noted how the smashing of pots occurred at 'holy places' and I reflected on how the broken vessels did not appear on the tarmacked path.[95] I also drew upon the findings of Korpisaari and Pärssinen, who suggested that within Shamanic ceremonies, the intentionally smashed ceramic vessels were later placed within 'offering pits', as an explanation of why the broken pots were found at the base of a tree.[96] This could imply that the pots were smashed elsewhere and the remaining vessels transported to an 'offering site' within the woodland. By perceiving the smashed pots as ritualistic offerings within this sacred space and latent with ceremonial intent, this allows the vessels to take on an animistic quality, therefore entering the realm of Levy-Bruhl's 'mystic participation'.[97]

When examining this interaction between person and pottery, I drew on Sundarum's findings regarding attitudes of ownership towards servicescapes, ranging from self-expression, ideological turn and symbolic play, which mirror my findings that physical practices are outward expressions, used to 'stamp their imprint on place'.[98] By leaving behind their imprints on the landscape, I observed that the stones and pottery became the vessels that connected the internal, personal experience of the numinous with the social, external construct of the person. This fitted in with Ujang and Zakariya's assertion that 'developing the sense of "ownership" and "territoriality" reflect(ed) the self and group identity'.[99]

In summarising this theme, I found Lane's assertion that 'the sacred site speaks then with its own voice, even as that voice is heard by culturally conditioned ears' useful, and that it is my own perception that is 'inescapably' linked to sacredness and place.[100] It appears antithetical that I would regard a place I considered sacred as my own, the sense of ownership coming from a human construct which juxtaposes the numinous experience. My understanding of the animate stones signifying a marking of territory would also appear contrary to my experience of having a relationship with them. Yet, seen through my mythic filter, my limited vocabulary and my culturally conditioned worldview, the sacred connection I experienced cannot be separated from my pre-existing Western framework.

Frequent Visits

> Field journal excerpt: *'There is a compulsion to return, this is only a physical return for I feel that I do not even have to take one footstep to reach the essence of this sacred place. Even though I carry this place within, it is through the frequent visits that I make, that a renewal of both the material and the immaterial is experienced. A strong bond repeatedly draws me back to this place, a place I have made my own'.*

Though I did not visit daily, I did visit three or four times a week, which is in keeping with the frequency of visits Tilley and Cameron-Daum recorded in their research on the Pebblebed heathlands.[101] Amongst my own various reasons for frequently visiting this area of woodland, I identified with the potent adjectives used by visitors when attempting to elucidate their reason for visiting the Pebblebed heathlands and how the landscape 'acts like other' and is a place 'to achieve a different kind of experience'.[102] Like Tilley and Cameron-Daum's visitors to the heathlands, I also experienced the sacredness that erupted out of the landscape, and this resulted in an inner attraction to the place.

> Field journal excerpt: *'There is the same rush of anticipation as I leave the main path and follow the familiar, overgrown track down to the ever-waiting threshold. I resist the temptation to have expectations and label all that I see. I just observe. Each visit brings a new discernment, a new wonder and understanding that I hadn't seen before'.*

When examining my frequent re-engagement with the woodland that aroused an emotional response, I regarded Ujang and Zakariya's findings that 'the special feeling towards a particular place (is) associated with elements of attraction, frequency of visits and understanding'.[103] By maintaining this affection through regular visits, I sustained place attraction and experience the sense of sacredness present. Tuan examined the concept of returning to place in terms of familiarity and a renewal through the 'familiar haven' within, which I certainly experienced when walking the familiar lines and crossing the threshold to what I experienced as a 'renewal of both the material and the immaterial'.[104]

Hashemnezhad, Heidari and Hoseini found that 'place attachment took place when people experienced powerful, long periods of time in that place', and I found that, with frequent visits, memories were developed and the reflection time within these memories served to increase my place attachment.[105] This could also be a factor in why I dreamt of this woodland. Observing that 'each visit brings a new discernment, a new wonder and understanding', fits in with Lane's understanding that each return visit should not be viewed as a return to a 'magical, imagined past where the landscape once pulsed with energy' but rather to experience afresh and without the 'dull predictability' of human constructs.[106] The numinous experience was fresh despite frequent visits to the landscape and further appeared as a natural phenomenon in which I was also a participant.

> Field journal excerpt: *'The night-time visits expand my awareness to the numinous quality found here. Only by coming here often in the daytime, do I know where to tread until I reach the liminal threshold of the entwined trees. The landscape looks different now, black, grey, and white replace the usual palette of colours that the daylight brings. In the dark, the veil between worlds appears thinner, more ethereal. I can't rely on sight here even with a torch and moonlight. I have to sense the familiar way.'*

My nocturnal visits were frequent, especially as the winter months push in and the dichotomous polarities of light and darkness, the visible and the invisible, the seen and the unseen, were apparent. Being a diurnal creature, my frequent visits occur mostly in daylight and with the company of others on the main

Figure 4: The carved-out tree, lines and the liminal threshold at night. Photos: Karen Hanson.

path. The experience of a night-time visit was powerful, as physical sight is constricted and therefore, uncertainty and foreboding can be felt. This drew upon Chevrier's findings regarding nocturnal visits to Catholic sacred places, in which the experience of the numinous was diminished once the nocturnal spaces are flooded with light.[107] Chevrier further considered that 'nocturnal ritual activities create new landscapes and new sights, based on the balance between light and dark' and this fitted in with my observations that 'the landscape looks different'.[108] (Fig. 4).

I found that the darkness added an 'ethereal' dimension to my frequent visits here, and that the 'veil between worlds appears thinner'. This was comparable to Moyes' assertion that the dark space within a sacred place was regularly used for ritual purposes, therefore allowing a crossing to the spiritual underworld.[109] In an earlier field journal entry, I noted that 'the carved-out tree was in the dream and by entering, I entered into the soul of the tree - another world'. At night, and with no torch or moonlight, there is only the dark space (Fig. 4) that Moyes proposed is the crossing to the spiritual underworld.[110] I felt the sacred quality when entering the tree during the day but much more heightened after dusk.

In closing this theme, I found, as Tilley suggested, that frequent visits 'become biographic encounters' and that present encounters are shaped by past memories and experiences of previous visits.[111] These are Inherent human constructs that mould the current visit. Regardless of seeing the landscape illuminated in the day or as dark shadows after dusk, the inner experience of the sacred was present with each frequent visit. My encounter with the carved-out tree during the day and at night further suggests the possibility that the experience moves beyond the construct of pre-existing beliefs and memories.

Conclusion

To conclude, the intention of this research project was to explore the concept of place attachment and from that attachment place becoming sacred, as being a human construct. By keeping a field journal to record and reflect upon my experience within the secluded area of woodland, I was able to examine my findings through a phenomenological and socio-cultural lens and compare them with prior work concerning place attachment. Over the course of conducting this research, I found that several enigmatic events such as the dream, personification of topographic features and night visits became commonplace and demonstrated the spatial relationship between the inner and outer realities of my perceptions. These events were experienced as mystical and coming from other realms of consciousness beyond the modification of behaviour and thinking that societal and cultural constructs have imposed.

I noticed that at times my behaviour and my actions were automatic, innate, and seemed to be 'driven' by something within the environment, while at other times, my thoughts and actions appeared rigid and from the mind. Yet both these paradigms of reality – the construct and the experience, are inexplicably intertwined and cannot be isolated when explaining place attachment. Whilst taking reflexive concerns into consideration regarding bias and assumptions, my emotion-laden experiences were clearly fundamental in understanding place attachment. I found that I cannot leave myself behind and be fully present with the landscape. I can only reconcile that within me which is sacred and that which is moulded through the social constructs of the collective. Since I have used an autoethnographic method to focus on my own individual experience, it would be interesting to repeat this research using the same heuristic lens to further explore the subjective experience of others within a similar landscape.

Notes

1 Jennifer Cross, 'Processes of Place Attachment: An Interactional Framework', *Symbolic Interaction*, vol. 38, no. 4 (2015), p. 574.

2 Leila Scannell and Robert Gifford, *The Psychology of Place Attachment: A Tripartite Organizing Framework*, cited in *Environmental Psychology: Principles and Practice* (Optimal Books, 2014), pp. 274–76.

3 Scannell and Gifford, *The Psychology of Place Attachment*, pp. 274–75; Alexander Kuo and Yotam Margalit, ' Measuring Individual Identity: Experimental Evidence', *Comparative Politics* 44, no. 4 (2012), p. 474.

4 Bernardo Hernández, M. Carmen Hidalgo and Cristina Ruiz, *Theoretical and methodological aspects of research on place attachment*, cited in *Place Attachment: Advances in Theory, Methods, and Applications*, eds. Lynne Manzo, Patrick Devine-Wright (London: Routledge, 2020), p. 95.

5 Christopher Tilley, *A Phenomenology of Landscape: Places, Paths and Monuments* (Oxford, 1994), p. 12.

6 Tilley, *A Phenomenology of Landscape*, p. 31.

7 Sheila Trahar, 'Beyond the Story Itself: Narrative Inquiry and Autoethnography in Intercultural Research in Higher Education', *Forum Qualitative Sozialforschung Forum: Qualitative Social Research* 10(1) (2009), p. 2.

8 Beldon C. Lane, *Landscapes of the Sacred: Geography and Narrative in American Spirituality* (The John Hopkins University Press, 2002), p. 59; S Kushner, *Personalising Evaluation* (London: Sage, 2000), p. 12.

9 Lane, *Landscapes of the Sacred*, pp. 42–45.

10 Jean D. Clandinin and Shaun M. Murphy, 'Relational Ontological Commitments in Narrative Research', *Educational Researcher*, vol. 38, no. 8 (2009), p. 601.

11 Edmund Husserl, *Ideas Pertaining to a Pure Phenomenology and to a Phenomenological Philosophy*, trans. F. Kersten (Dordrecht: Kluwer Academic Publisher:, 1983), p. 135.

12 Lane, *Landscapes of the Sacred*, p. 53.

13 Nan Shepherd, *The Living Mountain: A Celebration of the Cairngorm Mountains of Scotland* (Edinburgh: Canongate, 2011), pp. 8, 15.

14 Darrelyn Gunzburg and Bernadette Brady, *Space, Place and Religious Landscapes: Living Mountains* (London: Bloomsbury, 2020), pp. 1–2.
15 Emile Durkheim, *The Rules of Sociological Method,* ed. Steven Lakes, trans. W. D. Halls (The Free Press, 1982), pp. 4, 143–4; Emile Durkheim, *The Elementary Forms of Religious Life,* trans. J. W. Swain (London: Allen & Unwin Ltd., 1915), pp. 119–20.
16 Patrick Mooney, 'The Physical and Social Aspects of Place Attachment: Their Role in Self-Sustaining Communities', *TOPOS,* vol. 2 (2009), pp. 28–31.
17 Mircea Eliade, *The Sacred and the Profane: The Nature of Religion* (Harcourt and Brace, 1957), pp. 9, 11, 22, 26.
18 Yi-Fu Tuan, *Space and Place: The Perspective of Experience* (The University of Minnesota Press, 2001), pp. 161–78.
19 Yi Fu Tuan, *Topophilia: A Study of Environmental Perceptions, Attitudes and Values* (New York: Columbia University Press, 1990), pp. 93, 214.
20 Barbara B. Brown, Irwin Altman and Carol M. Werner, *Place Attachment* (International Encyclopaedia of Housing and Home, 2012), p. 1.
21 Jennifer Eileen Cross, 'Processes of Place Attachment: An Interactional Framework', *Symbolic Interaction,* 2015), pp. 9–12.
22 R. A. Woldoff, 'The Effects of Local Stressors on Neighbourhood Attachment', *Social Forces,* 81, (1) (2002), pp. 88–116.
23 Lee Cuba and David M. Hummon, 'A Place to Call Home: Identification with Dwelling, Community and Region', *The Sociological Quarterly,* vol. 34, no. 1 (1993), pp. 126–7.
24 David L. Haberman, *Faces of the Goddess* in *People Trees: Worship of Trees in Northern India* (Oxford Academic: New York, 2013), p. 152.
25 Paul Devereux, 'Dreamscapes, Topography, Mind and the Power of Simulacra in Ancient and Traditional Societies', *International Journal of Transpersonal Studies* 32 (1) (2013), p. 61.
26 Monica Janowski, 'Stones Alive! An Exploration of the Relationship between Humans and Stone in Southeast Asia', *Journal of the Humanities and Social Sciences of Southeast Asia and Oceania,* vol. 176, no. 1 (2020), p. 105.
27 Lucien Levy-Bruhl, *How Natives Think,* trans. Lilian A. Clare,(Routledge, 1926), p. 304.
28 Patricia J. Knobloch, 'Wari Ritual Power at Conchopata: An Interpretation of Anadenanthera Colubrina Iconography', *Latin American Antiquity* 11 (2000), pp. 388–89.
29 Julia Budka, *Egyptian Impact on Pot-Breaking Ceremonies at El-Kurru? A Re-Examination* (British Museum Publications on Egypt and Sudan, 2014), p. 646.
30 Knobloch, *Wari Ritual Power at Conchopata,* pp. 388–89.
31 Antti Korpisaari and Martti Pärssinen, *Pariti: The Ceremonial Tiwana Ku Pottery of an Island in Lake Titicaca,* (Helsinki: Academia Scientiarum Fennica, 2011), pp. 90, 125, 154.
32 Lane, *Landscapes of the Sacred,* p. 241.
33 Usha Sundarum, *Theorising Place as Practiced Object of Consumption: A Street Ethnographic Story,* (Unpublished doctoral thesis, University of Exeter, 2016), p. 37.
34 Sundarum, *Theorising Place,* p. 37.
35 Joy Whiteley Ackerman, *Walden: A Sacred Geography* (Unpublished doctoral thesis, University of New England, 2005), pp. 137, 173–5, 295.
36 Tuan, *Topophilia,* p. 69.
37 Tilley, *A Phenomenology of Landscape,* p. 48.
38 Mircea Eliade, *The Sacred and the Profane: The Nature of Religion* (Harcourt and Brace, 1957), p. 26.

39 Norsidah Ujang and Khalilah Zakariya, 'Place Attachment and the Value of Place in the Life of the Users', *Procedia: Social and Behavioural Sciences*, 168 (2015), p. 377.
40 Irwin Altman and Setha M. Low, *Place Attachment* (New York and London: Plenum Press, 1992), p. 109.
41 Tuan, *Topophilia*, p. 156.
42 Scannell and Gifford, *The Psychology of Place Attachment*, p. 4.
43 Hui-Ming Kuo, Jung-Yao Su, Cheng-Hua Wang, Pinyapat Kiatsakared and Kuan-Yuo Chen, Place *Attachment and Environmentally Responsible Behaviour: The Mediating Role of Destination Psychological Ownership,* (Sustainability 2021), pp. 3–5.
44 Annie Rischard Davis, 'The Cultural Property Conundrum: The Case for a Nationalistic Approach and Repatriation of the Moai to the Rapa Nui', *American Indian Law Review*, vol. 44, no. 2 (2019), footnote 31, p. 337.
45 Alfred Irving Hallowell, *Ojibwa Ontology, Behaviour and World View*, in *Culture in History*, ed. Stanley Diamond (New York: Columbia University Press, 1975) pp. 19–50.
46 Tim Ingold, *The Perception of the Environment: Essays on Livelihood, Dwelling and Skill* (London and New York: Routledge, 2000), p. 54.
47 Tilley, *A Phenomenology of Landscape*, p. 75.
48 Tilley, *A Phenomenology of Landscape*, p. 74.
49 Christopher Tilley and Kate Cameron-Daum, *An Anthropology of Landscape: The Extraordinary in the Ordinary* (London: UCL Press, 2017), pp. 165–6, 174.
50 Durkheim, *The Elementary Forms of Religious Life*, p. 342; Durkheim, *The Elementary Forms of Religious Life: A New Translation*, p. xivii.
51 Lane, *Landscapes of the Sacred*, p. 11.
52 Hashem Hashemnezhad, Ali Akbar Heidari and Parisa Mohammad Hoseini, '"Sense of Place" and "Place Attachment"', *International Journal of Architecture and Urban Development*, 3 (2013), p. 11.
53 Marie-Hélène Chevrier, 'Nocturnal Ritual Activities in Tourist Development of Pilgrimage Cities', *Journal of Policy Research in Tourism, Leisure and Events*, vol. 11, no. 3 (2019), p. 17.
54 Holley Moyes, *Sacred Darkness: A Global Perspective on the Ritual Use of Caves* (University Press of Colorado, 2012), p. 7.
55 Lane, *Landscapes of the Sacred*, p. 19; Levy-Bruhl, *The Notebooks on Primitive Mentality*, pp. 2–3.
56 Gunzburg and Brady, *Space, Place and Religious Landscapes*, p. 2.
57 Eliade, *The Sacred and the Profane*, p. 125.
58 Durkheim, *The Elementary Forms of Religious Life*, pp. 121–22, 133.
59 Tilley, *A Phenomenology of Landscape*, p. 11.
60 Haberman, *Faces of the Goddess* in *People Trees*, p. 152.
61 Haberman, *Faces of the Goddess* in *People Trees*, pp. 153–56.
62 Hallowell, *Ojibwa Ontology*, pp. 154–55; Haberman, *Faces of the Goddess* in *People Trees*, pp. 153–56.
63 Haberman, *Faces of the Goddess* in *People Trees*, p. 155.
64 Devereux, *Dreamscapes, Topography, Mind and the Power of Simulacra*, p. 60.
65 Devereux, *Dreamscapes, Topography, Mind and the Power of Simulacra*, pp. 59–61.
66 Devereux, *Dreamscapes, Topography, Mind and the Power of Simulacra*, p. 51.
67 Devereux. Dreamscapes, Topography, Mind *and the Power of Simulacra*, p. 61.
68 Devereux, *Dreamscapes, Topography, Mind and the Power of Simulacra*, p. 61.
69 Devereux, *Dreamscapes, Topography, Mind and the Power of Simulacra*, pp. 60–61.
70 Shepherd, *The Living Mountain*, pp. 88–98.
71 Shepherd, *The Living Mountain*, p. 1.

72   Tilley, *A Phenomenology of Landscape*, pp. 28–30.
73   Tilley, *A Phenomenology of Landscape*, p.30.
74   Lane, *Landscapes of the Sacred*, p. 17.
75   Scannell and Gifford, *The Psychology of Place Attachment*, p. 5.
76   Devereux, *Dreamscapes, Topography, Mind and the Power of Simulacra*, p. 60.
77   Kuo and others, Place *Attachment and Environmentally Responsible Behaviour*, p. 3.
78   Ackerman, *Walden: A Sacred Geography*, pp. 137, 173–5, 295.
79   Tuan, *Space and Place*, p. 194.
80   Scannell and Gifford, *The Psychology of Place Attachment*, p. 4.
81   Lane, *Landscapes of the Sacred*, p. 241.
82   Hallowell, *Ojibwa Ontology*, p. 39.
83   Levy-Bruhl, *How Natives Think*, pp. 102–3.
84   Tim Ingold, *Hunting and Gathering as Ways of Perceiving the Environment* in Roy Ellen and Katsuyoshi Fukui, *Redefining Nature: Ecology, Culture and Domestication* (Oxford: Berg, 1996), p. 40.
85   Tim Ingold, 'Towards an Ecology of Materials', *Annual Review of Anthropology*, 41 (2012), p. 432.
86   Janowski, *Stones Alive*, p. 105.
87   Hallowell, *Ojibwa Ontology*, pp. --50; Kuo and others, Place *Attachment and Environmentally Responsible Behaviour*, p.3.
88   Lane, *Landscapes of the Sacred*, p. 241; Scannell and Gifford, *The Psychology of Place Attachment*, p. 4.
89   Davis, *The Cultural Property Conundrum*, p. 337.
90   Levy-Bruhl, *How Natives Think*, p. 302.
91   Eliade, *The Sacred and the Profane*, p. 211.
92   Devereux, *Dreamscapes, Topography, Mind and the Power of Simulacra*, p. 60; Levy-Bruhl, *How Natives Think*, p. 302.
93   Lane, *Landscapes of the Sacred*, p. 25.
94   Knobloch, *Wari Ritual Power at Conchopata*, p. 646–48.
95   Budka, *Egyptian Impact on Pot-Breaking Ceremonies*, p. 646.
96   Korpisaari and Pärssinen, *Pariti*, pp. 90, 125, 154.
97   Levy-Bruhl, *How Natives Think*, p. 304.
98   Sundarum, *Theorising Place*, pp. 40–1, 357.
99   Ujang and Zakariya, *Place Attachment*, pp. 377–78.
100 Lane, *Landscapes of the Sacred*, p. 56.
101 Tilley and Cameron-Daum, *An Anthropology of Landscape*, p. 166.
102 Tilley and Cameron-Daum, *An Anthropology of Landscape*, pp. 171–73.
103 Ujang and Zakariya, *Place Attachment*, pp. 375, 380.
104 Tuan, *Topophilia*, pp. 127-128.
105 Hashemnezhad, Heidari and Hoseini, *"Sense of Place"*, p. 10.
106 Lane, *Landscapes of the Sacred*, pp. 69, 226.
107 Chevrier, *Nocturnal Ritual Activities*, p. 17.
108 Chevrier, *Nocturnal Ritual Activities*, p. 8.
109 Moyes, *Sacred Darkness*, pp. 6–7.
110 Moyes, *Sacred Darkness*, pp. 6–7.
111 Tilley, *A Phenomenology of Landscape*, p. 27.

6

THE ART OF LISTENING TO STONES: ENCOUNTERING A JAPANESE GARDEN

Berna Lee 李映晴

A sacred place is a geographical phenomenon that gives meaning to existence, while 'feeling out of place' is something one encounters when not being present. To be able to connect with a place, presence is essential – one must actually 'be there', whether the place is considered to be a sacred one or an ordinary one. Martin Heidegger described the human experience of being as 'being there' (dasein),[1] a state of 'being-in-the-world' that is spatial and relational.[2] Heidegger's understanding of presence highlighted the interconnected relationship between the human realm and the natural realm (Heaven and Earth) that is also described in Daoist cosmology.[3] This idea opens up the inquiry to understand what constitutes the sacredness of a place and how presence – or 'being there' – becomes an anchor to knowing our placement in the world. The aim of the paper is to investigate if a sacred place can be an ordinary place, intentionally made extraordinary with presence, rituals, and myths. For the purpose of this paper, it is human experience that is explored and discussed, without the intention to exclude the possible experience of non-human living beings. Using a phenomenological approach as a methodology, the paper studies the Portland Japanese Garden in Portland, Oregon, as a sacred place in an attempt to understand the way the place came to impose itself on my consciousness.

Portland Japanese Garden is situated on top of a hill in Washington Park in Portland, Oregon, in the United States. The land is located at the confluence of the Columbia and Willamette Rivers, and has been part of the traditional Indigenous Native Americans' homeland since time immemorial. Tribes included the Multnomah, Wasco, Cowlitz, Kathlamet, Clackamas, Bands of Chinook, Tualatin, Kalapuya, Molalla, and many more living along the Columbia River.[4] Since the 1800s, the land has been a city park, a golf course, and a zoo, prior to the founding of the Portland Japanese Garden in the 1960s. Initiated by Mayor Terry Schrunk and the Portland community, a collective effort was made to transform the place into the Portland Japanese Garden. The intention was to provide the local community with a garden of healing between the United States and Japan after WWII, building cultural understanding and connections through nature.[5] The Garden invited Japanese garden designer Professor Takuma Tono of Tokyo Agricultural University to work on the landscape. With the intention of the Garden in mind, Tono innovatively built the place by joining five separate gardens into one. Presenting a diverse style of traditional Japanese gardens in one place, the five gardens were linked intuitively by meandering streams and stone paths. The five gardens are the Flat Garden, the Strolling Pond Garden, the Tea Garden, the Sand and Stone Garden, and the Natural Garden. Constructed based on traditional Japanese garden-making philosophy, the Garden was built with the local topography in mind. Using local rocks and plant materials, the Garden developed in a secular way with influences of Shintoism and Buddhism, uniting the cultures of the two worlds. As a community, the Garden welcomes visitors from all walks of life across all ethnicities. Through the years, the place as a garden space developed into a community and a cultural centre. With their vision growing into a communal force, the Portland Japanese Garden initiative provided a sacred voice to the physical garden as well as resounding peace in nature to the world.

As one's embodied experience of a place is essential to understand the qualities and characteristics of a sacred place, my personal experience participating in the Portland Japanese Garden is the primary source of data for this paper. Through direct engagement with the correspondences and interactions moving through the landscape, the paper uses the first-hand perspective I personally lived through; as Edmund Husserl described, this lived perspective is an engine of intentionality in acts of consciousness.[6] The approach facilitates an understanding of how a sacred place is perceived by investigating the internal (presence) and external (rituals, myths, culture) dimensions of the human experience through its intricate dance with all living beings and natural forces in the place, meditating on the idea of an individual's participation and intention as a form of presence resonating through the garden space.

Sacred and Profane

The theory of the sacred and profane was discussed by Emile Durkheim and Mircea Eliade. Although they perceived these concepts differently, both theorists came to a similar conclusion that participation is necessary in the experience of a sacred place. This pair of terms – sacred and profane – is paralleled in the context of place with two Greek terms, *chora* and *topos*.[7] *Chora*, as described by Belden Lane, is a place that carries its own energy, having the power to 'summon its participants to a common dance, to a choreography'.[8] *Topos*, on the other hand, means topography, a neutral and measurable place. Durkheim's notion of a sacred space was a *chora* transformed from a *topos* by the participation of rituals or culture of a community. To Durkheim, all sacred space has a social origin, including religion – they were seen as communal experiences having shared practices, beliefs, and histories.[9] Therefore, anything that was expressed in society as a representation was considered to be sacred or described as 'the real'.[10] For Eliade, the sacred place also means *chora*, yet it is different from Durkheim's social approach. Eliade's sacred place embodies a supernatural force that breaks into the homogeneity of space, something he refers to as a hierophany.[11] The sacred place is a portal to the divine, activated by rituals to re-enact the 'return to origins'.[12] It speaks or resonates with those who participate to engage with it. Whether it is a social experience or a supernatural experience, both theories agree that participation creates sacredness or an extraordinary presence in a place.

Presence

To further investigate the quality of a sacred place and the moment of sacredness, one needs to understand the concept of presence and the nature of time within participation. The concept exists across cultures throughout history. The paper looks more deeply into the Japanese concept of space and time, *ma*, as well as known theories in the West. As Levy-Bruhl defined it, this nature of time is an event 'localized in space and time or better said, has its own space and time'.[13] Levy-Bruhl's argument supports that presence happens in the here and now, during the act of participation. One can see a glimpse of the breakdown of the concept of time in the Greek terms *chronos* and *kairos*. *Chronos* refers to a temporal boundary of chronological time. Aristotle referred *chronos* as the 'number of motion with respect to the before and after' (Physics, 219b IV. xi). *Kairos*, on the other hand, was described by Plato (Laws, 709b) as an occasion or a form of time that was perceived as an accomplished moment when the conditions are right. In theory, *chronos* time is quantitative while *kairos* time is a qualitative experience. Presence here occurs in *kairos*, an occasion made possible with participation that arises in a particular situation. In the context of the experience of a place, one can rely on participation to facilitate presence, transforming the profane or ordinary into the sacred. Participation becomes the key to transforming places from *topos* into *chora*.

Participation

The paper analyses the sacred place of the Portland Japanese Garden starting from the intention of its creators, identifying the characteristics of a sacred place perceived from within (interactions with all living beings and natural forces), from outside (rituals and culture), and from above (mythical narratives and supernatural).[14] Levy-Bruhl stated that participation is felt in the body before it becomes a thought.

He defined the process as a feature of the human mind that 'does not need to be the surety of visible casual order but rather on assemblages, of solidarities, of membership to a place of common participation'.[15] It is a Durkheimian way to sense any sacred elements that are perceived as larger than the self as a social expression. However, Levy-Bruhl did not deny the Eliade way of sacredness revealed by the supernatural. He believed that 'One lives in two worlds... the natural world, is imposed on them... the supernatural world, is revealed to them'.[16] Participation in both worlds was seen as a part of the phenomena of existence, and is independent and not in conflict with the logic of the mind. To understand the multidimensional experience of sacredness in the two worlds, the holistic approach of 'blurred genre' suggested by Clifford Geertz is used to identify how a sacred place is perceived.[17] As inspired by Belden Lane, his four axioms of identifying the landscape of the sacred are used for the experience.[18] While they are characteristics of a sacred place identified mainly for the geography and narrative in Indigenous Native American spirituality, all four would not necessarily be applicable to the subject matter – they are mainly used for reflections for the study. The four axioms are: 'sacred place is not chosen, it chooses'; 'sacred place is an ordinary place, ritually made extraordinary'; 'sacred place can be tred upon without being entered'; and 'the impulse of a sacred place is both centripetal and centrifugal, local and universal'.[19]

Figure 1: Google Satellite Map of Portland Japanese Garden with author's notes on the locations of the separate gardens visited[20]

The Sacred Intention

As a descendant from generations of Fengshui and astrology advisors since the Tang Dynasty (618–907 CE) in China, it has been my family's practice to assess different landscapes whenever we travel. While being a practitioner offers me techniques and knowledge, my experience as a Buddhist meditation instructor allows me to practice presence as I relate to my environment. This opened my curiosity to the understanding and embodiment of sacredness in different cultures across geography.

As a traveller from Hong Kong to Portland, I did not expect that the Portland Japanese Garden would leave a deep impression on my heart. I could not quite describe the sense of awe the first time, but with clear intention the second time, the garden truly spoke with me in its own unique voice. I visited the Garden twice, once in the summer of 2022, and the second in the following winter. The first time, without being aware of what I intended to experience, it felt as if the place 'chose me', as Lane described in his first axiom.[21] As I passed through the entrance of the Antique Gate at the foothill, the spatial experience of physically transitioning from the 'outside' shifted something inside of me. It was, as Eliade described, a sacred experience breaking into the homogeneity of a place.[22] I stepped into the magic of a *shakkei*, a Japanese term for 'borrowed scenery', a design concept originating in the Chinese *Garden Treatise Yuanye* in the seventeenth century.[23] It described garden-making that merges distant scenery into a part of the composition, obscuring spatial depth intentionally.[24] Through the gate, the garden path, secluded in the native forest, opened up, leading towards the main entrance on the top of the hill. A step at a time, the gentle slope and stairs prepped my breath and my mind as I climbed up like a respectful pilgrim. For a moment I thought I was in Kyoto, Japan. The mindfully curated and maintained path intuitively guided me as a ritual without words. Like falling in love, a surge of joy, excitement, and curiosity arose, and everything felt so pristine. The sacredness of our first encounter was powerful and spiritual, it was as Eliade described, a hierophany.

On my second visit, the feeling of the sacredness of the very same place changed its quality with an intention. From the striking feeling of a hierophany in the summer, the sense of awe shifted to an immense presence and peace. It was a rainy winter Saturday morning; the sky was grey, and the garden became more monotone. My sister and I arrived early; the day stretched out like a blank canvas of *chronos*. Starting the journey with the intention to embody the landscape, I took time to take in every moment felt in my body and my mind. As Levy-Bruhl described, when I moved through the natural world and interacted with my surroundings, the 'supernatural world' revealed itself in my sensations. I was immersed in the *shakkei* framed by each gate. As I was moving through, my sister surprised me with a comment echoing my own thoughts; she said, 'never have I looked back through the frame of the gate upon crossing'. It was in that moment that I realised my own participation interacts with others in the garden as I moved consciously from one scenery to another. Fresh discoveries were revealed to me through all senses. Everything became so much more alive. The touch of the mosses on the rocks, the sound of rain, and the aroma of the plants, my senses heightened. I was relating to the place and its topography as if I was having an intimate conversation with a friend. Presence was felt as joy of both moving through the place and in the serenity of being still. Sacredness presented itself as a deep sense of contentment and relational understanding.

Listening to Stones

One of the ways to engage or encounter presence is stillness, a concept contained in the Japanese notion of *ma*. *Ma* as a concept of space and time is also a core practice in Japanese garden making and means a pause or a space.[25] This pause pinpoints a *kairos* that makes a *chora* (physical or mental) possible. To me, it feels like a space that offers a state of potentiality that is similar to the formlessness described in the Daoist philosophy.[26] *Ma* is evoked through a variety of Japanese rituals and artistic practices. *Sakuteki*, the traditional way of Japanese garden design, is one of the ways rooted in *ma*.[27] Translated as 'setting stones' in the treatise *Sakuteki, Records on Garden Making,* in the eleventh century, it is a way to 'listen' to the power of a stone or natural material as a piece of *chora*. As a way to design, *Sakuteki* guides designers to 'listen' and interact with the materials throughout the process of garden making.[28] This resonates with the Japanese garden master Shiro Nakane who was a speaker at the 1996 International Symposium of Japanese Gardens. Nakane regarded the Portland Japanese Garden as a design response to the surrounding topography.[29] In the *Sakuteki* tradition, designers do not dictate the design plan. As intended, they start by interacting with a chosen piece of stone as a centre, and then 'following the request of the stone' to reveal the rest of the placements of the natural materials.[30] In the Portland Japanese Garden, the designer applied a similar process with local rocks and plant materials. This sensitive approach was not only a creative process but an act of listening and communicating with the natural world. One of the examples of 'listening' to stones was the Zagunis Castle Wall (Fig. 2). It is a Japanese medieval-style castle wall located at the west end of the main courtyard. The massive stone wall is stacked with large local Oregon blue granite stones. Placed by a communal area of benches, each stone was individually selected by the artist and shaped to be put in place. The touch of the hand-shaped stones evoked the thought of the mindful care given to the construction of the place. As Levy-Bruhl would agree, the intention instilled in each of the uniquely selected stones continues to interact with both humans and non-humans dwelling in the garden space.

Figure 2: Zagunis Castle Wall[31]

As a design application, *ma* can also be seen on a larger scale. The *karesansui* (Fig. 3) technique, 'dry-mountain-water', is a demonstration of space.[32] *Karesansui* is a seemingly empty space in the garden that represents an imaginary landscape. Composed of stones and white raked sand, they symbolize mountains and oceans, respectively, and were intentionally spread out in large areas in the design to engage participants for contemplation. This technique is similarly applied in Japanese and Chinese ink-wash paintings, leaving pieces of empty space for viewers to pause and create their own experiences as they participate in the art. Throughout the Portland Japanese Garden, *karesansui* is especially evident in the Flat Garden (Fig. 3) and the Sand and Stone Garden (Fig. 4). In both of the gardens, *ma* invokes the embodiment of the landscape with our inner interactions with the garden. Supported by Lane, the experience of the moment of sacred presence is, 'a situation to experience oneself simultaneously in a situation of *chora* and a moment of *kairos*'.[33] It allows the participants to correspond with the place and create meaning in their own experiences.

Figure 3: Summer view of the Flat Garden from the west veranda at the Garden Pavilion demonstrated with the Karesansui technique[34]

According to the garden docent, the three main elements of nature that form the body of the garden are the rocks, water and plants.[35] The significance of the three elements in Japanese garden making is that they are natural forms representing the lifeforce of the garden. Similar to the workings of a human body, rocks represent bones, water as water features or paths represent blood, and plants represent growth. The concept reminded me of the notion of *Fengshui* (風水) mentioned in verse 19 in *Zangshu*葬書, *the Book of Burial*, by Guo Pu 郭璞, written in the Han Dynasty (206–220 CE), China.[36] *Fengshui*, meaning 'wind and water' is a term in *Zangshu* that refers literally to the two natural forces of wind and water that express of the flow of *Qi*. Landscape is seen as a living manifestation of the lifeforce, *Qi*, and all myriad things or structures, including landscapes; all life forms grow or dissolve through the manifestation *Qi*. As I participated in the garden through the expressions of the three main elements of the Japanese garden, the lifeforce or the Qi within the landscape came alive, moving through my senses. Different compositions presented their unique body forms, each bringing their own textures, colours, smells, and shapes that expressed a unique world of its own. As already stated, Levy-Bruhl regarded that participation is first felt before it is thought.[37] *Qi* flows through the lush summer green to the bare 'bones' in the winter, and continued to move through my felt senses as I contemplated my similar body makeup and mortality in the changing of seasons.

As a sacred place, the presence of *ma* is evident in the Portland Japanese Garden from the design to the embodiment of the place. Each garden was created from an intention and a centre, each step was revealed through an epiphany of the materials. As Eliade would describe, the creation of the garden would be considered a sacred hierophany itself. The garden plan reveals itself as a participatory cosmos co-creating a web of harmonious interaction between living beings and the natural world. In the light of cosmogony and participation, the study will examine this concept through rituals practiced in the Garden.

Rituals

The rituals I encountered in the garden provided additional perspectives to the Eliadean and Durkheimian views. Eliade defined ritual as a practice to re-enact a cosmogony so as to achieve 'returns of origins',[38] while Durkheim defined ritual as a communal practice to fulfil the needs of human nature, and ultimately to help the individual transcend from death to rebirth.[39] In the Japanese garden, there are rituals practiced cyclically with the Eliadean concept of 'return of origins', while there are also ritual practices aligning with the Durkheimian concept of transcending life and death. My experience of the rituals in the garden extended its function further into the participation of our everyday lives. Some examples, such as *wabi sabi* and *haiku*, act as both an individual and a communal practice, utilising rituals as an agent of participation. Rituals engage participants to be present in the immediate surroundings and in their own lives. As stated earlier in Lane's suggested axioms, 'a sacred place is an ordinary place, ritually made extraordinary'.[40] The Portland Japanese Garden makes use of rituals in the design and maintenance of the garden to transform the land into a sacred place with presence. This was achieved by the mindfully curated and maintained space and paths – every aspect of the garden is a ritual, from tea meditation, breathing meditation, to walking through the garden. They are all different ways to engage participants to respond and interact with the environment by 'being there'. Therefore, each visit would feel like a ritual of its own. However, traditionally speaking, there are also a variety of historical rituals that are introduced and performed in the garden. The selected few I witnessed include the cyclical New Year ritual *shimenawa*, the day-to-day ritual *wabi sabi,* and the artistic ritual of *haiku*.

Shimenawa is a cyclical ritual. It is a rope hung on the inner roof of the main garden gate at the beginning of the New Year. These blessed ropes are made of twisted rice straws used for ritual purification. Placed at the gate, it indicates a border of sacred space, warding off evil spirits from entering the place. The supernatural element and the periodical re-enactment of the 'returns of origins' resonate with Eliade's theory. The use of the ritual announces the start of the new year as a sacred time and reveals the garden as a sacred place with a clear border separating the outside from the inside.

Besides annually repeated rituals, there are also a variety of rituals practised regularly in the garden. *Wabi sabi* is one of them. *Wabi sabi* is a constant practice seen in the technical maintenance of the garden. The concept resembles part of the Durkheimian ritual as a way to fulfil the nature of human needs. Unlike the Durkheimian ritual, *wabi sabi* is not limited to the idea of transcending death to rebirth, rather it celebrates the concept of aging. It is a way to appreciate the strength and beauty of things being impermanent. From a perspective of perfectly imperfect, there is beauty in all things including the broken, the worn out and the ordinary. Pondering on my own mortality in the garden during winter, *wabi sabi* was seen re-enacted everywhere throughout the place. An artistic example of *wabi sabi* that came to mind is the art of ceramic restoration or golden joinery – making use of gold lacquer to join and transcend broken pieces into new forms. Like golden joinery, the Portland Japanese Garden itself was reborn from the old Oregon Zoo. Parts of the zoo structure are still preserved and blend seamlessly into the environment, intentionally. Antique architecture and structures are well maintained but natural wear and tear is also allowed. As seen in the Sand and Stone Garden (Fig. 4), minor cracks are intentionally kept and seen as a part of the interactions of the environment. It is an aesthetic of *wabi sabi*, and a reminder that life and wonder exist in all things including the ordinary.

Figure 4: Winter view of the Sand and Stone Garden[41]

Japanese rituals are also very often practiced in various art forms for contemplation, one of them being the practice of *haiku*. Haiku is a practice of poetry writing that was also adopted as a Zen Buddhist tradition in Japanese culture. On an ordinary sidewalk close to the balcony overlooking the Sand and Stone Garden, a *haiku* was found on a stone among the lush evergreen. The intent of a *haiku*, as stated by Garry Eaton, is to present 'an illuminating moment or perception, a satori' that is experienced in nature.[42] With a limit of seventeen syllables, the short poem allows *ma* or space for imagination and the creation of meanings. This *haiku* was not placed on a pedestal or in a particular spotlight, it appeared as a part of the interactions that popped up in the garden. Written by the well-known Japanese poet Mizuhara Shuoshi (1892–1981) during his visit to the garden, the brief *haiku* gives a snapshot of his visit. It read,

> Here, miles from Japan
> I stand as if warmed by the
> Spring sunshine of home

The present tense reproduces the moment in time as if it was replaying again in the reader's presence. *Haiku* usually expresses a few images to ignite 'soft explosions' of universal truths in the reader's mind.[43] For this poem, the explosion for me was the idea of home as a 'place' that could be felt under the sun as sacredness. Eagleton described culture as 'what comes naturally, bred in the bone rather than conceived by the brain'.[44] Japanese rituals practised in the garden demonstrated the way Japanese culture is ingrained in the design and as a way of living. Through constant participation in rituals and the re-enactment of the practices, the garden has become a practice ground for presence, transforming itself from an ordinary place into a sacred place.

Myths

Myths can be referred to as something that may be true or otherwise. As characterized by Walter Burkert, a myth is a story that is repeatedly told and retold, 'Its themes are often surprisingly constant, in spite of the many fantastic and paradoxical motifs that shape its unmistakable identity; even though slightly distorted...'.[45] In the garden, myths are presented as a cultural phenomenon with *ma*, they appeared as allusions integrated into the architecture and garden arrangements. Without much explanation and with only minimal description, it is a way to allow the space to inspire engagement and the creation of meanings by the participants themselves. As Durkheim would argue, 'To exist at all, all communities must be imagined'.[46] *Ma* in the myths of the garden provides space for imagination, the formless *ma* activates a creative power contributing to the experience of participation. Just as Durkheim considered all forms of communities to be representations of 'the real',[47] the Portland Japanese Garden presents myths and rituals as forms of social expression, representing 'the real' by a shared cultural creative power that deems them to be sacred.[48] Ingvild Gilhus suggested that myths are themselves rituals that are intended to induce 'an altered state of consciousness'.[49] Mythical references at the garden therefore can evoke the sense of 'the real' through participation and imagination. In the garden, three spots spoke to me, one deeper than the other, through my physical sensations as well as my culturally conditioned ears. The experience guided me on a journey of interacting with the myths of Daoist cosmology and Chinese astrology. They were the Garden Pavilion, the Sapporo Lantern, and the Lower Pond of the Strolling Pond Garden.

The Garden Pavilion is a place elevated on the top of the hill. The traditional Japanese wooden architecture is surrounded by wide verandas all around. Soft natural light penetrates the main building through the large *shoji* (translucent paper) panels, giving it an ethereal ambience. On the west side lies the Flat Garden, while on the east, Mount Hood and the city can be seen on a clear day. With Japan being 'the land of the rising sun', the Mount Hood borrowed scenery to the east was designed to resemble the significance of Mount Fuji in Japan. The Flat Garden felt grounded and intimate, while the east side felt close to the sky. As Levy-Bruhl wrote, 'participation is created by *sympatheia*… reproducing one in order to create the other'.⁵⁰ The architecture and location correspond with cultural and cosmological symbols of Heaven and Earth. Sitting in the pavilion, the juxtaposition gave me a sense of dwelling between the two in Daoist cosmology. The idea expanded in more detail at the second location at the pagoda of the Sapporo Lantern. A pagoda is traditionally built with a religious function related to Buddhism; here in the garden, it symbolizes the friendship between Portland and Sapporo. The Pagoda is 18 feet tall with five tiers and nine rings on the top. As a form of *sympatheia*, the design symbolizes the five elements, Earth, Water, Fire, Wind, and Sky (Emptiness), and the nine rings of the heavens in Buddhism; a stone map of Sapporo is set in the front and a pair of asymmetrical sculptures on either side. The arrangement, like a riddle, seems to correspond further with Daoist cosmology, with hints of elemental force and duality. Filled with curiosity, the space engaged my attention to further contemplate what was beyond these sacred representations. Walking along, the path brought me to the third location of the Lower Pond, situated in the Strolling Pond Garden. According to the garden docent, the design inspiration was mainly from the royal palaces of China and the estates of aristocrats and feudal lords in the Edo Period (1603–1867 CE) in Japan.⁵¹ The setup here is secluded and more colourful than the rest of the garden. As the path moved towards the central pond, it finally showed me the main features of the area. They were the Heavenly Falls, the Zig-Zag bridge, and the stones patterning the northern constellation of Ursa Major. As imitation can manifest as a form of participation, as described by Levy-Bruhl, the setup reminded me of the astrological references of the ancient Chinese imperial centre. With a focus on the circumpolar position indicated by the Ursa Major, the ancient Chinese rulers would orient palaces and capital cities following this religiopolitical cosmology and astrology.⁵² They believed in a participatory cosmos and that there are cosmic correspondences with all earthly events. Mirroring the sky and orienting with the Ursa Major was one of the ways used to leverage celestial power, fulfilling the king's cosmo-magical role or the Mandate of Heaven.⁵³ The Lower Pond Garden here was revealed to me as a place that patterned the sky, with the Heavenly Falls being the Milky Way, the Zig-Zag Bridge as the constellation Cassiopeia, and Ursa Major in the middle. I was surprised by what I saw. Even though the official description of the Ursa Major stones was featured to honour the bear who lived in the old zoo, I realized my mind was interacting with the surroundings on its own as the garden spoke to me in a familiar voice.

Reflecting on Lane's first axiom – 'sacred place is not chosen, it chooses' – my experience here asserted that there was mythical power in a sacred place, yet the sacred place seems not to be the one who chooses. The revelation of sacredness was, as Levy-Bruhl suggested, the supernatural world revealing itself and one does not need to look further. From my experience with the garden, it is not the responsibility of the sacred place to choose whom to reveal its power to. Rather, it is the choice of the participant as to whether they want to choose to participate in the experience. Therefore, in the case of the gardens in discussion, the sacred place leans more on the third axiom by Lane, where presence is the key to interacting with a place. However, the quality of the 'voice' of the place we hear varies according to our own level of presence, cultural conditioning, and how all participants in the environment interact. Each of the three examples in the garden has its own voice as a sacred place. With *sympatheia* and imitations, the place was telling a myth as a form of ritual. Through the participation of humans and the environment, our own meanings were generated and presented themselves as a unique voice in the place.

Conclusion

The Portland Japanese Garden became a sacred place for me starting from within (presence). The voice of the garden changed from time to time and from one location to another according to my own state of presence. Through my personal participation in each garden space, my experience gradually deepened through my felt senses, communal rituals, myths, and the different cultures. They intertwined with each other as my body and my mind interacted and tangled with all the living beings and natural forces in the garden. Just like the art of *Sakuteki*, all natural material contains its own voice and each piece is a member of a *chora*. Like an orchestra, all living beings and natural forces in a place contribute to the unique voice of the *chora*. As one realizes all places contain their own texture of voice or power, this 'supernatural world', as Levy-Bruhl would describe, can be revealed to the participant when they choose to 'be there'. To my own felt sense, sacredness is of relational understanding, and presence was a way to access it.

My encounter with the garden suggested to me that the multidimensional perspectives of a sacred place, participation, and presence (internal) are the foundations in understanding a place, while rituals, myths, and culture (external) can act as agents to engage with the power of place. As Lane understood Heidegger's meaning of 'being there', 'place' places humanity in a way that 'it reveals the external bonds of his existence and at the same time, the depths of his freedom and reality'.[54] Like the participatory cosmos described in Daoist cosmology, with my experience of sacred placement in the world being rooted in space, time, and culture, these external bonds can also become practices to identify my own sacred place.

Through my participation in the garden, both the external and internal bonds contributed to identifying sacredness, and was felt in my body as 'being in place'. This study suggests that a sacred place requires a holistic perspective and openness to experience the interconnectedness of the whole of life. While the external bonds were agents for imagination and participation, yet without presence, the sacred place could only, as Lane stated, 'be tread on without being entered'.[55] The study reflects the idea that a sacred place is more than a geographical location; any ordinary place can potentially be transformed into an extraordinary one when one truly listens and participates with presence.

Notes

1. Martin Heidegger, *Being and Time*, first edition 1962 (Blackwell, 2001), pp. 172–73.
2. Heidegger, p. 148.
3. N. J. Girardot, 'Myth and Meaning in the "Tao Te Ching": Chapters 25 and 42', *History of Religions*, 16.4 (1977), pp. 294–328 (p. 319) <https://doi.org/10.1086/462770>.
4. Janet Eastman | The Oregonian/OregonLive, 'The Fascinating History of the Portland Japanese Garden', *Oregonlive*, 2017 <https://www.oregonlive.com/hg/2017/04/portland_japanese_garden_histo.html> [accessed 7 January 2023].
5. 'History -Portland Japanese Garden', *Portland Japanese Garden* <https://japanesegarden.org/about-portland-japanese-garden/history/> [accessed 7 January 2023].
6. Edmund Husserl, *Logical Investigations*, translated by J. N. Findlay from the second edition of Logische Untersuchungen, ed. Dermot Moran (London and New York: Routledge, 2001), II, p. 83.
7. Belden C. Lane, *Landscape of the Sacred: Geography and Narrative in American Spirituality, Expanded Edition* (John Hopkins University Press, 2002), p. 41.
8. Lane, p. 39.
9. Emile Durkheim, *The Elementary Forms of Religious Life* (New York: Free Press, 1995), p. xix.
10. Marco Orru and Amy Wang, 'Durkheim, Religion, and Buddhism', *Journal for the Scientific Study of Religion*, 31.1 (1992), p. 47 (p. 52) <https://doi.org/10.2307/1386831>.
11. Lane, p. 13.
12. Mircea Eliade, *Myth and Reality* (Harper & Row, 1975), pp. 34–35.
13. Lucien Levy-Bruhl, *The Notebooks on Primitive Mentality Trans. Peter Rivere* (San Francisco: Harper & Row Publishers, 1975), p. 59.
14. Lane, p. 59.
15. Levy-Bruhl, p. 59.
16. Levy-Bruhl, p. 139.
17. Clifford Geertz, 'Blurred Genres: The Refiguration of Social Thought', *THE AMERICAN SCHOLAR*, 49 (1980), pp. 165–79 (p. 165).
18. Lane, p. 19.
19. Lane, p. 19.
20. 'Google Satellite Map of Portland Japanese Garden with Author's Notes' (Google, 2023) <https://www.google.com/maps/@45.5184913,-122.7078983,81m/data=!3m1!1e3!5m1!1e4>.

21 Lane, p. 19.
22 Lane, p. 13.
23 Ji Cheng, *Yuanye: Craft of Gardens*, translated by Alison Hardie (Yale University Press, 1988).
24 Kevin Nute, *Place, Time and Being in Japanese Architecture* (Psychology Press, 2004), p. 21.
25 Marc Peter Keane, 'Listening to Stones', *A Journal of Place*, 4.1 (2008), pp. 9–11 (p. 11).
26 Girardot, p. 308.
27 Keane, p. 9.
28 Keane, p. 9.
29 Fran Nolan, 'Japanese Gardens - Places of Authenticity?', *Architecture Media Pty Ltd.*, 19.2 (1997), p. 186.
30 Keane, p. 9.
31 Berna Lee, *Winter Zagunis Wall at Portland Japanese Garden*, 2023.
32 Keane, p. 11.
33 Lane, p. 41.
34 Berna Lee, *Flat Garden at Portland Japanese Garden*, 2023.
35 Sonia Sabnis, 'Portland Japanese Garden Guided Tour' (Portland Japanese Garden, 2023).
36 Guo Pu, *A Translation of the Ancient Chinese: The Book of Burial (Zang Shu) Translated by Juwen Zhang and Guoliang Pu* (Edwin Mellen Press, 2004).
37 Levy-Bruhl, pp. 2–3.
38 Mircea Eliade, *Myth and Reality* (Harper & Row, 1975), p. 30.
39 Emile Durkheim, *The Elementary Forms of Religious Life* (New York: Free Press, 1995), p. 231.
40 Lane, p. 19.
41 Berna Lee, *Winter Sand and Stones Garden Portland Japanese Garden*, 2023.
42 Garry Eaton, 'A Note on Haiku', *Oxford University Press*, The Cambridge Quarterly, 38 (2009), pp. 328–37 (p. 328).
43 Eaton, p. 330.
44 Terry Eagleton, *The Idea of Culture* (Oxford, Blackwell, 2000), p. 28.
45 Walter Burkert, *Homo Necans The Anthropology of Ancient Greek Sacrificial Ritual and Myth* (University of California Press, 1986), pp. 31–32.
46 Durkheim, p. xxxiii.
47 Durkheim, p. xvii.
48 Orru and Wang, p. 52.
49 Ingvild Gilhus, 'Gnosticism: A Study in Liminal Symbolism', *Numen*, 1984.
50 Levy-Bruhl, p. 63.
51 Sonia Sabnis, 'Portland Japanese Garden Guided Tour' (2023).
52 David W. Pankenier, 'The Cosmic Center in Early China and Its Archaic Resonances', *Proceedings of the International Astronomical Union*, 7.S278 (2011), pp. 298–307 (pp. 298–304).
53 David W. Pankenier, 'The Cosmo-Political Background of Heaven's Mandate', *Early China*, 20 (1995), 121–76 (pp. 121–23).
54 Lane, p. 7.
55 Lane, p. 19.

7

GATHERINGS, LINES AND ENCHANTMENT: ENGAGEMENT WITH A BUTTERFLY GARDEN

Kim Corrall

My research explored the Butterfly Garden at The Living Desert in Palm Springs, California, asking whether it an inherently sacred space (for myself and the creatures that dwell there) or is its sacred nature a social construct? My enquiry was carried out through observation of the garden, which was captured in field notes, drawings, and photographs. This chapter sets out to review the results of the field study through the three main themes that emerged: the gathering of elements and life, the lines of life and movement, and the enchantment by the place through its song. Within these themes, the agency of the garden is explored, along with that of its human tenders, its non-human inhabitants and possible divine aspects.

Belden C. Lane pointed out that scholarship on the idea of sacred place has developed in three directions since the mid-twentieth century: ontological, cultural and phenomenological.[1] In the ontological view, as expressed by Mircea Eliade, space is largely unformed chaos out of which the sacred, in the form of 'hierophanies,' irrupts.[2] In contrast, from a cultural viewpoint, as detailed by Émile Durkheim, the sacred is a purely social construct that does not exist independent of mankind's projections.[3] In the phenomenological view, as summarized by Lane, 'places themselves participate in the perception that is made of them'.[4] This process was described by Sean Kane as the 'song of the place to itself, which humans overhear'.[5] Lane went on to contend that, taken individually, each of the aforementioned approaches is lacking, and that all three of them 'are necessary in grasping the diverse character of any particular place'.[6]

Thus, a field-based exploration of the potential sacred nature of the Butterfly Garden required a multi-faceted approach to acknowledge its many aspects: the possibility of the inherent sacredness of the land on which the garden was created, the human-constructed nature of the garden, the gathering of both human and non-human life in the garden, and the expression by the garden of its own story or song.

The research methodology for this study was observation in the field over the course of seven visits to the Butterfly Garden, ranging from one to four hours in length, and recorded through field notes, drawings, and photographs. My observations were grounded in a phenomenological approach, which Christopher Tilley described as 'the understanding and description of things as they are experienced by a subject', involving 'perception (seeing, hearing, touching), bodily actions and movements, and intentionality, emotion and awareness residing in systems of belief and decision-making, remembrance and evaluation'.[7] During my visits, I strove to reach a state of phenomenological 'participation' with the garden, explained by Lucien Levy-Bruhl as feeling the place or experience, rather than encumbering it with mental activity.[8] This method was chosen because, as Sarah Bell, Leslie Instone, and Kathleen Mee argued, 'by more directly championing non-human agency in research methods, we shift away from anthropocentric research practices to explore the interconnections between humans, non-humans and place'.[9] Phenomenological participation allowed me to expand my awareness out to the garden and its non-human elements and inhabitants and, thus, better explore these interconnections.

To reach a state of participation I employed various methods of engaging with place. I walked the land while listening to and feeling 'whatever emotions arise in you as you put your energy into the ground with the intention of "hearing" the feelings of the earth', as suggested by Mary Reynolds.[10] I also engaged by drawing parts of the garden, allowing the drawn lines to 'unfold in a way which responds to its immediate spatial and temporal milieu', as described by Ingold.[11] This enabled me to sink more deeply into the place and separate somewhat from conscious thought about it. While doing photography, I attempted to let the lines of the place travel off the edges of the frame to capture the paths of motion, both natural and constructed, and thus use photography more like a drawing tool than a full-frame capture, in keeping with Tim Ingold's statement that 'to observe is not so much to see "what is out there" as to *watch what is going on*'.[12] In this sense I used both my drawings and photographs to augment my written notes on what was going on at the time of observation. In all these activities, I focused on observing the entirety of the Butterfly Garden through the lens of 'engaged witnessing', defined by Bell, Instone, and Mee as taking 'into consideration the affective nature of encountering non-human actors, and involv[ing] a concerted attempt to accept or be open to being changed, moved, or shifted through paying close attention and becoming immersed in more-than-human engagements'.[13]

To learn about the creation of the Butterfly Garden and the preservation of the surrounding land managed by The Living Desert, I researched the history of the site as a whole. Previously published, detailed historical timelines of The

Living Desert were no longer available on their website, so I visited the Palm Desert Historical Society in Palm Desert, CA and went through the physical archives with its curator, Rochelle McCune. We found archived newspaper articles and old website printouts, which are referenced in the discussion of the site below. Additionally, I verified the timeline of the creation of the Butterfly Garden with the executive assistant of The Living Desert, Angela Woods.

An important aspect of this phenomenological study was my own reflexivity. As Kim Etherington states, we 'need to be aware of the personal, social and cultural contexts in which we live and work and to understand how these impact on the ways we interpret our world'.[14] As a white woman of British heritage, living and working on native Cahuilla land in the United States, I remained aware of how my background and worldviews influenced what I experienced in the field. I have lived in the southern California desert for over twenty years and have visited the Butterfly Garden regularly since its inception, often when I needed to find some peace in nature. I generally hold an animistic view of the world, described by Graham Harvey as recognizing 'that the world is full of persons, only some of which are human, and that life is always lived in relationship with others'.[15] In keeping with this view, I often observe and talk to plants, animals, rocks, the wind, and other fellow inhabitants of the world. The Butterfly Garden has been a sacred sanctuary to me as I have watched it develop and grow over time and I feel I have a close relationship with the place and its many dwellers, which affects how I interact with and experience them. In addition to the above considerations, I am an amateur nature photographer and have, over time, developed a methodology initially suggested by one of my teachers, Ralph Nordstrom, where I sit in the field in silent observation prior to picking up the camera. I noticed over the course of my fieldwork that this method, along with my longtime meditation practice, has honed my ability to be still and notice things that I otherwise might have missed in the midst of doing.

In the literature, there are several different theories regarding the sacred and the concept of sacred place. In the late 1800s, Durkheim, suggested that 'what defines the sacred is that the sacred is added to the real… and exists only in [one's] thoughts'.[16] Robert Trubshaw echoed this theory in the context of place when he stated that 'the significance of place has less to do with the physical landscape than with the meanings we give to that location'.[17] In this argument, that the sacred is purely a construct of the human mind and emotions, neither the place itself, nor its non-human inhabitants – nor any theological conception of spirit – have any agency in the creation of the sacred. Eliade, by contrast, asserted instead that the sacred emerged out of the profane, or the non-sacred, in the form of 'irruptions of hierophanies, which define a center point from which man can orient himself'.[18] In this model, agency is transferred onto a theological entity – the place and its non-human inhabitants have no real agency and humans can only recognize and honour the existing hierophany, not create it.

In both these Western academic models, the place itself, apart from human projection or divine emergence, is a spiritual blank canvas. Indeed, as Bernadette Brady pointed out, 'in contemporary thought landscapes tend to be viewed as inert in that it is a place upon which humanity acts'.[19] The phenomenological view rejects this notion by recognizing the importance of the interaction between the human body and its non-human surroundings. As Lane described, 'to be fully present to any locale is to recognize the reciprocity involved in touching and being touched by its particular array of rocks, trees, animals and geographic features'.[20] Lane went on to assert that none of these models alone were sufficient, but rather the reality of sacred space was some combination of all three.[21] Yet, Lane's view still involves some interaction between the human and the non-human in the creation or recognition of sacred space.

In many indigenous world views, this is not necessarily the case. In his discussion of myth, Sean Kane noted that 'the myth teaches that these sacred places are to be respected for their own sake, not for what human beings can make of them'.[22] Along these same lines, Patrick Curry posited that 'places are particular… therefore places are also sensuous, qualitative, and unique, each with its own personality which becomes unmistakable when they enchant us'.[23] In this line of thinking, places can act independently of humans. Christopher Tilley and Kate Cameron-Daum described how places 'gather', to use Heidegger's term. They gather topographies, geologies, plants and animals, persons and their biographies… so landscapes are… always in the process of being and becoming'.[24] This notion of 'gathering' has echoes of Aristotle, summarized by Brady as 'how a body is drawn to its proper place, a place where it finds a sense of wholeness, completeness and stillness, is a form of phenomenological gravity'.[25]

In this field study, the object of study was a garden, which has the potential to be at once a human-created landscape, an irruption of the divine, and an actively gathering sacred place of its own. A mature garden is an eco-system, defined by Jack Hunter as 'a complex system of interactions between living organisms (plants, animals, microbes, fungi and more), and the 'non-living' environment (water, minerals, gases, sunlight, and so on)'.[26] These interactions take place with or without the presence of humans, but the lines along which they occur may be constrained or encouraged by the human gardeners, who create, and then trim and tend the garden. As Ingold noted, all life is lived along lines that weave and intersect, and thus 'an ecology of life must be one of threads and traces… and its subject of inquiry must consist not of the relations between organisms and their external environments, but of the relations along their severally enmeshed ways of life'.[27] In a human-created and visited garden, built on a formerly open stretch of desert, humans form a portion of the lines that contribute to the life and tenor of the place and thus, an exploration of the garden as sacred space must take that into account. As David Cooper described, 'to experience the garden as a gift is not only to have a sense of nature as a gift, but of ourselves as belonging to this gift'.[28]

The Butterfly Garden

The McDonald Butterfly Garden is a part of the Living Desert Zoo and Gardens, which straddles the towns of Indian Wells and Palm Desert in the Coachella Valley of southern California, USA. The Living Desert was first formed as a reserve on wild desert land in 1970 through the Palm Springs Museum and a group of local citizens and conservationists, who stated that its 'purpose is to preserve and interpret the local desert in view of a future time when the Coachella Valley will be so extensively developed, the original features of the area – its wildflowers and foliage, wildlife, and geographical features – will be a thing of the past'.[29]

The reserve began with 360 acres of land and consisted at first of interpretive trails through the natural desert landscape; it has since grown to over 1,200 acres, 1,000 of which are still undisturbed nature preserve.[30] Fifty years after it began, The Living Desert is today an important advocate for desert conservation and is involved in multiple projects, breeding programs and partnerships around the world.

The Butterfly Garden was created in 2002 as part of the Tennity Wildlife Hospital construction project. The open land around the hospital was disturbed and graded considerably during construction. Afterwards, it was re-formed as an unenclosed garden, designed to attract wild, local butterflies and other desert life. Over time the garden has grown and flourished: the trees provide rare points of desert shade, the flowering plants have intertwined and expanded out as far onto walkways and over sidewalls as they are allowed, and the underbrush has grown thick and provides shelter for local wildlife. Based on my observations, the garden is rarely pruned, and the plants are allowed to grow and interact freely off the main pathways. The Butterfly Garden is one of the lushest areas of The Living Desert, which is itself a large collection of plant and animal life in the midst of the surrounding human-inhabited neighbourhoods. As such, it has developed into a powerful attractor, not only for the butterflies it was designed to shelter, but also for hummingbirds, quail, robins, lizards, bees, rabbits, and other non-humans.

Discussion

Gathering

A recurrent theme that came up in my field notes was that of 'gathering' or 'proper place'. From the first time I entered it some twenty years ago, it has been clear to me that the Butterfly Garden draws me in. Brady's summary of Aristotle's theory of 'proper place' as being where 'a body experiences wholeness, completeness, and stillness' is an apt description of how I feel when I sit in the garden.[31] I experience no need to do anything more than be present. he 'threshold' that Eliade described that sets a sacred place apart from the profane was tangible to me as I turned off the main path and moved into it.[32] Especially noticeable when I visited the garden at the end of a long work week, my body and mind relaxed immediately upon entry and I often ended up feeling just how tired I was – something I had not been consciously aware of until I settled onto my bench.

There were, however, several times where I noted feeling self-conscious just sitting in the garden, as opposed to doing something or being headed somewhere. The Living Desert is a zoo and botanical gardens; for most people it is a place to pass through, to see something and then move on to the next thing to be seen. I have rarely observed people sitting on one of the many benches in the garden or taking a pause to connect with the place. While the Butterfly Garden is undoubtedly sacred to me, this is not necessarily the case for other humans who pass through it. This juxtaposition is reminiscent of Lane's third axiom: 'sacred place can be tred upon without being entered'.[33] I remark upon it during my visit on 23 November:

> The mesquite shading me gifts me with a spray of tiny yellow leaves as a woman in a bright red dress sweeps by in a flash of color, intent on seeing everything before the day is done. Is it seeing, though, when we fly from point to point, taking in the world in a blur of awareness, reading the signs about the elusive butterflies and moving on, disappointed, when they fail to appear, missing the glorious beauty of the plants in their golden afternoon glow?

As I observed the other inhabitants and features of the garden, I noticed how many of them the garden had also gathered there in what Tilley and Cameron-Daum described as the ongoing 'process of being and becoming'.[34] Even the large rocks were brought in by humans from the surrounding area and placed in strategic locations. These rocks then attracted plants, which used them as a support structure as they spread and grew and this in turn drew insect and animal life to eat and shelter in the green shade (Fig. 1). The flowers that were planted specifically to attract the garden's namesake butterflies are also favourites of hummingbirds. Costa's hummingbirds are non-migratory and native to the desert. They were drawn in by the tubular flowers and happily spend the whole year feasting on the sage, fairy duster and milkweed blossoms, even while the butterflies migrate or slumber in the colder months. Bees and other insects are also attracted to the year-round flowers, while jackrabbits burrow in the lush undergrowth (Fig. 1). I had to wonder on my visits if the formerly arid land had had a dream of more lush vegetation and diverse life that it then enlisted humans in helping to gather.

Figure 1: Left (descending): A butterfly in flight; a jackrabbit hopping and frequently pausing on the path; a hummingbird perched on a nearby branch. Right: A placed rock supporting plant and animal life in the garden. November/December 2022. Photos: Kim Corrall.

Although I had often sat enjoying the garden in the past, I found that the longer observation periods of the field study and my deliberate stance of 'engaged witnessing' as described by Bell, Instone, and Mee afforded me richer glimpses of the abundant life there than I had previously seen.[35] On 4 December, I wrote:

> I found that only when I became perfectly still could I discern the movement all around me. One big tree had about twenty birds hidden in its branches, hopping periodically to higher or lower levels... The butterflies were enjoying the fairy duster and milkweed, moving about, being still and then fluttering up together. The hummingbirds zipped past my ears and flitted from flower to flower. Even the jackrabbit came out and investigated the path. The bees hummed along in their work and swarms of tiny insects danced and glistened in the sunlight.

It also seemed that some of the birds and animals recognized me through my more frequent visits. As I became better at embodying stillness, the hummingbird came several times and hovered just in front of my face or perched nearby, while the jackrabbit drew nearer and stayed out longer during my later visits.

Thus, the garden is a combination of many of the elements used to describe sacred place. It is a formerly wild place, now human-constructed and maintained, ala Durkheim, and my long association with it has layered it with personal meaning for me, as described by Trubshaw.[36] I can, though, perceive the existence of Eliade's 'threshold' and can wonder if there was an existing 'hierophany' or agency of the land that drew the humans to construct the garden in this particular spot.[37] The garden seems to be a powerful attractor for rocks, plants, local wildlife and humans such as myself, in its process of 'being and becoming', as put forth by Tilley and Cameron-Daum.[38] In this way, it exhibits a form of Brady's 'phenomenological gravity'.[39]

Lines

Throughout my fieldwork, I was very conscious of Ingold's premise that 'to be a place, every somewhere must lie on one or several paths of movement to and from places elsewhere. Life is lived... along paths, not just in places, and paths are lines of a sort'.[40] The more I considered this idea, the more I was aware of the multiple layers of lines in the Butterfly Garden – lines of bodily movement, yes, but also of sound, growth, wind, sunlight, and time. On 23 November I observed:

I look at the lines of the paths, the plants crossing them, the branches making tangles of lines in the air, intertwining with their neighbors, stretching out to intercept rays of sun. A small line of seedlings marches out of the underbrush to ford the path, mesquite pods curling round and in-between them. Lines of sounds cross each other, increasing and fading away in turn. The sun sinks lower in the sky, etching the leaves and branches in shadows on the ground. I sit and let the lines of my thoughts wander and peter out.

When I first began contemplating the crisscrossing lines in the garden, the most obvious ones were the walkways and the flight lines of birds and bees. As I spent more time there, though, I became fascinated by the entangling of the branches, vines and leaves, the curling forms of the mesquite pods and the growth trajectories of the plants. As so much of the garden is made up of lush, overlapping plants, I was drawn to the idea of lines of growth and made a few drawings over several visits in an attempt to capture them (Fig. 2). Additionally, I focused my photography on capturing some of these lines, their interconnections, and the sense of movement that arose when I allowed them to travel into or out of the frame (Fig. 2).

To capture the lines of non-plant life, I was inspired by Bell, Instone and Mee's descriptions of their field work where they followed the movements of the local creatures and let themselves be led by them.[41] I used this technique several times to trace the varying movements of the different inhabitants of the garden. I was struck by how different they all were. The butterflies were rather staid, settling into a flower and then staying there soaking up the nectar for long periods of time before fluttering up and coming to rest on the next one. The bees were steady and worked their way from one flower to the next in an industrious rhythm. The robins were the most communal, perching in a large group in a single tree, rustling up into the higher branches when humans walked by underneath and then dropping down beneath the tree to gather seeds when the danger had passed. The solitary hummingbird had by far the most energy, zigzagging adroitly from blossom to blossom, flying up to perch on a high branch and then divebombing the next patch of flowers at breakneck speed. It was challenging to capture these lines of motion in photographs, as a photograph is but a moment in time, but I drew upon Ingold's descriptions of drawings and worked to capture 'what was going on' in that moment (Fig. 3).[42]

Thus, lines are an important aspect of the interweaving of life in this place. The Butterfly Garden is a well-developed eco-system, which, in accordance with Hunter's description, is an interwoven series of interactions between

Figure 2: Left (descending): Flower lines of growth; mesquite leaves and pods against the sky; parallel lines of growth. December 2022. Photos: Kim Corrall.
Right (descending): Lines from the Bench; Plant Lines on Stone. November/December 2022. Drawings: Kim Corrall.

living and "non-living" elements.[43] Many of these interactions take place along Ingold's weaving and intersecting lines, and involve not only the visible, human-constructed pathways, but also the lines of sound, sun, wind, growth, and movement.[44]

Enchantment and The Song of Place

Over time the hummingbird has captured its place as one of the premiere residents of the garden. Although the signage clearly names the place the Butterfly Garden, engraved on the stone at its entrance is not a butterfly, but a hummingbird (Fig. 4). This is significant, as the hummingbird is present in the

Figure 3: Clockwise from upper left: A butterfly settled on a flower for a long drink; robins in the tree waiting for the humans to pass; bee in flight; hummingbird in flight. December 2022. Photos: Kim Corrall.

garden through all seasons. Especially in the colder months when the butterflies are dormant, the hummingbird is the primary pollinator of the tubular flowers that cover much of the space.

The Butterfly Garden has been growing and developing over the course of twenty years. From its arid desert origins to a newly planted, fledging garden, built with the aspiration to attract wild butterflies, it has now become a mature, verdant sanctuary to many forms of life. This sanctuary aspect of the garden has been recognized by designating the garden as a 'quiet zone' within The Living Desert, complete with a formal sign and benches for contemplation (Fig. 4). Another development is related to the associations of its namesake. As Curry

Figure 4: Clockwise from upper left: A bench for contemplation at the center of the garden; newly erected tribute wall in the Butterfly Garden; carved stone at the entrance to the garden; signage for the Butterfly Garden.
November/December 2022. Photos: Kim Corrall.

pointed out, 'the Greek word for the soul, *psūchê,* anglicized as 'psyche,' also refers to a butterfly'.[45] Last year, the Butterfly Garden received a memorial wall where visitors can have a tile mounted to honour their departed loved ones. This is the only such memorial wall in The Living Desert and fits well with the soul aspect of the butterfly (Fig. 4).

In these ways and with the help of its human tenders, the land seems to be drawing in further aspects of itself over time, a portrayal of Kane's 'song of the place to itself, that humans overhear'.[46] Curry posited that 'enchantment is personal'.[47] He then went on to break down the etymology of the word 'enchantment' as a combination of the preposition 'in' and the verb 'to sing', concluding: 'It thus means the experience of being, or finding oneself, in a song. Whether it is a song that one hears or that one is singing, one finds oneself both listening to it and experiencing it from the inside'.[48] When married with Kane's 'song of the place to itself', it is not surprising that Curry highlighted nature as one source of enchantment in modern life, explaining that 'places too can cast a spell'.[49]

In my field work, I made a concerted effort to pay attention to the song of the garden and the underlying land and to 'invite conditions for enchantment… and then let it do its thing, perform its wonders as it will', as Curry suggested.[50] I walked the boundaries of the garden and listened for 'the feelings of the earth', as suggested by Reynolds, sat in engaged witnessing like Bell, Instone, and Mee, followed, drew and photographed Ingold's lines and opened myself up to experience Lévy-Bruhl's 'participation'.[51] Throughout all of this, I tried to remain aware of what I was bringing to the mix from the perspective of the garden, and to not only experience the garden as a gift, but myself 'as belonging to this gift', as Cooper expressed.[52] On one of my last field study visits to the garden, I felt I had fully entered a state of belonging and enchantment:

> Today, I am… too tired to do much of anything. Instead, I lie down on my favorite bench and stare up though the branches at the sky, listening to the song of the place. I wonder if the leaves make sounds imperceptible to me as they fall or as they grow. A few leaves drift down on me as I lay, and I thank the tree. The birds converse from opposite ends of the garden, and I hear the unmistakable thrum of the hummingbird's wings as he whizzes by. I observe the many layers of the tree branches and the tiny straight leaves of the mesquite as the sun lights them on its way down to the horizon. I see a pair of birds flying far overhead and I wonder how high the garden goes – where does it end and the sky begin? does it end at all? After a time, I sit up to write before I have to leave. My long hair is full of tiny leaves – I have become entangled in this place.

Throughout its twenty-year development, the Butterfly Garden has been developing and singing its song. The humans who maintain the garden have added features, incorporating the symbology of the butterfly and the importance of the hummingbird. As I spent long stretches of time deliberately connecting with the garden, I felt I could hear the song the place was singing and enter into it.

Final Thoughts

In doing this phenomenological field study, I have been aware of my animistic view of the world and my love of the Butterfly Garden, a place I have been visiting since its inception. Spending long immersive periods in the garden for this study has only deepened those tendencies. At the same time, I was aware of the many people who passed me and the garden by with interest, but without any outward signs of the enchantment and reverence that I was feeling. At times I was saddened by the rapid pace of the visitors, even in a place designed for relaxation, education, and connection with desert life. he many benches in the garden offer the chance to sit and immerse oneself in the wonder of its abundant life, but few take it. I find this tendency to be endemic to modern society as a whole. Rushed by commitments, pushed to go faster and do more, many of us have disconnected from the very idea of taking a moment to sit and watch the leaves grow. I agree with the view of many indigenous cultures that all land, all life is sacred – this garden included. Through my engagement with the Butterfly Garden, I found that it is possible to reel in our accelerating life paths long enough to enter that sacredness.

Conclusion

This phenomenological enquiry explored the question: Is the Butterfly Garden at The Living Desert, CA an inherently sacred space (for myself and the creatures that dwell there) or is its sacred nature a social construct? The field study was carried out through onsite observation of the garden, which was captured in notes, drawings, and photographs. Three main themes emerged: the gathering of elements and life, the lines of life and movement, and the enchantment by the place through its song. I found that the garden is a combination of many of the elements used to describe sacred place. It is human-constructed, it appears to have a threshold, which demarcates it as sacred space, and it is a powerful attractor for rocks, plants, local wildlife, and humans, exhibiting tendencies of 'gathering' and 'phenomenological gravity'. Lines are an important aspect of the interweaving of life in this place. As a developed eco-system, many of its interactions take place along the weaving and intersecting lines of human and non-human movement, along with sound, sun, wind, and growth. Throughout its lifespan, the Butterfly Garden and the wild land it was built on have been developing and singing their own song. The humans who created and now maintain the garden have added features to enhance this song and, as I spent long stretches of time there, I felt I could hear the song and enter into it.

In response to the original question posed, I concluded that the sacred nature of the Butterfly Garden is a combination of elements that are constructed, inherent, phenomenological, and driven by the song of the place itself, perhaps one it was singing long before humans were drawn to create a garden there. I observed that, while the non-human inhabitants of the garden seem to recognize the garden as a place of deep comfort and are drawn to it, many humans appear to move through it too quickly for it to affect them. I found this to be connected less to the power of the place and more to the increasing speed at which modern human life is lived. As Lane pointed out, 'sacred space can be tred upon without being entered'.[53] The Butterfly Garden attracts many people to tred upon it, but few humans seem to take the time to enter its sacredness or connect with the land and its inhabitants. As I noticed my ability to enter the garden improve over the course of the study, I concluded that this is a learned skill. One area for future research would be to study if the development and practice of this skill by humans, utilizing the methods explored in this study, alters their perception of the sacredness of a natural place over time.

Notes

1 Belden Lane, *Landscapes Of The Sacred: Geography And Narrative In American Spirituality* (Baltimore: The Johns Hopkins University Press, 2002), p.42.
2 Mircea Eliade, *The Sacred And The Profane: The Nature Of Religion* (New York: Harper & Row, 1961), p.21.
3 Émile Durkheim, *The Elementary Forms Of Religious Life* (New York: The Free Press, 1995), p.424.
4 Lane, *Landscapes*, p.44.
5 Sean Kane, *Wisdom Of The Mythtellers* (Ontario, Canada: Broadview Press, 1998), p.50.
6 Lane, *Landscapes*, p.44.
7 Christopher Tilley, *A Phenomenology Of Landscape: Places, Paths And Monuments* (Oxford: Berg Publishers, 1994), p.12.
8 Lucien Lévy-Bruhl, *The Notebooks On Primitive Mentality* (New York: Harper & Row, 1975), pp.1–3.
9 Sarah J. Bell, Lesley Instone, and Kathleen J. Mee, 'Engaged Witnessing: Researching With The More-Than-Human', *Ethics In/Of Geographical Research*, 50 (2018), p.136.
10 Mary Reynolds, *The Garden Awakening: Designs To Nurture Our Land And Ourselves* (Cambridge: Green Books, 2016), p.30.
11 Tim Ingold, *Being Alive: Essays On Movement, Knowledge And Description* (London: Routledge, 2022), p.221.
12 Ingold, *Being Alive*, p.223.
13 Bell, Instone, and Mee, 'Engaged Witnessing: Researching With The More-Than-Human', *Ethics In/Of Geographical Research*, 50 (2018), p.137.
14 Kim Etherington, *Becoming A Reflexive Researcher: Using Our Selves In Research* (London: Jessica Kingsley Publishers, 2004), p.19.
15 Graham Harvey, *Animism: Respecting The Living World* (New York: Columbia University Press, 2006), p.xi.

16   Durkheim, *Forms*, p.424.
17   Robert Trubshaw, *Sacred Places* (Loughborough: Heart Of Albion Press, 2005), p.3.
18   Eliade, *Sacred And Profane*, p.21.
19   Bernadette Brady, 'Mountains Talk Of Kings And Dragons, The Brecon Beacons' in *Space, Place And Religious Landscapes: Living Mountains*, ed. by Darrelyn Gunzburg and Bernadette Brady (London: Bloomsbury Academic, 2021), p.183.
20   Lane, *Landscapes*, p.44.
21   Lane, *Landscapes*, p.44.
22   Kane, *Mythtellers*, p.50.
23   Patrick Curry, *Enchantment: Wonder in Modern Life* (Edinburgh: Floris Books, 2019), p.84.
24   Christopher Tilley and Kate Cameron-Daum, *An Anthropology of Landscape* (London: UCL Press, 2017), p.20.
25   Brady, 'Mountains Talk,' p.183.
26   Jack Hunter, 'Greening The Paranormal: Re-Wilding And Re-Enchantment,' in *Greening The Paranormal: Exploring The Ecology Of Extraordinary Experience*, ed. by Jack Hunter (USA: August Night Press, 2019), p.16.
27   Tim Ingold, *Lines* (London: Routledge Classics, 2016), p.106.
28   David E. Cooper, *Senses of Mystery: Engaging With Nature And The Meaning Of Life* (London: Routledge, 2018), p.80.
29   Daily News, "Living Desert Center Near," 1966, from the archives of the Palm Desert Historical Society, Palm Desert, CA (photo of article in Appendix).
30   The Living Desert, 'Our History',
    2014, printout of website page in the archives of the Palm Desert Historical Society, Palm Desert, CA (photo of printout in Appendix).
31   Brady, 'Mountains Talk', p.183.
32   Eliade, *Sacred and Profane*, p.25.
33   Lane, *Landscapes*, p.19.
34   Tilley and Cameron-Daum, *Anthropology of Landscape*, p.20.
35   Bell, Instone, and Mee, 'Engaged Witnessing', p.137.
36   Durkheim, *Forms*, p.424; Trubshaw, *Sacred Places*, p.3.
37   Eliade, *Sacred and Profane*, p.21.
38   Tilley and Cameron-Daum, *Anthropology of Landscape*, p.24.
39   Brady, 'Mountains Talk', p.183.
40   Ingold, *Lines*, p.2.
41   Bell, Instone, and Mee, 'Engaged Witnessing', p.140.
42   Ingold, *Being Alive*, p.223.
43   Hunter, *Greening The Paranormal*, p.16.
44   Ingold, *Lines*, p.106.
45   Curry, *Enchantment*, p.83.
46   Kane, *Mythtellers*, p.50.
47   Curry, *Enchantment*, p.22.
48   Curry, *Enchantment*, p.22
49   Kane, *Mythtellers*, p.50; Curry, *Enchantment*, p.83.
50   Curry, *Enchantment*, p.123.
51   Reynolds, *Garden Awakening*, p.30; Bell, Instone and Mee, 'Engaged Witnessing', p.137; Ingold, *Lines*, p.106; Lévy-Bruhl, *Primitive Notebooks*, pp.1–3.
52   Cooper, *Senses*, p.80.
53   Lane, *Landscapes*, p.19.

8

THE GNOME, THE ROCK AND THE POOL – SACREDNESS IN A DOMESTIC GARDEN

Wendy Fey

The aim of this chapter is to examine the proposition that the rockery in my garden could be considered as a sacred space, and if so, whether that sacredness was a natural phenomenon or a human construct. This enquiry arose from a growing feeling that the area I live in has a strong sense of aliveness which had led me to the notion of creating a shrine in our garden to honour that spirit. While considering how to go about this, I noticed the rockery as a form of pre-existing shrine that my husband and I had already ornamented with various items that are meaningful to us, and which have rich stories attached. I had the sensation of a sacred, or at least alive place being actively revealed to me, as described by Belden Lane.[1] Lane also referred to sacred space as being 'storied': I was interested in exploring ways in which the stories attached to the objects on the rockery may be considered to add to the sense of sacredness.[2] The material will be considered under the headings of five themes: the potential sacredness of the rockery, the rockery as a focus for various pathways, the contribution of the gnome on the top of the rockery, a particular small boulder on the rockery, and the rockery's own perspective.

Methodology

My chapter is based on a written journal recording my phenomenological responses to time spent with the rockery, using the approach described by Christopher Tilley in which my subjectivity is fully acknowledged, yet what he calls 'narcissistic navel-gazing' is avoided, keeping the rockery itself as the main focus.[3] I aimed to follow the approach of Maurice Merleau-Ponty in providing a 'direct description' of my experience, including sensations of the body as well as the feelings and the mind.[4] The initial impulse for this chapter was based on my own feeling response to the space, therefore a phenomenological approach was the most appropriate. Since the rockery is sited just outside my back door, I have daily opportunity to observe it, and spent a little time with it every day for a period of some six weeks, between 9 November and 22 December 2021, writing down my observations and responses in a journal, and taking occasional photos with my phone. In addition to direct observations, I noted in my journal the stories attached to some of the items placed on the rockery, namely a small figurine of a gnome and a particular small boulder. This included conversations with my mother who is also linked to one of the items, as noted in my journal.

I am a retired English woman living on the edge of a small town in the southwest of England, not far from farmland and open countryside. The rockery is sited in a fairly large garden, which occupies a lot of my and my husband's time in tending it, partly for the pleasure of gardening and creating a beautiful environment, and partly for the satisfaction of producing food. The rockery and associated pond were in place when we arrived some years ago, and we have done little to change them, apart from weeding and embellishing, so they carry a sense of always having been there. I have a strong personal relationship, however, to the objects we have placed on the rockery, as they all have significance and memories attached to them. I have a secular background and am not a subscriber to any particular religious view, but I am aware of the earth by virtue of my activities as a gardener, and I do have a strong sense of the aliveness of the earth that prompted this investigation. I am also deeply concerned about the current ecological crisis, and this concern has formed a part of my wish to pay close attention to the environment. Since I feel it is important to respect the earth simply in order to mitigate the damage human civilization has done, an element of bias may have arisen, as viewing the earth as sacred could be a way of promoting this respect.

Literature Review

There is extensive academic debate over the nature of sacredness as experienced in particular places. This debate was explored with reference to my sense of the possible sacredness of the rockery in my garden, considering if it is purely imaginary, a social construct arising from the way it is set apart from the rest of the garden, or a truly numinous space. Sacred space has been defined in a variety of ways, several of which have been useful in illuminating my experience of my rockery. One of the earliest to address the academic definition of the sacred itself was Rudolf Otto, who in 1917 set out the notion of the sacred as a mystery in which an awe-inspiring experience of the 'Other' is perceived, an experience he described as 'numinous', meaning of the divine.[5] He described this as an experience of a 'mysterium tremendum' or 'the feeling of personal nothingness and abasement before the awe-inspiring object directly experienced'.[6]

Sacred space as a purely sociological factor was discussed by Émile Durkheim who described sacred space as being set apart from everyday profane society, but dependent for its establishment and maintenance entirely on the collective human society. He considered that social custom was sufficient to account for the experiences of sacredness reported by people in certain places, without the need to invoke any divinity, writing that 'society in general... undoubtedly has all that is required to arouse the sensation of the divine'.[7] This related to the case of the rockery, in that it is a space set apart from the rest of the garden, is man-made, and its potential claim to being special could clearly be considered as a human construct as it is not a natural feature.

Another academic perspective was provided by Mircea Eliade. He held that the source of the sacred was to be found in a sacred realm that transcended the ordinary, profane space we inhabit, yet could 'break through' and reveal the sacred to us, at a time and place of its own choosing, an event he termed a hierophany.[8] He made a very clear distinction between sacred and profane space, writing that sacred space was '...an irruption of the sacred that results in detaching a territory from the surrounding cosmic milieu and making it qualitatively different'.[9] This indicated that the same place could be profane at one time, and sacred at another. The work of Belden Lane also informed my consideration of the subject, by reference to his four axioms for the study of sacred place, to be discussed later, to inform my examination of the potentially sacred nature of our rockery.[10]

In Anthony Thorley and Celia Gunn's report on sacred sites, commissioned by the Gaia Foundation, an operational definition of a sacred site was developed. This included a stem definition of 'A sacred site is a place in the landscape, occasionally over or under water, which is especially revered by a people, culture or cultural group as a focus for spiritual belief and practice or likely religious observance'.[11] They further identified nineteen characteristics, one or more of which was also required to define a space as sacred. This reflected the very broad range of possible ways of understanding the sacredness of a given site, from being 'a specific focus within a wider and possibly dynamically interconnected sacred landscape' to being 'identified as a place where the ancestors are present'.[12] The breadth of this definition encouraged me to consider the possibility of regarding the very ordinary and mundane rockery in our garden as a sacred site.

Given my intuitive feeling of an inherent aliveness in the garden, and a sense of relationship with the items we had placed there, I also drew on the theory of New Animism outlined in the work of Graham Harvey.[13] New Animism was described by Harvey as 'the notion that all earth is living, and that it is perhaps even a singular organism'.[14] In addition to providing a way of considering the setting of the rockery in the garden and the wider landscape, this view also prompted an approach to what Irving Hallowell termed 'other than human persons'.[15] This related to the presence of the items we had placed on the rockery, ostensibly as decoration, but which could have a presence that contributes to the potential sacredness of the space. This approach is in clear distinction to earlier definitions of Animism, described by Stephan Harding as 'a projection of human feelings onto inanimate matter', in which a human misunderstanding of the world leads to a belief in non-existent spirits inhabiting inert objects.[16]

A sense of the whole land being in some way animate was extended by reference to the work of Thomas Berry, who emphasized the connectedness of everything on the earth, referring to the 'Earth Community', in which 'we understand the universe as composed of subjects to be communed with, not objects to be exploited'.[17] This idea was further explored in the light of the influential Gaia Theory, as set out by Harding.[18] He described an approach to the Earth as a living organism, in which 'life and the non-living environment are tightly coupled [and]… what happens to one partner happens to the other', and the 'sense that Gaia really is alive, not in some metaphorical sense, but really, actually, palpably'.[19] This was also described by Brian Goodwin in his foreword to Harding's book, referring to the Earth as 'an emergent dynamic unity'.[20] A sense of aliveness and unity in connection with the rockery was related to a sense of the sacred, informed by the work of David Abram, who referred to the 'the magic afoot in the land', and 'the other forms of sentience and sensibility that surround us in the open field of the

present moment'.[21] This aliveness was also examined by reference to the work of Tim Ingold, in particular his description of the world as consisting of pathways and lines of connection rather than of static and separate spaces. As he described it, 'Thus the self… undergoes continual generation along a line of growth'.[22] Although he did not relate this to any theory of the sacred, it was felt to be relevant to an understanding of the lively presence of the rockery, as representing a concentration of aliveness that could be thought to make the sacred more evident or accessible in that particular space. This aspect of the way in which the rockery could be considered special was also examined in the light of Christopher Tilley's work, in which he emphasized the social meaning and significance embedded in space through the involvement of people, and the way that disregard of those meanings can 'desanctify' the land.[23]

Field Work and Discussion

The potential sacredness of the rockery

The idea for this investigation arose as I was making rather elaborate plans for constructing a small shrine to the sense of aliveness present to me in our garden. However, the plans had been proving too ambitious, and as I happened to walk past the rockery, I noticed the gnome placed on a stump at the top of the rockery, almost as if for the first time. It made a very vivid impression of rich colour and vivacity, strongly reminiscent of Lane's experience of encountering a deer in a clearing in the woods, demonstrating his first axiom for studying the sacred, namely that 'sacred place is not chosen, it chooses'.[24] I would not go so far as to claim that this represented an hierophany as described by Eliade or an experience of the awe-inspiring 'mysterium tremendum' described by Otto.[25] Rather, I was aware of a communication of some sort, as if the gnome was pointing out to me that I had a ready-made shrine and no need to make another.

I had paid very little attention to the rockery in the decade or so that I had known it. I had not thought of it as particularly impressive, tucked away in a functional corner of the garden by the clothes line and bins. It is certainly a candidate for Lane's second axiom, that 'sacred place is ordinary place, ritually made extraordinary'.[26] The ritual activity required had mostly been provided by my husband in tending it, but in undertaking my field work I attempted to engage in rituals to explore ways in which it can be considered a household shrine. Being almost entirely inexperienced in performing any sort of formal ritual, I made very little progress. I attempted to make an offering of some biscuits to the gnome at the top of the rockery, only to feel very awkward, with a strong sense, as recorded in my journal that 'the gnome was glaring at me'. However as Jonathan Z. Smith, quoted by Amy Whitehead, pointed out, 'ritual is, first and foremost, a mode of paying attention' so in this sense it could be claimed that my daily ritual of observation to this very ordinary place had potential to 'make' it extraordinary, as Lane described.[27] I would argue however that the ritual attention of observation, while adding enormously to my sense of relationship and awareness, could be better understood as a way of uncovering or revealing the extraordinary nature of the rockery in an Eliadean sense, rather than manufacturing it as Durkheim would suggest.

Although easy to observe, sited as it is in the garden, it is difficult to physically access, as it is very steep, which also contributes to its sense of being set apart in a Durkheimian sense. In attempting to climb it, I had a strong sensation of trespass as it can only be done by trampling over the plants and running the risk of dislodging some of the stones. It is sited behind a small pond, so anything dislodged would fall into the pond. However, the pond itself adds to the sense of life, with the movement of fish and reflection of the ever-fluctuating sky. The gradual ritual of daily attention built a strong sense of relationship over the weeks. There were times when I felt unwelcome, especially when I focused on the expression on the gnome's face, noting in my journal that 'Today the gnome was a bit less forbidding, but still quite stern'. As time went on however, I was able to note that 'the gnome looked, if not pleased, at least not displeased. Perhaps I am making progress'.

Initially my focus was mainly on the gnome figurine and a particular small boulder, inherited from my parents, which I had placed on the already established rockery. However, as time went on, I became much more aware of the actual rockery. In line with Lane's third axiom, namely, 'sacred place can be tred upon without being entered', my previous interactions with the rockery had been indifferent noticing, rather than 'entering', which Lane also described as 'a quest for the holy that is fulfilled finally in accepting the ordinary'.[28] In fact, I had the clear understanding that my previous attentions and observations had been very superficial, failing to grasp its reality. My awareness deepened, until it dawned on me just how large and solid it is. I realised much I had missed about its size and bulk, and its sense of presence and power, until I felt that I had 'entered' the space. As I noted in my journal 'I finally grasped that it is really there, not just as something to be looked at', and 'it is becoming more solid by the day'. I had the sensation that I was being rewarded for my attention with this enriched sense of the rockery's presence.

A more vivid experience came to me on the morning after the winter solstice, which felt like a very special point in the year, at sunrise, with the pale just-past full Moon getting low in the west behind me. The dawn light was very beautiful, colouring the clouds salmon pink and violet, and the strong presence of the sky in association with the rockery made a very powerful impression. I felt very aware that the rockery and I were part of a magnificent Whole that was indeed awe-inspiring and sacred. However, I did not feel that the experience was sacred in the sense of Otto since it did not involve a sense of encountering anything 'Other'. Rather I was aware of a grand inter-connection and balance of the Whole, and though it could be framed in the sense of Eliade's 'communication with the transcendent', I felt that it was more simply a moment of seeing the sacred in the world as it is, without the need for any Other, or separate realm intruding.[29]

In considering the rockery as a sacred space, the theories of Otto, Eliade and Durkheim all contributed to my understanding without supplying a description that fully fitted with my experience. In Lane's axioms I found a more convincing way of thinking about the sacredness of the space, as three of the four described my relationship with the rockery, providing me with a way of framing the possible sacredness of the rockery. The most moving experience was associated with the powerful sense of connection that developed in a single moment of observation with myself, the rockery, and the whole earth and sky, which came closer to reflecting the theories of Otto and Eliade, though without the need for referring to anything 'Other'.

Pathways/Lines

During the process of observing the rockery, I noticed many details I had overlooked before, one of which was a large gap in the fence behind it, where it borders our neighbour's garden. I surmised that it had been left as a route for the badgers which sometimes visit, and which can be damaging if hindered. Certainly, it must be in use by the numerous local cats, which I have often observed crossing the rockery (treading much more lightly than me) or basking on it in the sunshine, and I have seen many birds on the rockery from time to time. This has the effect of concentrating and entangling a number of paths due to what I now think of as the 'badger gate', and I had the feeling of a concentration of aliveness from it. I recorded this in my journal as 'very much reminding me that the rockery is a pathway'. Tilley wrote that 'Paths form an essential medium for the routing of social relations', and I felt that this could be extended to the substance of the rockery itself, since every element of it is, in a sense, on a 'path' from past to future, and in physical movement, however slowly from the human perspective.[30] I was especially aware of this with the single small inherited boulder, distinct from all the other 'ordinary' rocks, which had followed a path all the way from Scotland, and gave the impression of being about to fall into the pond: I had the impression that it is seeking a home in water.

This gathering together of paths contributed to the sense of aliveness, both in terms of the comings and goings of creatures and in terms of the rockery itself as a point of congruence for these paths. This sense of animation recalled the views of Harvey, who wrote that 'the sacred .. is present in… the living, ongoing, life force'.[31] This view described quite clearly the position I felt myself to occupy by the end of this investigation, witnessing the movement of life on and within the earth, and feeling it to have a deep connectedness and sacredness.

The Gnome

Lane asserted that 'Above all else, sacred place is "storied place"', which I took to apply to the items on the rockery.[32] There are several items, placed there as a way of displaying them, but also because we intuitively and aesthetically felt that they belonged there. The richness of personal memory and feeling associated with the stories attached to these items greatly enhanced the sense that the rockery is special and contributed to what Tilley referred to as 'sedimented layers of meaning' inhering in the place.[33]

The small statue of a gnome referred to above, is roughly eighteen inches high and stands right at the top of the rockery, on the stump of an old bay tree which we cut down. It was a gift from me to my husband many years ago when

I decided to abandon my resistance to his desire for a garden gnome, which at the time I regarded as unbearably kitsch. It is in a very dominant position in the space of the rockery, and has a somewhat aggressive and forthright posture, as can be seen in Fig. 1. It also has a small figure of a moon-gazing rabbit apparently worshipping it, as placed by my husband.

Figure 1: Photo by Wendy Fey showing the gnome on the top pf the rockery. December 2021

It has been through phases of neglect, being mostly hidden in the foliage in the summer, but currently it is freshly painted (by my husband) and in full view as a focal point, especially at the time of writing, when the winter season has reduced the amount of foliage. Indeed, it was my perception of the gnome as an active agent that first prompted my interest in the potential sacredness of the rockery space. Whitehead wrote that 'material objects... can be active participants in encounters'.[34] Perhaps however, it would be more accurate to suggest that the gnome was the agent in revealing the potential sacredness of the space to me, rather than being the sole 'container' for the sense of the sacred, which was my initial impression. It could be said that the place itself used the gnome to reveal itself to me, or perhaps they were in partnership, drawing me into a community. I recorded this in my journal as follows, 'Went out to say hello to the gnome and the rockery on a bright cold morning. I stood in a patch of sunshine and shared my breath, steaming in the cold air. It felt like a sort of connection, pleasing'.

In considering the gnome itself as 'sacred' I do not mean in any formal religious sense, dependent on faith or belief, or as a representation of any sacred being. Despite its prominent position and initial role as 'spokesperson', my phenomenological experience was of the gnome as a part of the overall community of the rockery. Its human features perhaps made it more accessible to me, and the personal story attached to it added to its specialness. However, it did not appear to be qualitatively different or more sacred than the rest.

The Stone

Of deeper emotional significance to me is the small boulder that currently sits on the rockery. This was collected by my mother from Gruinaird Bay in the northwest of Scotland in the 1960s and has been in the family ever since. She described the encounter as 'bewitching', an extremely unusual word for her to use. I have always been fond of this stone, finding it beautiful, and rescued it from the bottom of my father's derelict pond where it had spent about a decade. As with the gnome, I had a strong sense of this stone as an 'other than human person', in Hallowell's influential phrase, cited by Harvey.[35] That is, although it is not animate in the biological sense, I felt that it partook of the general aliveness of the world, described by Harding as 'the animate community of organisms, air, rocks, and water that constitutes the very fabric of our living planet'.[36] According to the Scottish Geology Trust's website, referring to the area where the stone was collected, 'The Hebridean Terrane is famous for containing the oldest rock formations in Scotland and some of the oldest in the world' and I found the sense of its immense age, and the journey it has taken over its life as well as with my family, very awe-inspiring.[37] As I noted in my journal, 'The soft light on the stone seemed so poignant, making me think of how many millions of sunsets it has experienced. Made me feel giddy to think of the stone's journey from lava to ice age to river-rolled to beach and then to my rockery and pond'.

Certainly, the presence of the stone enhanced the sense of power I sensed in the rockery. It is venerable due to its great age and weight, as well as the fact that it is radically unlike any of the other stones in the garden, as can be seen in Fig. 2. As Eliade wrote, 'The hierophany of a stone is pre-eminently an ontophany; above all, the stone... strikes man by what it possesses of irreducibility and absoluteness and, in so doing, reveals to him by analogy the irreducibility and absoluteness of being'.[38]

This refers to the solid reality of the stone, which is unmistakable, and part of what makes it special to me. The fact that it has travelled so far in time and space, partly through the agency of my family, gives it a particular sense of having a strong and exotic story to contribute to the place, deserving of respect, and carrying a strong sense of both the sacred and solid reality at the same time.

My own story had become intertwined with it in the manner of Ingold's lines, as he put it, 'All life is social in this sense, since it is fundamentally multistranded,

Figure 2: Photo by Wendy Fey showing the small boulder on the left, poised above the pond, gleaming in the rain. November 2021.

an intertwining of many lines running concurrently'.[39] A sense of awe and privilege attached to the fact that my own life path has become entwined with that of such a splendid stone.

Several items are part of the 'rockery community' and add their own richly evocative stories to the experience of observing the place. Their paths, and their personal significance and emotional quality have added to the overall specialness of the rockery. Given that they are special to us, it seems possible that the sense of power inherent in the rockery itself made it an appropriate place for them. I developed a strong sense that they are part of the whole community, and a focal point for the sacredness inherent in our garden and the surrounding landscape. As Tilley wrote, 'A social space… is constituted by differential densities of human experience, attachment, and involvement', and I felt that the space of the rockery possessed a greater density of personal meaning than, for example, the middle of the lawn.[40]

The rockery's perspective

Gaia theory, as explained by Brian Goodwin in his foreword to Harding, holds that the Earth can be understood as 'a co-dependent and coherent whole'.[41] Thinking about the rockery and its inhabitants, biologically animate and otherwise, in the light of this theory has led me to relate to it less as 'my' rockery and more as a fellow dweller in the garden, or another part of what Berry called 'the Earth Community'.[42] However small and insignificant this ordinary feature in the garden may be, by virtue of existing, it is part of the Whole, and can be considered sacred because as Harding wrote, 'every speck of matter is sacred simply because it exists'.[43] While accepting this premise, I nevertheless had a sense of aliveness being concentrated or pooled, or perhaps more accessible in some places, such as the rockery.

My initial sense of the rockery, via the gnome communicating with me, made me wonder about its motives, as well as my own motives in undertaking the investigation. For myself, I confess to an element of simple curiosity in exploring an issue I had not considered deeply before. But beneath that lay an intuition that the land itself has aliveness, and I wished to both understand it better and strengthen my connection with it. It has been argued that there is a cost to humans from our estrangement and sense of separation from the world. Goodwin pointed out that 'quantities without qualities give us a world without beauty, and… without health': therefore the quality of sacredness may be understood to bring benefits to humans as well as to the place, spirit, and other-than-human persons we are acknowledging.[44] By paying attention to the qualities of the rockery, I felt I had enriched myself, and hopefully the rockery itself appreciated the sense of community.

If the rockery was to be considered a sacred space, which 'chose' to reveal itself to me, I was led to wonder why it would do that. Thorley wrote about 'the importance of sacred sites as foci in the landscape for continuity and maintenance of spiritual expression and nourishment of both society and the land'.[45] In my field notes I recorded a sense of being welcomed, slowly and cautiously, by the space of the rockery, developing a sense of relationship that I felt was rewarding for the space as well as myself. My field notes recorded on some days that 'the rockery seemed pleased to see me'. In addition, considering the rockery and all its inhabitants, living and otherwise, as persons, I felt a need for a level of etiquette, as described by Harvey as a way of 'inculcating good relations between persons of different species'.[46] My fumbling attempts at making offerings were motivated by the impulse to show respect and affection, however unsuccessfully. I wondered if the sacred as manifest in the rockery had an impulse to be recognized and appreciated, though I had no sense that it was requiring anything more from me than attention, and perhaps fellowship. After making daily observations for some weeks, I gradually became aware of just how physically big, solid, and weighty the rockery is. I was astonished that I hadn't really grasped this before and felt that the rockery itself was perhaps exasperated at my slowness to connect with it.

Conclusion

The aim of this chapter was to investigate the possibility that the rockery in our back garden could be considered as sacred space, and if so, whether it was a natural phenomenon or a human construct. This was a phenomenological study, based on my own observations over several weeks. The project was considered under five themes: the potential sacredness of the rockery, the pathways concentrated on the rockery, the gnome on the top of the rockery, a particular small boulder on the rockery, and the rockery's own perspective. Theories as to what may constitute the sacred from Otto, Durkheim, and Eliade were used to frame the enquiry. Both Durkheim's and Eliade's views, though very different, were found to apply to some extent to my phenomenological experience of the rockery in that it is a space 'set apart' and a human construct as Durkheim described sacred space, and also a place where I experienced a form of hierophany, as suggested by Eliade. Otto's more extreme concept of the sacred as a numinous feeling of awe was not felt applicable to this ordinary domestic rockery, except in one incident which included an awe-inspiring sense of connection with the whole earth and sky.

Three of Lane's four axioms for the study of the sacred were found to be descriptive of my experience: I had for years hardly noticed the rockery, let alone experienced any sense of sacredness; I had felt that the rockery itself initiated the sense of communication with me; and there were personally significant stories attached to the space due to the objects placed upon it. I discovered that my initial observations were superficial, allowing me a very minimal sense of the aliveness or sacredness of the space. However, over time I became much more aware of the physical presence of the rockery, and its connection to the general aliveness of the world as a whole. The approach of New Animism, as described by Abram and Harvey provided a framework for understanding a connection between this sense of aliveness and the sacred. In line with Lane's work, I found the personal significance of the stories attached to the objects we have placed on the rockery contributed to the sense of the rockery being a very special space. There was a strong sense of the gnome and the boulder in particular being 'other-than-human' persons with their own trajectories that I felt pleased and honoured to be sharing. A sense of community developed and contributed richness to the 'storied' space of the rockery.

My observations led to an understanding of the rockery as a site where many paths converge, which I considered in the light of Tilley's and Ingold's work on the importance of lines and pathways as a focus for life, providing a sense of concentration of life and therefore sacredness.

In the course of preparing to write this chapter, I began to think of the space as more of a community rather than as 'my' rockery, and I began to wonder about the rockery's own perspective and its motives. Applying the perspective of Gaia theory led me to feel that the rockery shared the aliveness of the whole earth and is sacred by the simple fact of existing. Its 'set apart' nature, and my experience of communion with it however resulted in my feeling that the aliveness was somehow more concentrated, or perhaps nearer the surface, in this particular space than elsewhere in the garden. Through pursuing this investigation, I developed a much fuller understanding of how the sacredness of our rockery could be defined and found in the end that its sacredness was not just a human construct, but that it was partaking of the sacredness of the whole world and providing a focal point for the experience and expression of the sacred.

Notes

1   Belden C. Lane, *Landscapes of the Sacred : Geography and Narrative in American Spirituality*, Expanded edn (Baltimore, MD: London: Johns Hopkins University Press, 2002), p.19.
2   Lane, *Landscapes of the Sacred: Geography and Narrative in American Spirituality*, p.15.
3   Christopher Y. Tilley and Kate Cameron-Daum, *An Anthropology of Landscape : The Extraordinary in the Ordinary*, (London: UCL Press, 2017), p.viii.
4   Maurice Merleau-Ponty, *Phenomenology of Perception*, trans. Donald A. Landes (London: Routledge, 2012 [1945]), p.lxxi.
5   Rudolf Otto, *The Idea of the Holy : An Inquiry into the Non-Rational Factor in the Idea of the Divine and Its Relation to the Rational*, 2nd edn, trans. John W. Harvey (Oxford: Oxford University Press, 1970 [1917]), p.7.
6   Otto, *The Idea of the Holy : An Inquiry into the Non-Rational Factor in the Idea of the Divine and Its Relation to the Rational*, p.12.
7   Emile Durkheim, *The Elementary Forms of Religious Life*, trans. Karen E. Fields (New York: London: Free, 1995 [1912]), p.208.
8   Mircea Eliade, *The Sacred and The Profane : The Nature of Religion*, trans. W. R. Trask (New York: Harcourt Brace, 1959), p.30; Eliade, *The Sacred and The Profane: The Nature of Religion*, p.21.
9   Eliade, *The Sacred and The Profane: The Nature of Religion*, p.26.
10 Lane, *Landscapes of the Sacred: Geography and Narrative in American Spirituality*, p.19.
11 Anthony Thorley and Celia Gunn, 'Sacred Sites: An Overview (Abridged)', (2008), p.12.
12 Thorley and Gunn, *Sacred Sites: An Overview (Abridged)*, p.12.
13 Graham Harvey, *The Handbook of Contemporary Animism* (Durham: Routledge, 2014).
14 Harvey, *The Handbook of Contemporary Animism*, p.22.
15 A. Irving Hallowell, 'Ojibwa Ontology, Behavior, and World View', *Readings in Indigenous Religions,* (2002), p.22.
16 Stephan Harding, *Animate Earth : Science, Intuition and Gaia* (Totnes, Devon: Green Books, 2009), p.21, loc. 401 (Kindle version).
17 Thomas Berry, *The Great Work: Our Way into the Future*, 1st edn (New York: Bell Tower, 1999), loc 90 (Kindle version); Berry, *The Great Work,* loc. 106 (Kindle version).
18 See Harding, *Animate Earth: Science, Intuition and Gaia*.
19 Harding, *Animate Earth: Science, Intuition and Gaia*, p.64, loc. 1153 (Kindle version); Harding, *Animate Earth: Science, Intuition and Gaia*, p.240, loc. 4214 (Kindle version).

20 Harding, *Animate Earth : Science, Intuition and Gaia*, p.12, loc 235 (Kindle version).
21 David Abram, *The Spell of the Sensuous*, 2nd edn (New York: Vintage, 1997), p.21; Abram, *The Spell of the Sensuous*, p.162.
22 Tim Ingold, *Being Alive: Essays on Movement, Knowledge and Description* (London: Taylor & Francis Group, 2011), p.221.
23 Christopher Tilley, *A Phenomenology of Landscape: Places, Paths, and Monuments*, (Oxford; Providence, RI: Berg, 1994), p.21.
24 Lane, *Landscapes of the Sacred : Geography and Narrative in American Spirituality*, p.19.
25 Otto, *The Idea of the Holy: An Inquiry into the Non-Rational Factor in the Idea of the Divine and Its Relation to the Rational*, p.12.
26 Lane, *Landscapes of the Sacred: Geography and Narrative in American Spirituality*, p.19.
27 Jonathan Z. Smith, 'To Take Place', in G. Harvey, ed. ,*Ritual and Religious Belief: A Reader* (London: Equinox, 2005). pp.26–50, p.33, quoted in Amy Whitehead, *Religious Statues and Personhood : Testing the Role of Materiality* (London: Bloomsbury Academic, 2013), p.108.
28 Lane, *Landscapes of the Sacred: Geography and Narrative in American Spirituality*, p.19; Lane, *Landscapes of the Sacred: Geography and Narrative in American Spirituality*, p.18.
29 Eliade, *The Sacred and The Profane: The Nature of Religion*, p.57.
30 Tilley, *A Phenomenology of Landscape: Places, Paths, and Monuments*, p.31.
31 Harvey, *The Handbook of Contemporary Animism*, p.23.
32 Lane, *Landscapes of the Sacred: Geography and Narrative in American Spirituality*, p.15.
33 Tilley, *A Phenomenology of Landscape: Places, Paths, and Monuments*, p.27.
34 Amy Whitehead, 'Appalachian Animism: Religion, the woods, and the material presence of the mountain', in Darrelyn Gunzburg and Bernadette Brady, eds, *Space, Place and Religious Landscapes: Living Mountains* (London: Bloomsbury Academic, 2020), p.162.
35 Hallowell, 'Ojibwa Ontology, Behavior, and World View', cited in Harvey, *The Handbook of Contemporary Animism*, p.2.
36 Harding, *Animate Earth: Science, Intuition and Gaia*, p.244, loc. 4564 (Kindle version)
37 https://www.scottishgeologytrust.org/lets-talk-geology-volunteer-blog-an/, accessed 15 December 2021.
38 Eliade, *The Sacred and The Profane: The Nature of Religion*, p.155.
39 Ingold, *Being Alive: Essays on Movement, Knowledge and Description*, p.221.
40 Tilley, *A Phenomenology of Landscape: Places, Paths, and Monuments*, p.11.
41 Harding, *Animate Earth: Science, Intuition and Gaia*, p.12, loc..234 (Kindle version).
42 Berry, *The Great Work: Our Way into the Future*, loc. 90 (Kindle version).
43 Harding, *Animate Earth: Science, Intuition and Gaia*, p.225, loc. 4174 (Kindle version).
44 Brian C. Goodwin, *How the Leopard Changed Its Spots: The Evolution of Complexity* (New York: C. Scribner's Sons, 1994), p.200.
45 Thorley and Gunn, *Sacred Sites: An Overview (Abridged)*, p.36.
46 Harvey, *The Handbook of Contemporary Animism*, p.5.

9

A WAR MEMORIAL IN THE NEW FOREST: LOOKING TOWARDS HOME

Kathy Vinton

The aim of this research is to investigate whether the Canadian War Memorial, located near Burley in the New Forest National Park, can be thought of as sacred space and, if so, whether this is a human construct or a natural phenomenon.

The New Forest National Park is a low-populated, mainly unfenced area, with a mixture of forest and heathland, and is popular with campers, walkers and cyclists. However, sited in a somewhat isolated, seemingly random location is a Canadian War Memorial. Unlike town or village war memorials whose positions may have been chosen by planners, or those erected on a battle field, this memorial is unusual in that it is located at the site where outdoor, multi-denominational religious services had been held for the Canadian servicemen billeted in this part of the New Forest for the three months leading up to their dispatch to Juno Beach in Normandy on D-Day, June, 1944.[1] Although very peaceful now, thousands of British, Canadian and American troops had been billeted in different parts of the New Forest due to its location on the south coast, close to the coast of France. The memorial commemorates the Canadian lives lost, which include those of the young men who had taken part in the services only days before D-Day. The dedication stone at the memorial displays this information as shown in Figure 1.

For this project, the question of sacredness with regard to this site has been considered with respect to its location, its previous use as a site for services, and its current use as a war memorial, incorporating the views of major theorists, including Emile Durkheim (1858–1917), Mircea Eliade (1907–86) and Belden Lane. Having carried out a literature review, a reflective phenomenological method was employed, following a programme of visits for fourteen consecutive days and maintaining a daily journal recording thoughts and feelings, with some photographs also being taken. Additionally, a qualitative observational approach was taken to record people's behaviour in the vicinity of the site. The notes from the journal were then related back to the views of the theorists.

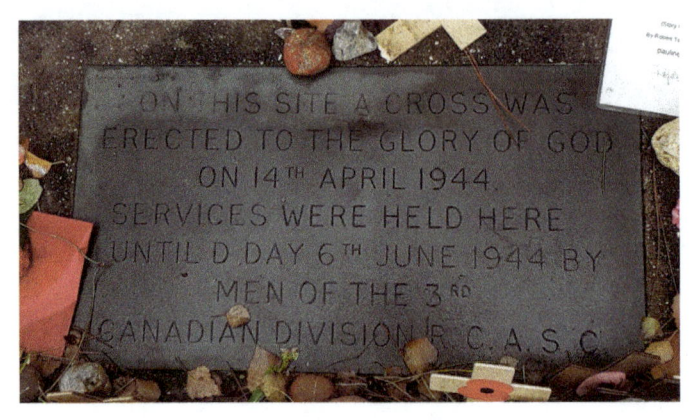

Figure 1: Canadian War Memorial Dedication Stone, Image: Photo by Author.

In the discussion, consideration is firstly given as to whether the site, just prior to being chosen for the outdoor services, could have been considered sacred in terms of Eliade's concept of hierophany.[2] As Lane has suggested, although perhaps unnoticed by many, a sacred landscape may exist but be dismissed 'because we have not learned to recognize them'.[3] Secondly, with all three theorists broadly in agreement that ritual action could create sacredness, the effect of the repetition of services held before D-Day is considered and, thirdly, the possibility of sacredness having been retained either through natural phenomenon or through its current use as a commemorative site is discussed. Conclusions are finally drawn as to the sacredness of the Canadian War Memorial site and whether this was as a human construct or a natural phenomenon.

Scholars still draw on the views of two of the earlier theorists on sacred space, Durkheim and Eliade. Linked through their use of the words sacred and profane (Durkheim fifty years before Eliade), their views, whilst ostensibly containing similarities, are polarised between Durkheim's atheistic, sociological standpoint and Eliade's religious one. In terms of sacred space, this is evidenced by Durkheim taking the stance that experience of certain natural phenomena could not be defined as 'outside the world of ordinary experience'.[4] Eliade, however, in direct opposition, has co-opted Rudolf Otto's idea that, indeed, something could have a quality 'felt as objective and outside the self' (numinous).[5] He further maintained that 'The sacred always manifests itself as a reality of a wholly different order from "natural" realities'.[6]

These two opposing views have been acclaimed and critiqued to different degrees due to the inevitable difficulty of categorising something which is outside of normal experience. As described by William Paden, some people have referred to the perception of sacredness as an 'a priori religious reality... wholly other, unknowable', which he described as conferring religious privilege and exempting it from analysis, whilst others have reacted to that view, wishing to avoid the idea altogether.[7] Durkheim's structuralist approach thereby found supporters, according to William Pickering, for giving weight to the scientific study of religion, deeming it to be more valuable than to consider sacredness 'in terms of relationship to god spirit or some transcendental force or existence'.[8]

However, the above stances would tend, then, to ignore the phenomenological, ethnographic research into the a priori religious reality, termed 'agency' in some instances, especially when referring to indigenous societies. Catherine Allerton has described that Southeast Asian people viewed agency as 'having the power to act in the world'.[9] Furthermore, her experience led her to suggest that claims that landscape has agency should be taken more seriously.[10]

It may appear, though, that the emphasis regarding sacred space has focused on indigenous peoples, a fact Anthony Thorley and Celia Gunn have acknowledged, describing how they tried to develop a definition to encompass such sites as cathedrals.[11] Denis Byrne highlighted this apparent division by purposefully describing numinous sites in Europe, in order to highlight the fact that people in all parts of the world spiritually engage with, and experience, their landscapes.[12] Lane, too, has encompassed this message, with his work into the sacred being described as ranging over 'religious traditions, literary landscapes, and personal experiences, illuminating a path to deeper understanding of the sacred meanings attached to places'.[13] Despite these efforts, it is currently apparent that, as Christopher Tilley and Kate Cameron-Daum succinctly reiterated, 'Notions of sacredness are fine to take seriously in relation to traditional indigenous societies but not amongst ourselves in the west'.[14] Therefore, with the subject of sacred space evidently presenting an on-going challenge, it is hoped that all investigations into sacred space, including this one, wherever or however carried out, are accepted as valid contributions to the body of research.

Methodology

The three processes employed in this research project were, first, to review relevant literature to create a framework, as suggested by Judith Bell and Stephen Waters.[15] This was carried out with respect to sacred spaces, together with the significance of war memorials. Secondly, phenomenological fieldwork on an auto-ethnographic basis was undertaken, whereby my own observations of, and feelings and reaction toward the site, were studied, as described by Elaine Campbell.[16] To allow a suitable time for perceptions to adjust and change, a programme of visits to the site for fourteen consecutive days was followed, incorporating observations and prayer, with notes being recorded at the time and some photos taken. The timing also established the advantage noted by Bell and Waters of being able to allow a variety of different emotions and beliefs come to the surface and be tracked.[17]

The involvement of prayer was designed to simulate the prayer experience of the servicemen. A minimum of seven minutes was maintained and included set prayers (from memory) and contemplative prayer, described by Amber Griffioen as not only seeking to increase understanding of the divine but also to 'arrive at important truths about one's own self and what one is'.[18] Although in this instance very limited in scope, José-Manuel González-González, Jesús Gerardo Franco-Calvo and Darío Español-Solana have described the value of re-enactment in research, despite the acknowledgement that the differences in time and circumstances inevitably restrict the extent to which the past can be replicated mentally or physically, thus risking a distortion to any response.[19] Finally, an analysis of my observations was made with reference to the theorists.

To further strengthen the research process, an initial pilot visit was carried out to ascertain any potential issues related to the process, as suggested by Bell and Waters.[20] Additionally, reflexivity was regularly focused on during the process in an attempt to carry out the task in an impartial manner, acknowledging the effect that my own views may have had on my observations. Although from a white, working-class, Roman Catholic family, I have questioned the existence of God in the form of Christianity since my late teens. I completed a BSc (Hons) degree in Applied Biology in my forties in order to gain a scientific perspective of the world and briefly taught science in secondary schools before returning to office work. I am married with two daughters and am now retired.

Sacred Space

Among the early theorists on sacred space, Durkheim and Eliade are prominent, having each presented detailed views regarding the creation and maintenance of the sacred in religion, including sacred space, albeit maintaining opposing views on its causality. Both views concurred that the perception of sacredness is an objective experience, however they both excluded experiences of awe and wonder as sacred if, as stated by Durkheim, it is not specific to religious feeling.[21] Eliade, meanwhile, maintained that sacred space cannot be chosen by non-religious man even if the experience of it is similar to a hierophany.[22]

With the above limitation, Durkheim's sociological view was that anything can become sacred if it is deemed so by collective feeling.[23] He went on to confirm that sacredness could only be constructed by a group of similar-minded people with one collective consciousness.[24] Furthermore, Durkheim maintained that the energy acquired by an object in this way could be transferred to the space around it by psychic contagion.[25] In contrast, Eliade claimed that sacred space resulted from the fact that some space was not homogenous, thus allowing for sacred space to manifest itself independently in a hierophany.[26] He described this as usually taking the form of an eruption 'that results in detaching a territory from the surrounding cosmic milieu and making it qualitatively different.'[27] He also clarified that sacred space was not accessible to everyone, being only accessible to religious man.[28]

However, Lane has expressed his discomfort with what he described as too simple a dichotomy between the religious aspect and the cultural aspect, describing that, for him, the cultural approach was taken from the outside compared to his own approach to the same phenomenon from the inside.[29] He expressed his concern regarding the difficulty of steering between 'the Scylla [monster] of the constructivists and the Charybdis [whirlpool] of the essentialists', claiming that each side missed some of the value of the other's stance.[30] His ideas have attempted to resolve this, evident in his theories regarding the creation and maintenance of sacred space wherein, together with his presentation of four axioms as a guidance to understanding its character, he appeared to combine both Durkheim's and Eliade's views.[31] His first axiom, that 'sacred space is not chosen, it chooses' is comparable to Eliade's concept of hierophany, although it could be thought that Lane has downplayed the reality of the numinous through his second axiom, that sacred place is ordinary place, ritually made extraordinary. This axiom concurred with Durkheim's view that religious ritual (by a group) created sacredness although for Durkheim this meant that when rites and rituals cease, any concept of sacredness disappears.[32] For Lane, however, the first axiom implied that sacredness would remain. Eliade also valued ritual, not in the creation of the sacred, but as a return to the sources of the sacred, claiming that through ritual, human existence could be saved 'from nothingness and death'.[33]

Lane has presented a path between the different views by, on one hand, acknowledging a transformation of consciousness at the point when an ordinary place becomes a place of extraordinary significance, whilst on the other hand he has included the concept of a simultaneous perception of earth and sky being joined in an 'otherworldly mystery'.[34] Having invoked words such as 'otherwordly', however, he has then proceeded to describe these experiences as being 'exercised on the human imagination', which has reduced the impact of the concept of numinous. Lane's combination of different views is again apparent in his perhaps contradictory contention that, whilst a sacred place is a construct of the imagination, it 'affirms the independence of the holy' going on to add that 'God chooses to reveal himself only where he wills'.[35]

Veronica della Dora has summarised the problem with the designation of sacred space in that it '... problematizes traditional binary distinctions, such as those between the spiritual and the material, the invisible and the visible...'.[36] However Lane's fusion of the concept of human construction with the designation of sacred space by God, concluded that sacred space is a combination of both human, more-than-human and divine interaction. This view is consistent with the idea that descriptions of sacred space appear to have moved on from being divided between Durkheim's and Eliade's ideas of the necessity of religious involvement and can now include non-religious sacredness.

Memorials

An example of the mixed public views on sacred space in the west has emerged from research carried out by Erika Svendsen and Lindsay Campbell with respect to nationwide local memorials created following the 9/11 event in New York. Their research found that 75% of the sites' stewards viewed the memorials as sacred, with half of these asserting that the two main reasons were that they either hosted rituals traditionally thought to confer sacredness, or the sites were connected to hallowed ground or religious practices.[37] Their longevity, together with memorial acts at the sites were also given as reasons.[38] Additionally, they found that the definition of sacred ranged from a formally consecrated space to a broader setting aside, including the leaving of relics (debris from the crash site and personal mementos) as well as through spiritual rituals, including prayer and the inscription of victims' names.[39] Patriotic symbols, such as flags, were also felt by some to create sacredness.[40]

Svendsen and Campbell also reported however that those stewards who did not feel their sites were sacred (25%), nevertheless felt they were special or important. The use of the word sacred was reserved for actual religious sites or the crash sites. Specifically, they noted that family members of the 9/11 victims did not believe that these memorials were sacred sites.[41] Additionally, James Mayo has claimed that the sentiments and the utilitarian purposes imposed on war memorials give them meaning, with memorials that perform public services contributing to sacredness.[42] However, when contrasting memorials to shrines, he described the difference being in the emphasis of the sacredness of the shrine or ritual, rather than the pure function of a memorial.[43]

A different experience of commemorative ritual, however, has been described by Edward Casey when, during the ritual of a remembrance parade, he recognised that he was not remembering the deceased or even really thinking of them at all and he suspected that most of the people there were in the same position.[44] The ritual act of remembrance had evidently been ineffective in creating a sense of sacredness. This is similar to Lane's description of his initial experience at the Vietnam Veterans Memorial in Washington, DC.[45] Although having felt touched by the mementos, he contrasted this feeling with his transformative experience of being drawn to the books listing the names of the dead, an old school friend's name randomly coming to mind, and finding this friend's name listed among the dead. He described that this caused him to experience a burst of deep emotion and that he felt the place become sacred for him in a way he had never expected and which he did not know how to explain.[46]

Comparing Lane's experience with Casey's, it is apparent that, from a position as described in Lane's third axiom, that sacred place can be tred upon without being entered, Lane's personal connection had revealed or created the sense of sacredness, without the need for ritual or setting aside. This, together with the views above, highlights that sacred space can be a deeply personal thing, or perceived as part of a group, with differing ideas as to how this is influenced. The results of the fieldwork, as recorded in the journal, can be compared to these ideas and an evaluation made as to whether they fit with the above ideas or add something new.

Fieldwork and discussion

Following the pilot day, the fourteen-day programme of visits commenced on Tuesday, 22 November 2022. Although conflicting ideas were evident from the literature review, key points were considered significant, with which to interpret the perception of sacredness during the fieldwork, as categorized below.

Sacredness inherent through nature

The Canadian War Memorial (Fig. 2) is situated close to the top of a hill, accessed by a three-mile, low gradient, cycle path through forest from Burley or, alternatively, a single-track road runs along the ridge of the hill at right-angles to the cycle path, passing approximately twenty metres away from the site.

The view from the ridge is instantly spectacular and had been noted on my previous trips but the area had not been considered in terms of sacred. During the fieldwork, however, I observed a deepening awareness and appreciation of the surrounding landscape as being sacred, noting a growing sense of commune with the trees, squirrels, ferns, sun, wind and rain, which conformed with Lane's description of sacred places which '... also participate in the entire array of sensory exchanges that play across the land' together confirming that they are more than just a construction of human imagination.[47] I noted in my journal

Figure 2: Canadian War Memorial, Image: Photo by Author.

that this would indeed have been a possible location for an Eliadian hierophany at some time in the past as well as Lane's first axiom, and may have guided the choice of location for the outdoor religious services in 1944. In addition to the magnetism of the location, however, the practicalities of the site were also evident in that it had the form of a small, natural amphitheatre, was protected from westerly wind and with the tree line providing cover from the view of German planes. A possible consideration may also have been given to the distant west-facing view on leaving the hollow, towards Canada and home, as shown in Figure 3. All these, however, could possibly have been interpreted as signs, attracting the men to that particular space, in accordance with Eliade's idea that a sign could be shown to indicate sacred space.[48] For these reasons, together with my own experience, I deduced that the site could constitute a natural sacred space, of itself containing sacredness, a natural phenomenon.

Figure 3: View West from the Memorial, Image: Photo by Author.

Sacredness acquired through design of the site

Surprisingly, rather late on in the fieldwork, I noted that the memorial itself was very understated and almost odd-looking with two tall white flag posts (one Canadian, one British) towering either side of a much lower (two metres) plain wooden cross, as can be seen in Figure 2. The flags contributed to a sense of Lane's fourth axiom concerning centrifugal force, driving thoughts away to Canada although, at the same time, echoing Svendsen's findings of the importance of patriotic signs. The flag poles are also reminiscent of Eliade's axis mundi, connecting the site with Eliade's thinking of three cosmic levels – earth, heaven and the underworld.[49] Additionally, during its use as a site for services, the cross itself, as a religious symbol, would definitely have connected the servicemen's prayers with the concept of sacred and may have simulated the axis mundi, as described by Eliade.[50]

From Figure 2, it can also be seen that there is no path to the memorial, and, with the picket fence surrounding it allowing space for only approximately ten people, the memorial is set apart, a commonly used criterion for sacred space, used also by both Durkheim and Eliade.[51] Interestingly, however, during the first few days, instead of communicating a sense of sacred space which pulled me in, my own experience was not centripetal, but of a sense that a commitment needed to be made which caused some hesitation. From my observations, this was also common to other people observed during the fourteen days. Out of eight sets of visitors, counting twenty-one people in all, only six went through the gate, with others, including members of the same group, remaining at what perhaps they may have considered a respectful distance. Although some carried on chatting after a brief silence, their reaction appeared to concur with the findings of Svendsen and Campbell. Following the first few days, however, I looked forward to the protection the fence seemed to supply, sensing Eliade's concept of entrance.[52]

The fencing off and the fact that the bolt from the original wooden cross made by the men had been purposely re-used in the making of a replacement cross, created more of a shrine-like effect, which has been described above by Mayo as increasing the sense of sacredness.[53] Taking the design together with my experience, sacredness was again indicated, but more through human construction and perception, my experience notwithstanding.

The part played by rituals

The services held for the servicemen at the site for the three months before D-Day constituted ritual action, described almost universally as designating the status of sacred as described above. In addition, the subsequent small memorial services which have been held on 11 November each year may also be said to preserve the sacredness with longevity found to be an important criterion for sacredness by Svendsen. Adding to this is the fact that, during the year, a small number of people attend independently, either in terms of having made a pilgrimage there, ritually placing flowers or artefacts.

The ritual aspect of my own visits also appeared to be a key to my perception of the sacredness of the site but, as it was undertaken alone with no group support as required by Durkheim for sacredness to be conferred, it could be said that this was more in line with Lane's and Eliade's views. I also perceived that my ritual of prayer became significant in directing my thoughts back to the possible thoughts of the young men, wondering if their prayer allowed them to sense or perceive more deeply the sacredness of the site, a concept referred to by Griffioen.[54] I recorded that I hoped that their prayer had given them reassurance and comfort, strengthening them in the face of battle, pertinently described by Jason McMartin as 'prayer links terrestrial life with participation in God's purposes in our post-mortem existence'.[55] Additionally, the prayer as a group not only conformed to Durkheim's criterion of ritual action, but, as Griffioen discussed, collective prayer focuses attention on the well-being of others, creating a bond between the people praying.[56] In the case of the Canadian soldiers, this may have united them with each other, but also provided a connection to their families at home. Thus the religious connotations, together with my experiences through the ritual visits, significantly contributed to the concept of the site being sacred, both as a human construct and a natural phenomenon, as described by Lane.

Changing perceptions of the sacredness of the site

Lane asserted, further to his third axiom, that sacred space is intimately related to consciousness.[57] From my personal stance, it is the case that my raised awareness of the site altered my consciousness, enabling my perception of sacredness to be experienced. My initial lack of awareness changed once within the enclosure, and similar to Lane, although moved by mementos, typical of many war memorials, I was significantly struck by three black and white photos supported on sticks in the ground of young men in uniform, on which their names and Canadian regiment had been written (Fig. 4). I could sense, as described in Lane's third axiom, my state of consciousness changing and the sense of sacredness growing.

Through my engagement with the landscape and the site itself, by the end of the fourteen days, I noted that I had become very aware of the sacredness of the site. The possibility of an original hierophany, the design of the site and

Figure 4: From the Site, Image: Photo by Author.

the ritual action all largely concurred with many of the descriptions of sacred space described in the literature. Durkheim's more restrictive criteria for sacred space, which only included the ritual action during the three months when the services were taking place, were the exception. Since, on his terms, the lack of, or minimal, more recent ritual action would have caused the site to lose its sacredness, the fact that I, at least, perhaps with other visitors, could still perceive its sacredness, might be seen as indicating that this part of his theory may not have been entirely accurate.

Final thoughts

As discussed, the concept of sacred space has raised many issues and polarized thoughts. Theorists' views differ at many levels and Lane has attempted to find an acceptable way forward whilst he acknowledged that 'What fascinated me most was the messiness, ambiguity, and the mystery of people's deeply personal experience of place'.[58] As an illustration of this, on the pilot day, before officially commencing the fieldwork but having arbitrarily driven to the War Memorial, I got out of the car and checked the time on my phone to start the seven minute prayer. It showed 11.11, significant as being instantly recognisable as Armistice Day or Memorial Sunday (11 November). My final visit to the War Memorial was on the way home following an overnight stay at a hotel. As usual, I checked my phone before the prayer and it showed 10.25. Having prayed, I then became lost in thought, reflecting on the fourteen-day experience. Finally, on returning to the car and taking off my jacket, the engine was switched on and the car radio lit up with the time – 11.11. I quickly double-checked my phone which also still showed 11.11. C.G. Jung (1875–1961) has described the concept of synchronicity as meaningful coincidence.[59] For me, each of these incidences of synchronicity, one right at the commencement of the fieldwork and the other right at the end, represented powerful incidences of Otto's numinous and were felt to be very significant for the project, being neither perception nor imagination. However, for the purposes of this project, and with respect to reflexivity, I isolated (as far as possible) the initial experience during the fourteen days, and both experiences in the writing up of this discussion.

Together with my religious history, despite being in the past, it is easy to see how criticisms can be made of phenomenological auto-ethnographic work, querying the representativeness and validity on the basis of bias, making it unlikely that someone else would experience the same results, as described by Bell and Waters.[60] However, in their paper, Wilma Koopman, Christopher Watling and Kori LaDonna Koopman have suggested that an improvement would be achieved if more effort could be made with regard to reflexivity, rather than allowing merely the reflexive paragraph to suffice.[61] More focus on this may be beneficial. However, although there are valid criticisms, as long as all possible influences are declared, according to Jo Pearson, it could be considered that certain backgrounds have an advantage in research.[62] An example of this may be seen in this project regarding the fact that, as prayer was included in an attempt to re-enact the prayer time of the servicemen, my own familiarity with prayer could have helped me identify with the servicemen more than someone who dismissed the idea of prayer.

There remained, however, the difficulty in distinguishing between my perception (involving belief or knowledge) and my imagination, with regard to the increase in sacredness. Lane described the recognition of sacredness as existentially, not ontologically, discerned.[63] However this should not mean that sacredness does not ontologically exist. The recent concept of the ontological turn has been described by Paolo Heywood as continuing the tradition in anthropology of aiming to take difference seriously and understand it on its own terms. He illustrated the challenge with a scenario where 'your interlocutor may "believe" the tree to be a spirit, and you may 'respect' this belief as much as you wish, but your own belief is... what you would think of as "knowledge". You do not think of yourself as "believing" it to be a tree, you *know* it to be so'.[64] This posits that our perceptions may be different and not always correct and highlights the inadequacy of merely 'respecting' someone else's views. The apparent reluctance of modernism to acknowledge the possibility of an objective spirituality has appeared to affect analysis of sacred space but the situation is hopefully changing in the post-modern world, supported by increased use of phenomenological, auto-reflexive accounts.

Conclusion

The aim of this research project was to explore whether the Canadian War Memorial, which had been formerly used as an outdoor worship site, could be described as sacred space. From Durkheim's era, the concept of sacred space has been constantly changing but has not lost any importance. In comparing the fieldwork results with the views of various theorists on sacred space and several papers on memorials, this project aimed to further that discussion.

Having been chosen and used as an outdoor place of worship for the three-month period before D-Day, 6 June 1944, by men whose lives would later be commemorated there, it was thought appropriate to consider sacredness at three levels, the first being whether this particular area in the landscape originally was in itself sacred, secondly whether sacredness had been established through the ritual of services and prayer by the servicemen, and thirdly whether, as a memorial, it could now be counted as sacred space. A literature review was carried out ascertaining different scholars' interpretations of sacred space, and to what degree War Memorials are generally deemed to be sacred. Having decided upon a phenomenological approach, field research in the form of a programme of visits on fourteen consecutive days was carried out during which, following a brief period of prayer undertaken as a re-enactment of the activity at the site prior to D-Day, thoughts and feelings were recorded in a diary. These notes were subsequently discussed and compared with other scholars' accounts and opinions from the literature.

The initial discussion focused on the possibility of the site having already been sacred, referencing concepts described by Eliade and Lane Had this been the case, the site could then be said to have attracted the servicemen to it. It was acknowledged that the site physically would have offered protection from wind and from German planes, as well as offering distant views west to their homes and families in Canada, however it was thought that these features may also have been signs from the landscape itself, following Eliade's concept. My own perception of the landscape's sacredness at the location increased during the fourteen days.

The ritual of outdoor prayers and services for the servicemen over the three month period, with the wooden cross as a focus, was thought to concur with many theorists' ideas of what makes a place sacred. Although there is now less ritual at the site, mainly once a year on Memorial Sunday, considering the location, the re-use of the bolt from the original wooden cross in its replacement and the cross's current position between the two national flag poles, it was concluded that the site did warrant the status of sacred, as a combination of both human action and spiritual phenomena.

The fieldwork, based on phenomenological auto-ethnographic experiences, exposed my changing perceptions of the site from, initially, an outsider viewpoint, as described by Lane, with no personal sense of the sacred, to an insider viewpoint, eventually perceiving the landscape itself to be sacred through my own ritual activity. Although from Durkheim's secular view, there could have been no sacredness inherent in the site, the ritual during the time when it was used for worship would have created sacredness and, currently, the setting aside of the area together with group, annual ritual in front of the cross, would have maintained some sacredness, even on Durkheim's terms. My overall conclusion was that the area itself was and always had been sacred, due to some natural phenomenon, in accordance with Lane's axioms and descriptions. The natural, spiritual and human element, together with the services held and memorial creation, intensified my experience of the site as sacred, accepting, as well, the possibility of Eliade's hierophany having drawn the young servicemen and their chaplain to the site in April, 1944, for prayer and, knowingly or unknowingly, facing towards home as they left.

Notes

1   Newforestknowledge.org. https://nfknowledge.org/contributions/history-of-the-memorial-at-mogshade-hill/#map=10/-1.66/50.88/0/24:0:0.6|39:1:1|40:1:1. [Accessed 31 December 2022]

2   Mircea Eliade, *The Sacred And The Profane The Nature Of Religion* (W.R. Trask, Trans.) (San Diego: Harcourt Brace Jovanovich, 1987), p. 11.

3   Belden C. Lane, *Landscapes Of The Sacred, Geography And Narrative In American Spirituality*, (Baltimore: The John Hopkins University Press, 2002), p. 254.

4   Emile Durkheim, *The Elementary Forms Of Religious Life* (K. E. Fields, Trans.) (New York: The Free Press, 1995 [1912]), p. 84.

5   Rudolf Otto, *The Idea Of The Holy An Enquiry Into The Non-Rational Factor In The Idea Of The Divine And Its Relation To The Rational* (John W. Harvey, Trans.) (Oxford: Oxford University Press, 1924), p. 11.

6   Eliade, *The Sacred And The Profane*, p. 10.

7   William E. Paden, 'Before 'The Sacred' Became Theological: Rereading The Durkheimian Legacy', *Method & Theory in the Study of Religion* 3, no. 1 (1991), pp. 10–23, p.10.

8   William S. F. Pickering, 'The Eternality Of The Sacred : Durkheim's Error?', *Archives De sciences Sociales Des Religions* 35, no. 69 (1990), pp. 91–108, p. 91.

9   Catherine Allerton, 'Introduction: Spiritual Landscapes Of Southeast Asia', *Anthropological Forum*, 19 (3) (2009), pp. 235–51, p. 11.

10   Allerton, 'Introduction: Spiritual Landscapes', p. 1.

11   Anthony Thorley and Celia M. Gunn, *Sacred Sites: An Overview. A Report For The Gaia Foundation (Abridged Version)*, 2008, (London: Calverts, 2008), p. 11.

12   Denis Byrne, 'The Enchanted Earth: Numinous Sacred Sites', *Sacred Natural Sites, Conserving Nature and Culture*, ed. by Bas Verschuuren and others (London: Earthscan, 2010), pp. 53–62, p. 55.

13   Timothy Hessel-Robinson, *Interdisciplinary Studies in Literature and Environment* 10, no. 1 (2003): 281–82, p. 282.

14   Christopher Tilley and Kate Cameron-Daum, *An Anthropology Of Landscape, The Extraordinary In The Ordinary* (London: UCL Press, 2017), p. 12.

15   Judith Bell and Stephen Waters, *Doing Your Research Project, A Guide For First-Time Researchers*, 7th Edn (London: Open University Press, 2018), p. 127.

16   Elaine Campbell, 'Exploring Autoethnography as a Method and Methodology In Legal Education Research', *Asian Journal of Legal Education*, Volume 3, Issue 1, 2016, pp. 95–105, p. 96.

17   Bell and Waters, *Doing Your Research Project*, p. 26.

18   Amber L. Griffioen, 'Are You There, God? It's Me, The Theist, On The Viability And Virtue Of Non-Doxastic Prayer', *Analyzing prayer : Theological And Philosophical Essays*, 1st edn, ed. by Oliver Crisp, James Arcadi and Jordan Wessling (Oxford: Oxford University Press, 2022), pp. 38–58, p. 43.

19   José-Manuel González-González, Jesús Gerardo Franco-Calvo and Darío Español-Solana, 'Educating in History: Thinking Historically through Historical Reenactment', *Social Sciences*, 11: 256, (2022), pp. 1–18, p. 13.

20   Bell and Waters, *Doing Your Research Project*, p. 254.

21   Durkheim, *Forms*, p. 81.

22   Eliade, *The Sacred And The Profane*, p. 24.

23   Durkheim, *Forms*, p. 416.

24   Durkheim, *Forms*, p. 426.

25   Durkheim, *Forms*, p. 281.

26   Eliade, *The Sacred And The Profane*, p. 11.

27   Eliade, *The Sacred And The Profane*, p. 28.

28   Eliade, *The Sacred And The Profane*, p. 20.

29   Lane, *Landscapes Of The Sacred*, p. 6.

30   Lane, *Landscapes Of The Sacred*, p. 5.

31   Lane, *Landscapes Of The Sacred*, p. 19.

32   Karen E. Fields, 'Translator's Introduction', in E. Durkheim, *The Elementary Forms of Religious Life* (K.E. Fields, Trans.) (New York: The Free Press, 1995 [1912]), p. xliv.

33   Eliade, *The Sacred And The Profane*, p. 107.

34   Belden C. Lane, 'Giving Voice to Place: Three Models For Understanding American Sacred Space', *Religion And American Culture: A Journal Of Interpretation*, Vol. 11, No. 1 (Winter 2001), pp. 53–81, p. 53.

35   Lane, *Landscapes Of The Sacred*, p. 58.

36   Veronica della Dora, 'Engaging Sacred Space: Experiments In The Field', *Journal Of Geography in Higher Education,* 35:2, (2011), pp. 163–84, p. 165.

37   Erika S. Svendsen and Lindsay K. Campbell, 'Living Memorials: Understanding The Social Meanings Of Community-Based Memorials To September 11, 2001', *Environment And Behavior*, Vol.42 (3), (2010), pp.318-34, p. 326.

38   Svendsen and Campbell, 'Living Memorials', p. 327.

39   Svendsen and Campbell, 'Living Memorials', p. 326.

40   Svendsen and Campbell, 'Living Memorials', p. 327.

41   Svendsen and Campbell, 'Living Memorials', p. 330.

42   James M. Mayo, 'War Memorials As Political Memory, *Geographical Review*, Vol. 78, No. 1, (1988), pp. 62–75, p. 64.

43 Mayo, 'War Memorials', p. 63.
44 Edward S. Casey, *Remembering, A Phenomenological Study*, 2nd edn (Bloomington: Indiana University Press, 2000), p. 216.
45 Lane, *Landscapes Of The Sacred*, p. 54
46 Lane, *Landscapes Of The Sacred*, p. 55.
47 Lane, *Landscapes Of The Sacred*, p.4.
48 Eliade, *The Sacred And The Profane*, p. 27.
49 Eliade, *The Sacred And The Profane*, p. 36.
50 Eliade, *The Sacred And The Profane*, p. 32.
51 Fields, 'Translators Introduction', p. xlvi; Eliade, *The Sacred And The Profane*, p. 26.
52 Eliade, *The Sacred And The Profane*, p. 25.
53 Mayo, 'War Memorials', p. 63.
54 Griffioen, 'Are You There, God?', p. 39.
55 Jason McMartin, 'Prayer And The Meaning Of Life', *Analyzing prayer: Theological And Philosophical Essays*, 1st edn, ed. by Oliver Crisp, James Arcadi and Jordan Wessling (Oxford: Oxford University Press, 2022), pp. 202–19, p. 216.
56 Griffioen, 'Are You There, God?', p. 46.
57 Lane, Landscapes Of The Sacred, p. 19.
58 Lane, Landscapes Of The Sacred, p. 6.
59 C.G. Jung and Roderick Main, 'Synchronicity', *Jung On Synchronicity And The Paranormal*, (Princeton: Princeton University Press, 1997), pp. 93–102, p. 97.
60 Bell and Waters, *Doing Your Research Project*, p. 244.
61 Wilma J. Koopman, Christopher J. Watling and Kori A. LaDonna Koopman, 'Autoethnography as a Strategy for Engaging in Reflexivity', *Global Qualitative Nursing Research*, Vol. 7, (2020) pp. 1–9, p. 7.
62 Jo Pearson, '"Going Native in Reverse": The Insider as Researcher in British Wicca', *Nova Religio: The Journal of Alternative and Emergent Religions*, 5, no. 1 (2001), pp. 52–63, p. 58.
63 Lane, *Landscapes Of The Sacred*, p. 19.
64 Paolo Heywood, 'The Ontological Turn', *The Cambridge Encyclopedia of Anthropology*, ed. by Felix Stein (2017), pp. 1–12, p. 9.

10

THE HIROSHIMA PEACE PARK; IS IT POSSIBLE FOR A NUCLEAR WEAPON TO CREATE A SACRED SPACE?

Andrew Spencer

The aim of this chapter is to examine the role that a nuclear weapon might have played in the creation of a sacred space. While the question is potentially too vast to answer definitively, the research presented here is focused specifically on the sacred geography of a small area in Hiroshima, southern Japan known as the 'Peace Park'. The question was explored through a limited amount of personal fieldwork in 2018, combined with feedback from friends and colleagues who had visited the Park in previous decades. These personal observations and experiences are then put into dialogue with the work of a number of key scholars, as described below in the literature review section.

The Peace Park is mostly located within a few hundred metres' radius of the hypocentre, or exact location, of the world's first use of a nuclear weapon in wartime. This was detonated at an altitude of 600 metres on the 6th of August 1945 at 8.15 in the morning.

As can be seen in Figure 1, in addition to the iconic 'A-Bomb Dome', or Genbaku, there are about fifty different shrines and memorials to those who died directly, and indirectly, as a result of the bombing. The main shrines and buildings are named on this map.[1]

Figure 2 gives a visual idea of the relatively small scale of the Peace Park and shows a view from the south towards the Genbaku in the distance with the Cenotaph in the foreground. The arch of the Cenotaph covers a stone box which contains a register of all those who died directly, or later on, as a result of the bombing (see Fig. 3). While the Park is not specifically oriented to any particular religious tradition, Benedict Giamo describes the Cenotaph Arch as being in the style of the Shinto religion, intended to 'shelter the souls of the victims'.[2] To the north of the Cenotaph is the Flame of Peace. This was lit from the flame in the Shinto shrine on Miyajima Island to the south of Hiroshima. Reputedly that flame has been burning continuously for over one thousand years. The Genbaku itself (Fig. 4) was finally designated as a UNESCO World Heritage site in 1996

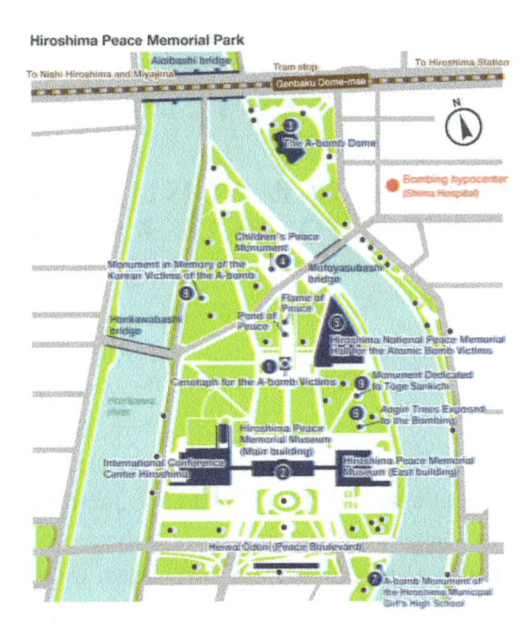

Figure 1: Map of the Hiroshima Peace Park (scale is about 600 metres north to south) – courtesy nippon.com

Figure 2: The Hiroshima Peace Park: The Cenotaph and Genbaku ('A bomb dome') – courtesy nippon.com

with the Peace Park as a 'buffer zone… defined both as a place of prayer for the atomic bomb victims as well as for permanent world peace'.[3]

In addition to serving as an introduction to the Park, this chapter begins with a literature review and a description of my research methodology. The findings and discussion are centred around a number of key themes aimed specifically at answering the research question, which itself can be broken down into several subsidiary questions. It should be clearly noted that this study does not deal directly with the ethics of the bombing, which is an extensive, still controversial and very definitely far from clear-cut topic in its own right.

Figure 3: The Cenotaph and casket containing the register of names – image by author, August 2018

Figure 4: The Genbaku (view from the south east – image by the author, August 2018

There are several key scholars whose theories can be usefully applied to this field of research. Randall Studstill in his paper 'Eliade, Phenomenology, and the Sacred' emphasises Mircea Eliade's (1907–1986) phenomenological approach to understanding how sacred space is differentiated from the profane.[4] Eliade describes three main concepts that might be applicable to the Peace Park. The first is the notion of a hierophany, or manifestation of the divine in a wider sense. As Eliade said: 'Every sacred space implies a hierophany, an irruption of the sacred that results in detaching a territory from the surrounding cosmic milieu... making it qualitatively different' from the land around it.[5] Might the explosion of the bomb at Hiroshima represent a form of hierophany?

Eliade also employed the concept of the 'Centre of the World' in reference to 'one of the deepest meanings of sacred space'.[6] He proposed that a hierophany can create a breakthrough or connection between some, or all, of three cosmic planes – between Earth, Heaven and the Underworld. As Eliade noted, 'this communication is sometimes expressed through the image of a universal pillar, *axis mundi*, which at once connects and supports heaven and earth and whose base is fixed in the world below (the infernal regions)'.[7] Sacred space, which can take many forms, essentially lies around this cosmic pillar, or *axis mundi*, which is at the centre of that particular world.[8] The third concept is theophany, or the manifestation of the divine in an individual, personal sense. Eliade described a number of examples illustrating how crossing the threshold into a sacred space may result in a theophany, or the appearance of a sign for some, but not all individuals.[9]

Émile Durkheim's (1858–1917) arguments could be regarded as providing an alternative perspective on the creation of sacred space. t can be argued that Durkheim viewed sacred spaces as being made and re-made by human action, rather than as a consequence of divine hierophany. In the introduction to her translation of Durkheim's work, Karen Fields notes that his key observation regarding sacred space is that it is 'set apart and forbidden'.[10] That is to say sacred space is set apart and surrounded by taboos by groups of people who may paradoxically encounter sacredness as a 'ready-made' phenomenon.[11] It is also important to bear in mind that Durkheim was essentially a social scientist rather than a phenomenologist, so his emphasis is primarily on the social.[12] He was also researching in a different era to Eliade and, as Steven Lukes suggests, 'philosophy, science and art existed in nothing like today's isolation from one another'.[13]

Belden C. Lane offers another way of considering the role of the atomic bomb and the creation of the Peace Park. He suggested 'four different rules or "axioms" to understand the character of sacred space'. He regarded these as largely phenomenological in nature. All four are perhaps applicable, but, for example, the first axiom, 'that sacred place is not chosen, it chooses' seems to be particularly important in this context.[14] Tim Ingold's ideas on the anthropology of lines also have relevance here, and can be applied to map making. The Peace Park is obviously now defined by maps which have particular shapes and lines that may be important in the context of this research question, guiding and influencing the visitor's experience.[15] Clearly the wartime circumstances also point to the Peace Park as a contested space, therefore Barbara Bender's theory of contested spaces also has relevance here, and will be discussed later in this chapter.[16] Vera Zolberg's paper on contested remembrance is a reminder that the

Peace Park was a source of controversy even in the 1990s.[17]

In terms of Japanese secondary sources, the most important of these is perhaps the work of Yuki Miyamoto, a Japanese American scholar whose mother, at age 6, was a survivor of the bombing.[18] In particular, her book *Beyond the Mushroom Cloud*, written in English, is based on an extensive study of Japanese primary sources and interview materials.[19] As with translations of Eliade and Durkheim and the lexical constraints of the English language, it is necessary to be aware of even more challenging issues when making translations from Japanese to English. My youngest son, who is now a near-native Japanese speaker, summarised it as follows: 'In written prose, there may often be no subject which might be stated only once, or assumed, or omitted altogether depending on the context. There is a much larger vocabulary than English, for example, as with ancient Greek, the word love in Japanese can be represented by six different words, each with its own subtle nuance. In the end it is about trying to achieve the best fit of transmission from Japanese to English'. As Bryan Rennie observed about Eliade's thinking, 'in the complex arena of religious belief small inaccuracies [in translation] can develop into major misunderstandings'.[20] A number of official Japanese websites such as that of the Peace Park Museum were also consulted as part of the research for this chapter, and these are listed in the bibliography.

Reflexive Considerations and Methodology

I am a male born in 1953 at the start of what is considered to be the beginning of the 'cold war,' and thirty years later was very aware of the nuclear standoff in Europe at that time between the United States and Europe on one side and the Soviet Union on the other. Recently, military historians such as Tom Nichols confirm that the NATO exercise 'Able Archer' (1983) came very much closer than the Cuban missile crisis (1962) to triggering a nuclear conflict with the Soviet Union.[21] Consequently, I do have a bias in my thinking about these issues, whereby I still regard the world's nuclear arsenal as a potentially greater threat to humanity than, for example, the effects of climate change. As Miyamoto notes in *Beyond the Mushroom Cloud*, the 2010 world inventory of nuclear weapons exceeded twenty thousand, most of which have substantially greater power than that used on Hiroshima.[22]

My trip to Japan in August 2018 was primarily to see my youngest son, who happened to be studying at the University of Hiroshima during most of 2018. Therefore, visiting the Peace Park felt for me like a kind of pilgrimage. I took notes and photographs during the day I spent there, but was not aware at that time that it would later become the focus of my academic research. Consequently, this project also draws on the extensive fieldwork that Miyamoto carried out with survivors (hibakusha) and religious leaders in Hiroshima. Her work was on a scale that would not be possible to replicate in a project of this size.[23]

This study uses a substantial amount of literature related to the bombing, the Peace Park, relevant concepts in sacred geography and additional visual material that is available from Japanese websites. Although I did not conduct interviews specifically for this research, feedback from friends and former work colleagues who visited the Park in previous decades has been incorporated into the discussion. I have also drawn on ideas and thoughts from my youngest son who was a student at the University of Sheffield, recently graduated with a BA degree in Japanese and East Asian studies in 2019 and has returned to Japan as a language teacher. In summary, the research methodology employed what Monique Hennink and colleagues might describe as 'mixed research methods' with some fieldwork and an emphasis on literature surveys and digital sources.[24]

Findings and discussion

This section contains a number of themes that progressively address various components of the research question. The discussion begins with personal reflections and then moves on to consider several perspectives from a more collective level.

Theophany

As noted above, Eliade proposed that sacred spaces can show themselves as distinct from the profane through a number of signs.[25] One of these he described as theophany, or divine manifestation, in the form of a personal experience.[26] For myself, I experienced an intense theophany when visiting the Park in August 2018. Normally I am not significantly affected by places that appear to have been set apart from the profane. On this occasion, however, on stepping across the southern boundary into the Park and catching sight of the 'A-Bomb Dome' in the distance, an unstoppable wave of sadness started sweeping up through my body, manifesting itself as a flow of tears. This was not crying in the normal sense, and the feeling was definitely one of sadness rather than anger or guilt. Having travelled widely since 1974 I have never felt such strong emotions on entering other places that would normally be considered as sacred.

Subsequent to that experience, this year, in completely separate conversations, I learned from two of my former work colleagues that they had experienced virtually the same theophany over twenty years ago. Similarly, a friend from San Francisco who was in London in recent days had been there in the 1980s and experienced the same type of emotions on entering the Park. At least anecdotally, then, the area associated with the atomic bomb hypocentre appears to have an unusual and consistently powerful energy. Could this be considered a form of theophany, and as a sign of sacredness?

Eliade's thesis that sacred space reveals itself as a hierophany or 'irruption' which sets it apart from the profane provides another way of looking at the research question.[27] The detonation of the bomb itself could, perhaps, be considered as a higher, more intense form of irruption or hierophany which has defined the space as sacred. As Eliade suggested 'the hierophany reveals an absolute fixed point, a centre' – in this case the hypocentre as shown in Figure 1.[28] Perhaps this hierophany could be considered as similar in intensity to volcanic eruptions or other natural earth energy events.

Eliade links a hierophany to the 'axis mundi' or 'centre of the world' of the place in question and in this case, it could be said that the hypocentre marks such a place.[29] Further, it could be argued that the column of smoke, ash and the mushroom cloud that followed, acted as a visible form of what he refers to as a 'cosmic pole,' connecting at least the Earth and Heaven. Given the nature of this weapon, this particular axis might have connected to the underworld as well. A smaller-scale but interesting comparison is Eliade's observation of the Achilpa tribe in Australia. In their mythology, the divine being, Numbakula, created a sacred pole from a gum tree which he used to ascend to the higher worlds. Ritually, a replica of the pole serves as a portable 'axis mundi'.[30]

Human action and sacred space

Notwithstanding the Eliadean perspective that the Peace Park, as a sacred place, could have been the result of the eruption of divine forces, it might also be seen as due to human action. Miyamoto describes in some detail how the Peace Park came to be designed and constructed in a way that Durkheim, as a social scientist, would have recognised. She records as early as February 1946 how the restoration council, led by mayor Hamai Shinzō, recognised that the city needed a new identity, having been a military base since the Sino-Japanese war of 1894. They unanimously agreed to develop a city of peace, and in the same year started working on a blueprint for what is now the Peace Park. Hamai led the effort to build the Park, which was completed in 1954, followed shortly after by the museum in 1955.[31] The inscription on the Cenotaph (Fig. 5) expresses the spirit of Hiroshima – 'enduring grief, transcending hatred, pursuing harmony and prosperity for all and a yearning for genuine lasting world peace'. In this sense Durkheimian principles apply to the Peace Park as it was set aside and forbidden (for other uses) as a separate and sacred place resulting from human actions after the atomic bombing.

Figure 5: English Inscription on the Cenotaph – image by author, August 2018

Contested sacred space

Regarding the Peace Park as a potentially contested space, Bender describes in her paper on Stonehenge an area that appears to have been a sacred space for millennia. However, she demonstrated that its collective ownership and spiritual or esoteric significance had changed several times over that period. In essence, there has been a continuing contest between different groups and their interpretations regarding that space.[32]

Therefore, a question in this context is: Did the atomic bombing initiate a sacred space in the near radius of the hypocentre, or was it already in existence? Immediately to the north of the Genbaku, literally on the other side of the road, was the torii, or main entrance gate of the Shinto Gokoku shrine. This was one of the more important Shinto shrines in Japan, having been established in 1869 to commemorate the *Han* victims of the *Boshin* war (Japanese civil war). In 1934 it was moved to its current position on the north side of the road opposite the Genbaku with the gate about 170 metres from the hypocentre.[33]

Perhaps more significant was the original location of the Pure Land Buddhist temple Jisen-ji, which had flourished in the northern promontory of what is now the Peace Park, where the river system divides (see Fig. 1). This was extant since the seventeenth century and was about 200 metres to the east of the hypocentre. Given the original target was the Aioibashi Bridge at the north of the Park it could be said that the temple most likely would have been the hypocentre of the explosion if the bomb had not drifted slightly to the east in the wind.[34]

It would therefore appear that both sites were already sacred places prior to WWII. As this study is restricted to the Peace Park it could be argued that the atomic bomb effected a 'remaking' of an already sacred place in a manner that might be recognised by both Bender (contested space) and Durkheim (human action). That it was a Buddhist sacred space is not so surprising; as Miyamoto notes that although both religions were and are similar and of major importance in Japan, it appears that Hiroshima could be classified as 80% Pure Land Buddhist.[35]

The element of contest has continued since the war. Miyamoto describes the controversy generated by the National Air and Space Museum (NASM) at the Smithsonian Institute in the US. An exhibit involving the original bombing aircraft (Enola Gay) was planned for 1995. The Smithsonian Director, Martin Harwitt, argued that the museum should exhibit sound scholarship. The plan was to present the exhibit with 'perspectives literally and metaphorically both above and beneath the mushroom cloud'.[36] This plan for a 'balanced exhibit' triggered such intense criticism amongst various organisations in the US that the Peace Park Museum withdrew its offer to loan items from its collection, and Harwitt had to resign his position.[37] All of that took place in spite of the Peace Park's message and ethos being one of reconciliation and world peace. In a separate paper, Miyamoto offers a critical review regarding what is known as the Hiroshima National Peace Memorial Hall in the east of the Peace Park. This was added in 2001, and while the intention of the government was to insert a secular memorial, Miyamoto argues that nonetheless it could be regarded as having a strong religious element.[38]

There also appears to be an ongoing – slow but perceptible – change in the meaning of the Peace Park as the generations move over time. According to my youngest son, for his generation in Hiroshima, the element of commemoration is gradually fading, but the ethos of world peace and reconciliation is still very strong.

Who picked the target?

Whether the Peace Park as a sacred space is considered to be the result of a hierophany, or human action, the next related question is: Was the targeting and ultimate hypocentre position solely due to human action? The US Army report on the immediate aftermath describes the general suitability of Hiroshima as a target due to the flat nature of the city, high population density with mostly wooden buildings, numerous small workshops in the residential areas, better weather conditions than the capital Tokyo and a clearly militaristic culture. In other words, it appears that the military planners were seeking potential for maximum effect in what was clearly considered to also be a scientific experiment, as well as an Allied military objective.[39]

Based on documentation in the Peace Park Museum, the detailed targeting instruction given to the aircrew of Enola Gay carrying the bomb was to aim for the Aioibashi Bridge whose distinctive 'T' shape and bifurcation of the river delta system would be clearly visible from their height of 6000 metres. I can find no documentation that suggests cognisance of the Jisen-ji temple or Gokoku shrine on the part of the military planners.[40]

It might be argued that there was a component of what Ingold described as the anthropology of lines involved in the map making and targeting of Hiroshima.[41] Moreover, the clear 'T' of the bridge and the associated triangular shape of the Peace Park (see Fig. 1) points to the possibility that an element of sacred geometry was also involved, perhaps at a sub-conscious level. Lane's four axioms in identifying the phenomenology of a sacred place are also important when considering this issue, especially the first which is 'that *sacred place is* not chosen, it chooses'.[42] In other words, one has to hold open the possibility that the bomb was guided by something Eliade might have called 'ganz andere', or the 'wholly other', to an already visible sacred place.[43]

Conclusions

The primary question associated with this research project on the Peace Park in Hiroshima was whether it is possible for a nuclear weapon to create a sacred space. The simple answer in this case is probably 'not on its own,' but it almost certainly increased the visibility of an area that already had elements of a sacred space from one of local concern (the Jisen-ji temple) to a site of global significance (the Peace Park).

Taking Durkheim's perspective as a social scientist, then, it could be argued that the bombing was part of a process of human activity remaking sacred areas in the near vicinity of the hypocentre. In this case, the Peace Park, including the Genbaku, was conceived in 1946, and opened in 1954 with a range of shrines and memorials. More recently it was eventually 'set apart' as a World Heritage site by UNESCO in 1996 as a place of prayer for both the victims and world peace. It is clear that the atomic bomb also played its part in the history of the Peace Park as a contested space, analogous in some ways to the changes over time described by Bender for Stonehenge. As noted above, the contest continued long after WWII, partly as a result of very different paradigms held by the local survivors and numerous veterans' organisations in the United States. It is also possible that Ingold's anthropology of lines may provide useful insights into part of the process of the atomic bomb's ultimate transformation of the area into the Peace Park.

From a phenomenological viewpoint it can be seen how the detonation of the atomic bomb could have met Eliade's concept of a sacred place becoming visible through a hierophany. Further, it might be considered that the hierophany created an 'axis mundi' or cosmic pillar, focused on the Peace Park and its near vicinity. His idea of a sacred place creating theophany for individuals appears to be active as far as the Peace Park is concerned. Applying Lane's phenomenology of sacred landscapes to the Peace Park points to the possibility that the atomic bomb was 'chosen' [and guided to] the sacred space of the Peace Park, rather than the bomb creating a sacred space of its own accord.

Notes

1 Key introductory summary and pictures of the Peace Park: https://www.nippon.com/en/features/h00141/hiroshima-peace-memorial-park.html [accessed 19th December 2019].
2 Benedict Giamo, 'The Myth of the Vanquished: The Hiroshima Peace Memorial Museum'. *American Quarterly*, vol. 55, no. 4 (2003), pp. 703–28.
3 UNESCO documentation regarding World Heritage listing of the Genbaku and Peace Park: https://whc.unesco.org/en/list/775/ [accessed 19 December 2019].
4 Randal Studstill, 'Eliade, Phenomenology, and the Sacred.' *Religious Studies*, vol. 36, no. 2 (2000), pp.177–94.
5 Mircea Eliade, *The Sacred and the Profane; the Nature of Religion*, trans. Willard R. Trask (Harcourt, Brace and World Inc., 1959), pp.20–26.
6 Mircea Eliade, *The Sacred and the Profane*, p.36.
7 Mircea Eliade, *The Sacred and the Profane*, pp. 36–37.
8 Mircea Eliade, *The Sacred and the Profane*, pp.36–37.
9 Mircea Eliade, *The Sacred and the Profane*, pp.24–29.
10 Émile Durkheim, *The Elementary Forms of Religious Life*, trans. Karen E. Fields (New York: Free Press, 1995; 1st edn, *Les formes élémentaires de la vie religieuse*, Paris; F. Alcan 1912), p.xlvi.
11 Émile Durkheim, *The Elementary Forms of Religious Life*, trans. Karen E. Fields, p.xlvi.
12 Steven Lukes, *Émile Durkheim, His Life and Work: A Historical and Critical Study* (London: Penguin Books Limited, updated edition 1992), p.34.
13 Émile Durkheim, *The Elementary Forms of Religious Life*, trans. Karen E. Fields, p.xxii.
14 Belden C. Lane, *Landscapes of the Sacred: Geography and Narrative in American Spirituality*. Expanded edn (Baltimore, MD; London: John Hopkins University Press, 2001), pp.19–37.
15 Tim Ingold, *Lines: A Brief History* (Oxford: Routledge Classics 2016), pp.85–92.
16 Barbara Bender, 'Contested Landscapes: Medieval to Present Day', Stonehenge: Making Space (Oxford: Berg, 1998), (PDF).
17 Vera L. Zolberg, 'Contested Remembrance: The Hiroshima Exhibit Controversy', *Theory and Society*, vol. 27, no. 4 (1998), pp. 565–90.
18 Yuki Miyamoto, *Beyond the Mushroom Cloud: Commemoration, Religion and Responsibility After Hiroshima* (New York: Fordham University Press 2012), p.xiv
19 Academic biography of Yuki Miyamoto:

https://las.depaul.edu/academics/religious-studies/faculty/Pages/yuki-miyamoto.aspx [accessed 19 December 2019]; Academic review of Yuki Miyamoto's *Beyond the Mushroom Cloud:* https://www.h-net.org/reviews/showpdf.php?id=38017 [accessed 19 December 2019].

20   Bryan Rennie, *Reconstructing Eliade; Making Sense of Religion* (Albany, NY: State University of New York Press, 1996), p.19.

21   Tom Nichols 2014 article on NATO exercise 'Able Archer', http://nationalinterest.org/feature/five-ways-nuclear-armageddon-was-almost-unleashed-11044 (accessed 17 November 2019).

22   Yuki Miyamoto, *Beyond the Mushroom Cloud*, p.3.

23   Yuki Miyamoto, *Beyond the Mushroom Cloud*.

24   Monique Hennink, Inge Hutter and Ajay Bailey, *Qualitative Research Methods* (London: SAGE Publications Ltd. 2011), pp. 52–60.

25   Mircea Eliade, *The Sacred and the Profane*, pp.24–29.

26   Paul Larsen, 'Theophany', in D.A. Leeming, K. Madden, and S. Marlan, eds, *Encyclopedia of Psychology and Religion* (Boston, MA: Springer 2010).

27   Paul Larsen, 'Hierophany', in D.A. Leeming, K. Madden, and S. Marlan, eds, *Encyclopedia of Psychology and Religion* (Boston, MA: Springer 2010).

28   Mircea Eliade, *The Sacred and the Profane*, p.21.

29   Mircea Eliade, *The Sacred and the Profane*, p.36

30   Mircea Eliade, *The Sacred and the Profane*, p.33.

31   Yuki Miyamoto, *Beyond the Mushroom Cloud*, pp.31–33.

32   Barbara Bender, '*Contested Landscapes*': (PDF)

33   Example of material from the Peace Park Museum – evidence for the pre-bombing location of the Shinto Gokoku Shrine: http://www.pcf.city.hiroshima.jp/virtual/VirtualMuseum_e/exhibit_e/exh0702_e/exh070206_e.html [accessed 19 December 2019].

34   Remains of the Buddhist Jisen-ji Temple, evidence for its location in the Peace Park: http://www.pcf.city.hiroshima.jp/virtual/VirtualMuseum_e/tour_e/ireihi/tour_12_e.html [accessed 19th December 2019].

35   Yuki Miyamoto, *Beyond the Mushroom Cloud*, p.7.

36   Yuki Miyamoto, *Beyond the Mushroom Cloud*, p.17.

37   Yuki Miyamoto, *Beyond the Mushroom Cloud*, pp.18–19; Vera L. Zolberg, 'Contested Remembrance', pp.565–90.

38   Yuki Miyamoto, 'The Ethics of Commemoration: Religion and Politics in Nanjing, Hiroshima, and Yasukuni', *Journal of the American Academy of Religion*, vol. 80, no. 1 (2012), pp. 34–63.

39   L. R. Groves, *The Atomic Bombings of Hiroshima and Nagasaki*, The Manhattan Engineer District of the United States Army, June 29, 1946.

40   Description of aircrew's original target (see text for location 6): http://www.pcf.city.hiroshima.jp/frame/Virtual_e/tour_e/guide1.html [accessed 19 December 2019].

41   Tim Ingold, *Lines: A Brief History*, pp.85–92.

42   Belden C. Lane, *Landscapes of the Sacred*, pp.19–37.

43   Mircea Eliade, *The Sacred and the Profane*, p.9.

11

A LIMINAL HAVEN: EXPLORING THE SACRED GEOGRAPHY OF AN ENGLISH DROSSCAPE

Daniel Broadbent

Can a motorway flyover be considered a sacred place? This chapter records a programme of research aimed at assessing whether sacred space is a human construct or a natural phenomenon, through a phenomenological study of the area beneath a section of motorway flyover on the edge of the town of Taunton, Somerset, in the south west of England. The site is not of a type which would generally be regarded as sacred. Lying just north of Junction 25 of the M5, it is, rather, a piece of wasteland, of the kind Alan Berger termed a 'drosscape', largely ignored and existing only as a by-product of industrial or economic activity.[1] However, the recovery of a fragment of a Bronze Age sword from the riverbank nearby, indicative of a religious offering, suggests that the River Tone at this point may have been considered sacred in the prehistoric past.[2] Here too, on the evening of 4 November 2011, seven people lost their lives and a further fifty-one were injured in one of the worst road traffic accidents to have occurred in Britain.[3] A memorial to the victims is situated a short distance from the flyover. However, whilst the memorial is considered as part of this research, the main the focus of study is the flyover itself, the area directly beneath and adjacent to the crash site.

The flyover stands at the eastern edge of Hankridge Water Park, a narrow strip of urban green space which acts as a buffer between the Heron's Gate business park and the southern bank of the River Tone. It is an area popular with dog-walkers, joggers, and anglers, and provides one of the most direct walking routes from Taunton into the countryside. Forming part of the North Petherton by-pass section of the M5, the flyover was constructed between May 1973 and November 1975.[4] As part of the construction, bridges were built over the Taunton-Bridgwater canal, a four-track railway line, a farm access track and the River Tone, which was itself re-cut as part of the construction process.

Of particular interest are the liminal qualities of the site. Bjørn Thomasson defined liminality as the sensation of finding oneself at a boundary or 'in-between' position; it is 'the experience of inbetweenness itself'.[5] Berger developed the term 'drosscape', in part to describe the inherent in-between nature of waste landscapes.[6] In addition, the location of the flyover, at the point at which the M5 crosses the River Tone, marks the eastern edge of urban Taunton; it therefore forms a liminal boundary between urban and rural environments.

This study explores the liminal qualities of this site in the context of Christine Simmonds-Moore's work on 'boundary thinness' and 'participatory eco-consciousness', using a phenomenological approach adopted from Christopher Tilley's studies of landscape.[7] The findings suggest the area as a place of numerous liminal 'locales' which create the possibility for sacred experience.

Academic Rationale

For Emile Durkheim, non-physical attributes could only exist as a product of the human mind.[8] Accordingly, the natural world is in no way inherently sacred and sacred space can exist only as a mental construction projected onto the landscape. In contrast, for Mircea Eliade, every sacred space implied a hierophany, 'an irruption of the sacred that results in detaching a territory from the surrounding cosmic milieu and making it qualitatively different'.[9] Eliade understood the location of this hierophany as a point of breakthrough, at which the earth was put in communication either with heaven above, or the underworld below.[10]

However, Simmonds-Moore suggested that exceptional or spiritual experiences can be a product of the conscious mind and its environment working together.[11] She described a 'participatory eco-consciousness' in which human consciousness co-creates its spiritual realities in conversation with the physical and social environment.[12] This state of consciousness includes, 'connectivity to unconscious and preconscious aspects of mind, awareness of the body... and interpersonal and extrapersonal connectivity (via increased empathy and compassion)'.[13] Simmonds-Moore further argued that the liminal qualities of both the individual mind and its environment are important factors in the creation of such states of consciousness and the sense of 'boundary thinness' at the locations at which they occur.[14] There is, therefore, at least some degree of agency given to the location in which these experiences occur. Such thinking echoes Aristotle's conviction of the agency of place. As Edward Cassey wrote, for Aristotle, place was 'a unique and nonreducible feature of the physical world, something with its own inherent powers'.[15] Place became defined as *topos*, a vessel which imposes its own qualities onto that which it contains.[16] It is this relationship, between the human mind and its environment, that this study seeks to explore in determining whether the space contained beneath the M5 flyover as it crosses the River Tone can be considered sacred and, if so, if its sacredness is a human construct or a natural phenomenon.

Key Concepts

The Creation of Meaning

Simmonds-Moore is not alone in exploring the relationship between mind and environment. Edmund Husserl's concept of the life-world addressed the distinction between the materially 'real' world and the world as it is perceived, filtered through experiences, personal beliefs, and the senses.[17] Tilley advanced such thinking, his phenomenological approach emphasising the way in which neutral locations become transformed into places embedded with meaning, which he termed 'locales', as people engage with them, creating memories, experiences and stories.[18] Therefore, just as spaces can be used by different people or groups of people, so numerous locales can be created at the same geographical location. Lucien Levy-Bruhl wrote of a 'mystic symbiosis' at the heart of his law of participation, which similarly helps to explain why a given object, location. or phenomenon may be imbued with religious significance for some people but not for others.[19] The mythologist Martin Shaw similarly stressed that 'we make things holy, by the kind of attention we give them', whilst Nancy Wissers wrote of her reliance on metaphor as a means of conveying and helping to understand her own experience of engaging with the sacred.[20]

Liminality and Drosscapes

Arnold van Gennep identified a class of rituals which translate biological rites of passage into symbolic, cultural rites.[21] These symbolic rites consist of three stages – separation, transition and incorporation – designed to remove a person from their previous status and enable them to enter a new one.[22] During the transitional or 'liminal' phase, the person is caught between two states of being, removed from their past but not yet admitted into the future. Victor Turner subsequently developed this concept of liminality, allowing it to be applied to any 'betwixt and between' situation or object.[23] Thomassen argued that liminality is a concept with which to think, and which 'points toward a certain kind of interpretative analysis of events and experiences'.[24] He observed three distinct dimensions of liminality: subjective experience, ranging from individuals to whole societies; temporal liminality, ranging from moments to epochs; and spatial liminality, ranging from individual thresholds to borders between countries or larger regions.[25] Dag Oistein Endsjo and Damien P. Nelis, for example, have both argued that, for the ancient Greeks, the geographical periphery, was an essentially liminal area.[26]

Berger is credited with developing the term 'drosscape' to define areas of economically worthless waste ground, by-products of urban development which creates a liminal zone. C. Michael Hall is amongst those who have recognised the ecological significance of these economic wastelands as havens of urban biodiversity, a point re-emphasised by Paul Farley and Michael Symmons Roberts' explorations of English 'edgelands'.[27] Kevin Lynch has commented on the inherent 'otherness' of such landscapes, describing them as 'places for dreams, for antisocial acts, for exploration and growth', a view echoed by John Fulbright's interpretation of graffiti art as a 'ritual transgression'.[28]

Methodology

My first visit to the flyover site took place in the summer of 2019 and is described below. Intermittent further visits were made over subsequent months, with more focussed field research conducted for the purpose of this study taking place between October and December 2021. An autoethnographic method of research was adopted, utilising a phenomenological approach drawn from Tilley's studies of cultural landscapes. Tilley argued that an understanding of 'locale' cannot be achieved remotely, through the study of maps.[29] Instead, 'the experience of place is of fundamental significance'. Of particular relevance is the multi-sensory experience. Tilley adopted the term 'synaesthesia' to define a process of bringing multiple senses into play simultaneously, writing that, 'it is to an understanding of the multi-sensorial dimension of landscape and place, as encountered in the life-paths of individuals, that our analyses need to be directed'.[30] Tilley also argued for making multiple visits to a locale, approaching from different directions in order to 'observe in a much more subtle manner the way in which it is related to its physical surroundings'.[31]

Therefore, during the formal research period for this study, multiple visits were made to the flyover site, at varying times of the day and on different days of the week. Written notes and photographs were systematically taken, to record significant observations drawn from these visits. Particular attention was given to noting not just visual stimuli, but also the sensations of sound, touch, smell and even taste (from fruiting plants for example). Attention was also taken to record any emotional responses to the site, with attempts made to account for any external stimuli which might affect these, such as the weather or the degree of traffic noise.

During the autumn and winter of 2021, as fieldwork for this project was being undertaken, I was aware of a wider liminal context for the work. The world remained in the grip of the global Covid-19 pandemic, with great uncertainty about the future. At the same time, much of the news media was dominated by the Cop 26 United Nations Climate Change Conference in Glasgow, with great emphasis placed on the conference being 'the last chance' to avoid climate catastrophe.³² The outcome of the conference was largely derided as a failure – at the very least a disappointment – only adding to the liminal sense of being neither here nor there, separated from the past but with the future very much unknown.

Glenn Albrecht coined the term 'solastalgia' to describe a form of emotional anxiety caused by the inability to derive solace from one's home environment due to its physical degradation and a subsequent undermining of personal or community identity.³³ Along with the impacts of war, terrorism and gentrification, Albrecht identified the sense of isolation, and the disruption to personal relationships, brought about by health pandemics as one cause of solastalgia. However, he identified the prime sources of solastalgia as being related to environmental degradation. Along with the physical impact of bio-diversity loss and climate change, Albrecht also identified a more general sense of unease shared by many people about the current state of human relationship with the planet. Albrecht saw this unease as 'an expression of deep-seated solastalgia about non- sustainability' and identified an increasing desire for humanity to be reconnected with the natural world as, at least in part, an attempt to overcome this solastalgia.³⁴ This longing for connection with the natural world is evidence of what Val Plumwood previously identified as a 'hyperseparation' of humans from nature, in the industrialised world, a division which she saw as being the consequence of a subject/object dualism dominating Western scientific thought.³⁵

Given that the present study explored an area which, as I argue, embodied this tension between the human and natural worlds, the influence of solastalgia on its findings is not only difficult to deny but also, I believe, entirely relevant to them.

Findings

The Memorial

I first became aware of the flyover site in the summer of 2019. In an effort to get fit, I had recently taken up running and, one Saturday morning, I decided to run east along the southern bank of the River Tone where, according to my map, a public footpath led beyond the M5 motorway and out into the countryside. Jogging eastwards through Hankridge Water Park, I ran straight past an arrangement of wooden benches which, I would later realise, was a memorial to the victims of the M5 crash of 2011.

The memorial takes the form of seven carved benches, each one named for one of the victims of the tragedy, forming a semicircle around a modest split-tree carving (Fig. 1). It was unveiled on the first anniversary of the crash following a fundraising campaign amongst the local community.³⁶ For at least some of the

Figure 1: Memorial to the victims of the 2011 M5 motorway tragedy. ©Dan Broadbent

bereaved, the location provides a welcome place for remembrance. Tonia White, whose parents were among those who died, told the Somerset County Gazette that, 'I feel a connection down at the memorial... probably because it's close to where it happened. I don't feel anything when I go home (to Newport) where we interred the ashes'.[37] This would imply that the scene of the accident holds an inherent sacredness; that the crash itself may have given rise to an Eliadean hierophany, which marks out the site as sacred. Further to this, Thomassen argued that sudden tragedies can create a sense of liminality.[38] This can take the form of subjective liminality as the bereaved adjust to a life without their loved ones, or spatial liminality as the location continues to be associated with the event. Indeed, the memorialising of the event might prolong this liminal phase. As Mike Parker Pearson observed, by monumentalising the sites of such events 'death is engraved on the landscape. It is re-experienced by the living whenever we see (or even think about) the event and its location'.[39]

The Flyover

Despite my knowledge of the crash, I had not been aware of the memorial. As I approached it on that first morning, I did not feel a sudden outpouring of the sacred. On the contrary, I just kept on running, until I came to the flyover itself, around 60 metres further around the river bend. At this point, on the south bank of the river, having already crossed the canal and railway lines, the flyover

Figure 2: The area beneath the flyover, July 2019. © Dan Broadbent

is making its descent, enclosing an area approximately 35 metres by 20 metres and reaching around 7 metres at its highest point. The river itself is screened from view by a concrete wall, covered in graffiti art, which supports the road as it arches towards the ground. This area beneath the motorway is a largely empty concrete shell, the embodiment of urban waste ground (Fig. 2).

It is perhaps surprising then that my initial reaction to encountering the site was something approaching captivation. The most immediately startling impression was the juxtaposition of the urban and the rural. Approached from the west, the structure of the flyover forms a huge concrete frame, and in the early summer morning, the scene which it displayed was one of bucolic idyll, the sun rising in the east over wheat fields, with the medieval village of Ruishton beyond. On that first visit I was reminded of television programmes from my childhood such as *The Box of Delights* or *The Chronicles of Narnia*, where the protagonists are able to step through a picture frame and experience the enclosed painting as real.[40]

This had not been intended as the destination of my run. Nevertheless, I stopped to take photos and linger in the space. If Casey's insistence on an Aristotelian agency of place is accepted, this place seemed to be flaunting its 'inbetweenness', a liminal area through which one must pass in order to leave the urban and enter the rural.[41] More than this, I had the sense of being temporarily removed from the concerns of daily life. There was a surprising, almost cathedral-like sense of peace and calm beneath the flyover, despite the traffic roaring overhead. Being early on a weekend morning, the volume of traffic was perhaps less than it would be at other times, but on subsequent visits I have been struck by the relative quiet beneath the bridge, the concrete structure appearing to insulate the traffic noise.

People on the edge

I visited numerous times subsequently; the flyover often becoming the destination for my runs, a place which, once reached, I would begin to explore, often attempting simply to 'be', enjoying its meditative quality. However, there were unknown forces at play beneath the bridge, with evidence of rough sleeping along with alcohol and drug consumption in the form of discarded bottles, cans and empty packets of cigarette papers, all of which created a degree of trepidation when walking beneath the flyover. Perhaps the most obvious example of human activity was the frequently changing gallery of graffiti. The graffiti artist Crayone has described graffiti as a shamanic art, equating it with palaeolithic cave art, which some researchers interpret as spiritual in origin.[42] For Crayone, 'shamans were liminal beings who communicated with the gods and creatively transformed social forces through ecstatic ritual trance and symbolic artistic expression'.[43]

Lynch described wastelands as 'havens of rebellious, marginal, illegal people'.[44] However, Endsjo argued that, in ancient Greece, those people who lived on the geographical periphery of society, 'living in all respects on the very margins of the human world... were repeatedly said to be closer to the gods'.[45] These peripheral geographic areas were considered inherently liminal, reflecting 'a territorial parallel to the intermediate stage of Greek rites of passage', such as those identified by van Gennep and Turner.[46] Similarly, Nelis discussed a liminal area between the city and the land beyond, identifying this as 'the realm of Artemis', the goddess specifically associated with the transition from youth to maturity.[47]

A haven for wildlife

As well as providing refuge for humans living on the margins of society, drosscapes have been shown to be havens for wildlife. Christian Haid described such areas of urban waste, neither wild nor cultivated, as a form of 'interstitial wilderness with its spontaneous growth of vegetation'.[48] For Farley and Roberts these unmaintained areas were England's true wildernesses, allowing nature an unexpected opportunity to thrive.[49]

The water park to the west of the flyover is well-maintained. Indeed, during the course of this research, a substantial amount of tree and shrub clearance took place. This had the effect of making the space more open, brighter and safer, perhaps, for human users of the area. However, it also made the presence of the neighbouring business park much more apparent, both visually and audibly, and therefore, less inviting for non-human species. Beyond the flyover to the east is agricultural land, bringing its own disturbances and dangers to wild flora and fauna. In contrast, wildlife appeared to thrive in the area immediately adjacent to the flyover. As Berger has noted, 'drosscapes have few caretakers, guardians, or spokespersons',[50] and this area was less maintained, more overgrown and richer in biodiversity. Bramble thrived and examples of field-maple, lime, holly, elder, and blackthorn were amongst other species present adjacent to the flyover, these in turn supporting a range of insect and bird life. Indeed, one of the most striking features of the flyover was the preponderance of birdsong on either side, loud enough to be heard clearly over the traffic above. The sound-insulating effect of the flyover has already been noted and this may well have been another encouragement to wildlife.

The flyover then, acted as both a haven and a liminal place for nature. Largely ignored by humans, it lies 'betwixt and between' two differing anthropocentric landscapes, one providing an area of human leisure and recreation, the other human agriculture.

The River

On my early visits to the flyover, I avoided venturing beyond the concrete wall which shields the river from the public right of way. To do so, one must walk around the end of the wall, making oneself visible to whoever, or whatever, may be lurking behind. However, on a sunny autumn morning, I eventually found the confidence to explore this area. The sense of trepidation I had felt in the back of my mind when walking beneath the flyover was amplified here, as I moved off the public right of way and around the physical barrier of the wall. Doing so however, the sense of calm beneath the flyover was also amplified. There was a genuine sense of crossing a threshold into what could be termed an 'inner sanctum'. Eliade wrote of church architecture that, 'the threshold is the limit, the boundary, the frontier that distinguishes and opposes two worlds – and at the same time the paradoxical place where those worlds communicate, where passage from the profane to the sacred becomes possible'.[51]

Looking across the river, the graffiti-covered wall was mirrored on the northern bank. However, the presence of the river softened the impact of the flyover, increasing the sense of the natural meeting the human-made. There was a sense of separateness; on this side of the wall, hidden from the footpath, one was removed from the everyday. Being here required intent and there was

Figure 3: Looking north across the River Tone beneath the flyover.
© Dan Broadbent

evidence of both human and non-human actors utilising the space. The shallow riverbank was soft and silty; at various times human boot prints were present, sunk into the silt, accompanied by dog tracks. Fox prints and the prints of both egret and heron were also observed, emphasising the area as a place of safety for wildlife.

Despite the hidden nature of this location, however, there was a tangible sense that one might be being observed, that one's presence might be uncovered. I was aware that there may be human forces watching, those 'people on the margins' perhaps, or local anglers in camouflage gear, out of sight along the riverbank. But the possibility came to mind that whatever this intangible presence may be, it might not be of natural origin. Having crossed a threshold, I was reminded again of Eliade: 'within the sacred precincts, the profane world is transcended… here in the sacred enclosure communication with the gods is made possible'.[52]

I wanted to try and make some sort of sense of the *genius loci* of this area, the spirit of place which kept drawing me back. Nancy Wissers wrote of a childhood experience amongst nature, 'much like being with and communicating with someone, except that there was no tangible someone'.[53] Expressing the difficulty in trying to convey such experiences she argued that 'people in our culture who had this experience would be forced to make up metaphors'.[54] Standing beneath the flyover bridge, enjoying the sense of separateness, but at the same time with a lingering concern about who or what might find me here, an image came to mind of a troll, specifically the troll which lurked beneath a bridge in the children's fairy tale of *The Three Billy Goats Gruff*.[55]

Leonard Pronko described trolls as a large, powerful, supernatural creatures which 'represent the invisible, the world of the imagination'.[56] Jennifer Eastman Attebury identified two types of troll in traditional literature: Nordic ogre trolls and Scandinavian humanoid trolls.[57] The humanoid-trolls live away from human settlements, and emerge only occasionally to cause relatively mild acts of mischief; the ogre trolls, however, serve as 'an embodiment of maliciousness'.[58] Ogre-trolls can also be turned to stone if they are caught in sunlight.[59] Perhaps this is why, with the bright morning sun rising in the east, I was brave enough to venture into the inner sanctum of the flyover, although always with the sense that the troll might awaken.

Levy-Bruhl argued that in moments of participation, there is a sense of communion with something greater than oneself, and that during such experiences, though the laws of nature are not denied, 'they are put aside'.[60] At a moment of participation, 'one lives in two worlds without needing to understand either of them, the first, the natural world, is imposed on them, the other, the supernatural world, is revealed to them'.[61] Through such a participatory framework, might the fleeting presence of a troll be construed as something more substantial than a convenient metaphor? For Levy-Bruhl, myths were no less real than history, occurring in a place in time distinct, but not separate, from material reality.[62] Therefore, he wrote, 'there is nothing further to seek when the myth as spoken'.[63] The author Neil Gaiman has used the ogre-troll as a metaphor for loss in the modern world, including environmental loss, and Attebery noted that the actions of trolls can be 'spurred by human aggression'.[64] In this context, perhaps the *genius loci* of the flyover reflects the damage to nature caused by the construction of the motorway, and the recutting of the River Tone to accommodate it.

The recovery of a fragment of Bronze Age sword from the riverbank close to the flyover suggests that the River Tone in this area may once have been considered sacred.[65] Hutton described the casting of precious objects into rivers and pools as 'arguably the principal trace of religious activity in the late Bronze Age' and, in England, the rivers into which such items were deposited were all, like the Tone, major trade routes flowing eastwards.[66] A religious significance to these finds has been inferred from their being deliberately broken prior to deposition, rendering them 'incapable of further use'.[67] Interpretations of such activity range from a funerary rite; an offering of plunder to the gods; and even as a response to Bronze Age climate change.[68]

Whatever the intention behind such activity, the deposition of a sword into the River Tone fits Hutton's interpretation of a religious offering. Over recent centuries however, the river has been treated with far less respect. The first major recutting of the Tone commenced in 1638, in order to improve the navigation of the river for the movement of coal.[69] Its course has been altered several times since, most recently as part of the construction of the motorway flyover in the early 1970s.[70] By way of comparison, in New Zealand in 2017, the Whanganui River became the first river in the world to be granted the same legal rights as humans, the new status meaning the law now sees no distinction between harming the river or harming the Whanganui tribe who claim it as an ancestor.[71] Graham Harvey related examples of other tribal cultures undertaking rites and rituals before attempting to make any mark on the natural world.[72] One assumes such actions were not undertaken by the Taunton navigators or the builders of the M5.

Discussion: liminal minds, liminal places

Like Wissers' childhood experience, my overwhelming sensation when exploring the flyover, amongst seemingly contradictory feelings of peace tinged with unease, was one of unspoken communion with the spirit of the place, and that this spirit in some way represented the uneasy relationship between the human and natural worlds.[73] Was this sensation the result of an Eliadean hierophany, the result of centuries of violence against nature at this location? Or was it the Durkheimian product of my own mind? Is it possible that deliberately exploring the flyover site in this way actually encouraged a sense of the sacred? Martin Shaw has suggested that we create sacredness in that to which we give our attention, and Levy-Bruhl's law of participation would similarly suggest that, through attachment and investment of time, anywhere can become sacred.[74] Thomassen also wrote that liminal experiences can be artificially induced, through rituals.[75] In this context, my repeated visits and exploration of the flyover site might constitute a form of ritual. If so, this might suggest a Durkheimian understanding of the flyover site, my experiences being, therefore, a human construct.

Furthermore, Simmonds-Moore argued that, 'liminality can be experienced as psychological sensitivity; a fluidity of thoughts and feelings, a tendency to see agency and causality and a heightened tendency towards experiencing exceptional experiences'.[76] It can also be experienced as an enhanced recognition or empathy for the plight of another and, Simmonds Moore believed, such insight might also extend to the environment or environmental issues.[77] In the context of the media attention on Cop 26, I found it difficult to avoid feelings of solastalgia whilst exploring a landscape which in many ways embodied the tension between human and nature. Thomassen argued that whole societies can experience liminality during crises or the 'collapse of order'.[78] In this context, the environmental crisis can be viewed as a liminal time in Earth's history. We are now separated from the certainties of the past while the future remains unknown. It is not unreasonable to suggest that a sense of global liminality may have influenced my experiences beneath the flyover. I may not have experienced a literal troll beneath the bridge, but it seems to serve as pertinent symbol for the precariousness and unpredictability of humanity's current relationship with nature.

However, it does not necessarily follow that these experiences existed only in the mind. Simmonds-Moore wrote of numerous ways in which environmental factors can affect conscious perception.[79] For example, spaces containing living organisms, physical features and still or running water, all of which are present beneath the flyover, are likely to have an influence on the observer.[80] In particular, Simmonds Moore noted that water-like sounds can create 'pink noise' which is recognised as having therapeutic effects on both the human mind and body.[81] Not only is moving water present beneath the flyover, but the sound of traffic, especially beneath the flyover where it is insulated and softened, may have a similar pink noise effect. Such influences, however, are not limited to physical factors. Spaces may also be considered liminal because people have experienced strong emotional states in the past. Simmonds-Moore wrote that 'the localisation of prior meaning and experience might then become accessible to some (sensitive) observers who are physically present in the same'.[82] In regard to the flyover site, such an interpretation might be construed as relating to the grief experienced as a result of the 2011 crash; to the environmental damage caused to the site over hundreds of years; or even, in some way, to the ritual deposition of a Bronze Age sword. Echoing Levy-Bruhl's law of participation, Simmonds-Moore described participatory eco-consciousness as a means by which the mind and location, the liminality of each serving as an influence on the other, combine to create exceptional experiences, which can be interpreted as a sense of the sacred.[83]

Conclusions

This research aimed to assess whether a piece of urban waste ground beneath a motorway flyover could be considered a sacred space and, if so, whether that sacredness was based on an Eliadean model of hierophany or a Durkheimian understanding of the sacred as a projection of the human mind. Explored through the lens of liminality, using a phenomenological approach, the findings suggest this particular drosscape exists as a palimpsest of co-existing liminal 'locales', embedded with meaning for both human and non-human actors.

According to Thomassen's framework, the flyover can be viewed as a liminal locale both for the bereaved and for the memory of those who, as a result of the 2011 crash, never reached their intended destination, but whose names are now memorialised at the site. Viewed as a drosscape on the geographical periphery, the site has an inherent liminality, existing on the boundary of the planned and unplanned; the urban and rural; the human and the natural; the managed and the ignored. Those humans who retreat to the site as a refuge from public gaze exist in a tradition of marginal people who, both Endsjo and Nelis argue, have been recognised as liminal beings since the time of ancient Greece. From the point of view of Crayone, the graffiti artists too, engaging in acts of 'ritual transgression', have a claim to a tradition of sacred liminality.[84] And for wildlife, the unmaintained nature of the site provides a liminal haven, in-between two differing anthropocentric landscapes.

Simmonds-Moore's study of participatory eco-consciousness suggests that liminal sites have the potential to co-create extraordinary or spiritual experiences.[85] However, while such thinking can be understood as restoring agency to place, Simmonds-Moore argues that places can only be considered truly liminal if a co-participating consciousness is present.

Whereas, the River Tone may have been considered sacred in late prehistory, over the course of the last 400 years it has been periodically re-cut and re-routed, most recently during the construction of the flyover. The Whanganui might understand the River Tone to be wounded at the point of its most recent cut. Perhaps, beneath the M5 flyover on the edge of Taunton, the river is in need of healing and nurturing. If one accepts the agency of place on which Casey insisted, perhaps this explains why nature is drawn to this area, and why it stopped me in my tracks on a morning run. Conversely, by repeatedly, even ritually, exploring a place representative of nature's struggles with humankind, during a period when that struggle is creating a liminal moment in time, it is not surprising that my own mind might have been open to co-creating a sense of the sacred at the site, perhaps even building my own peripheral refuge. It is possible then, for an English drosscape, in the form of a motorway flyover, to be considered a sacred space. Not, perhaps, as a purely natural phenomenon, nor as an entirely human construct, but rather as a co-creation of the location itself, and the participating mind which explores it.

Notes

1   Alan Berger, 'Drosscape in the Landscape', in *The Urbanism Reader*, ed. by Charles Waldheim (Princeton: Princeton University Press, 2006), pp.197–217.

2   Ronald Hutton, *The Pagan Religions of the Ancient British Isles* (Oxford: Blackwell, 1993), p.184.

3   Lisa O'Carroll, 'Seven Dead and 51 Injured in Horrific M5 Crash', *The Guardian*, 5 November 2011. <https://www.theguardian.com/uk/2011/nov/05/m5-crash-motorway-pile-up> [accessed 7 January 2022].

4   The Motorway Archive, *M5 North Petherton By-Pass (J24 to J25)*, <https://web.archive.org/web/20070316122427/http://www.iht.org/motorway/m5edwischeme.htm> [accessed 8 January 2022].

5   Bjørn Thomassen, 'Thinking With Liminality: To The Boundaries Of An Anthropological Concept', in *Breaking Boundaries: Varieties Of Liminality*, ed. by Agnes Horvath, Bjørn Thomassen and Harald Wydra (Oxford: Berghahn Books, 2015), pp.39–58, (p.40).

6   Berger, 'Drosscape in the Landscape', pp.197–217.

7   Christine Simmonds-Moore, 'Liminal Spaces And Liminal Minds: Boundary Thinness And Participatory Eco-consciousness', in *Greening The Paranormal: Exploring The Ecology Of Everyday Experience*, ed. by Jack Hunter (August Night Press, 2019); Christopher Tilley, *A Phenomenology Of Landscape: Places, Paths And Monuments* (Oxford: Berg, 1994).

8   Karen E. Fields, 'Translators Introduction: Religion As An Eminently Social Thing', in *Emile Durkheim, The Elementary Forms Of Religious Life: A New Translation* (New York: Free Press, 1995), pp.xvii – lxi (p.xliv).

9   Mircea Eliade, *The Sacred And The Profane* (New York: Harcourt, 1987), p.26.

10   Eliade, *The Sacred And The Profane*, p.36.

11   Simmonds-Moore, 'Liminal Spaces', p.120.

12   Simmonds-Moore, 'Liminal Spaces', p.125.

13   Simmonds-Moore, 'Liminal Spaces', p.125.

14   Simmonds-Moore, 'Liminal Spaces', p.126.

15   Edward S, Casey, *The Fate Of Place, A Philosophical History* (Berkeley: University Of California Press, 1998), pp.70–71.

16   Casey, *The Fate of Place*, p.51.

17   Edmund Husserl, *The Crisis Of European Sciences And Transcendental Phenomenology* (Evanston: Northwestern University Press, 1970).

18   Tilley, *Phenomenology*, p.34.

19   Lucien Levy-Bruhl, *How Natives Think* (Mansfield Centre: Martino Publishing, 2015), p.376.

20   Martin Shaw, *Smokehole: Looking To The Wild In The Time Of The Spyglass* (London: Chelsea Green, 2021), p.5; Nancy Wissers, 'This Moment Returns To Me: Childhood Reverie And A Lanape Idea Of Recruitment By The Earth', in *Greening The Paranormal: Exploring The Ecology Of Everyday Experience*, ed. by Jack Hunter (August Night Press, 2019).

21   Arnold van Gennep, *The Rites Of Passage* (Chicago: University of Chicago Press, 1960).

22   van Gennep, *Rites Of Passage*, p.21.

23   Victor Turner, *Dramas, Fields, And Metaphors: Symbolic Action in Human Society* (Ithaca: Cornell University Press, 1974).

24   Thomassen, 'Thinking With Liminality', p.42.

25   Thomassen, 'Thinking With Liminality', p.48.

26 Dag Oistein Endsjo, 'To Lock Up Eleusis: A Question Of Liminal Space', *Numen,* 47 (2000), pp.251–386, (p.351); Damien P. Nelis, 'Iphias: Apollonius Rhodius, Argonautica, 1.311-16', *Classical Quarterly,* 41 (1991), pp.96–105, (p.99).

27 C. Michael Hall, 'The Ecological And Environmental Significance Of Urban Wastelands And Drosscapes', in *Organising Waste In The City: International Perspectives On Narratives And Practices,* ed. by María José Zapata Campos and Michael Hall (Bristol: Policy Press, 2013), pp.21–39, (p.23); Paul Farley and Michael Symmons Roberts, *Edgelands: Journeys Into England's True Wilderness* (London: Vintage, 2021).

28 Kevin Lynch, *Wasting Away: An Exploration Of Waste: What It Is, How It Happens, Why We Fear It, How to Do It Well* (San Francisco: Sierra Club Books, 1990), p.153; John Fulbright, 'Graffiti as Ritual Transgression', *FoundSF,* <https://www.foundsf.org/index.php?title=Graffiti_as_Ritual_Transgression> [accessed 7 January 2022].

29 Tilley, *Phenomenology,* p,34.

30 Christopher Tilley, *The Materiality Of Stone: Explorations in Landscape Phenomenology* (Oxford: Berg, 2004) p.16.

31 Tilley, *Phenomenology,* p,74.

32 Rachel Amery, 'COP26: "Last chance" warning as UK climate change chief grilled on oil and gas, flights and rising temperatures', The *Courier,* 16 September 2021, <https://www.thecourier.co.uk/fp/politics/scottish-politics/2538890/cop26-last-chance-warning-as-uk-climate-change-chief-grilled-on-oil-and-gas-flights-and-rising-temperatures/> [accessed 7 January 2022].

33 Glenn Albrecht, 'Solastalgia', *Alternatives Journal,* 32.4/5 (2006), pp.34–36.

34 Albrecht, 'Solastalgia', p.36.

35 Val Plumwood, *Environmental Culture: The Ecological Crisis of Reason* (London: Routledge, 2002), p.54

36 *The Times,* 'M5 crash memorial unveiled', 4 November 2012. < https://www.thetimes.co.uk/article/m5-crash-memorial-unveiled-h7897qcmp3w?region=global> [accessed 7 January].

37 *Somerset County Gazette,* 'Fourth anniversary of M5 Taunton crash which killed seven - victims' daughter talks to the Gazette', 4 November 2015, <https://www.somersetcountygazette.co.uk/news/13931165.fourth-anniversary-of-m5-taunton-crash-which-killed-seven-victims-daughter-talks-to-the-gazette/> [accessed 7 January 2022].

38 Thomassen, 'Thinking With Liminality', p.50.

39 Mike Parker Pearson, *The Archaeology Of Death And Burial* (Stroud: The History Press, 2009) p.193.

40 *The Box Of Delights* (London: BBC One Television, 21 November – 24 December 1984); *The Chronicles Of Narnia* (London: BBC One Television, 13 November 1988 to 23 December 1990).

41 Casey, *The Fate of Place,* p.70.

42 Fulbright, 'Graffiti As Ritual Transgression'; David Lewis-Williams, *The Mind In The Cave: Consciousness And The Origins Of Art* (London: Thames and Hudson, 2002), p.143.

43 Fulbright, 'Graffiti As Ritual Transgression'.

44 Lynch and Southworth, *Wasting Away,* p.153.

45 Endsjo, 'To Lock Up Eleusis', p.372.

46 Endsjo, 'To Lock Up Eleusis', p.351.

47 Nelis, 'Iphias', p.99.

48 Christian Haid 'Landscapes Of Wilderness: Heterotopias Of The Post Industrial City' [Paper to CRESC annual conference] *Framing the City* (University of Manchester, 2011) cited in Hall, 'The Ecological And Environmental Significance Of Urban Wastelands And Drosscapes', p.23.

49 Farley and Roberts, *Edgelands,* p.26.
50 Berger, 'Drosscape in the landscape', p.213.
51 Eliade, *The Sacred And The Profane,* p.25.
52 Eliade, *The Sacred And The Profane,* pp.25–26.
53 Wissers, 'This Moment Returns To Me', p.75.
54 Wissers, 'This Moment Returns To Me', p.76.
55 George Webbe Dasent, *Popular Tales From The Norse* (Edinburgh: David Douglas, 1903), pp.264–65.
56 Leonard C. Pronko, 'Trolls, Trills, And Tofu: Ibsen, Verdi, And Kabuki', *Comparative Drama,* 29.3 (1995), pp.303–18. (p.308).
57 Jennifer Eastman Attebery, 'The Trolls Of Fiction: Ogres Or Warm Fuzzies?', *Journal of the Fantastic in the Arts,* 7.1 (1996), pp.61–74.
58 Attebery, 'The Trolls Of Fiction', p.63.
59 Attebery, 'The Trolls Of Fiction', p.63.
60 Levy-Bruhl, *The Notebooks,* p.134.
61 Levy-Bruhl, *The Notebooks,* p.139.
62 Levy-Bruhl, *The Notebooks,* p.63.
63 Levy-Bruhl, *The Notebooks,* p.109.
64 Neil Gaiman, *Troll Bridge* (London: Headline, 2016); Attebery, 'The Trolls Of Fiction', p.64.
65 Somerset Historic Environment Record, 44228: *Bronze Age Sword Find, River Tone,* <https://www.somersetheritage.org.uk/record/44228#> [accessed 8 January 2022].
66 Hutton, *Pagan Religions,* p.184.
67 Hutton, *Pagan Religions,* p.186.
68 Hutton, *Pagan Religions,* p.189-190.
69 Somerset Historic Environment Record, 22905: *River Tone Navigation,* <https://www.somersetheritage.org.uk/record/22905#> [accessed 8 January 2022].
70 The Motorway Archive, *M5 North Petherton By-Pass (J24 to J25).*
71 Eleanor Ainge Roy, 'New Zealand River Granted Same Legal Rights As Human Being', *The Guardian,* 16 Mar 2017. <https://www.theguardian.com/world/2017/mar/16/new-zealand-river-granted-same-legal-rights-as-human-being> [accessed 8 January 2022].
72 Graham Harvey, *Animism: Respecting The Living World* (London: Hurst, 2017), p.62.
73 Wissers, 'This Moment Returns To Me', p.75.
74 Shaw, *Smokehole;* Levy-Bruhl, *The Notebooks.*
75 Thomassen, 'Thinking With Liminality', p.50.
76 Simmonds-Moore, 'Liminal Spaces', p.112.
77 Simmonds-Moore, 'Liminal Spaces', p.117.
78 Thomassen, 'Thinking With Liminality', p.50.
79 Simmonds-Moore, 'Liminal Spaces', p.112.
80 Simmonds-Moore, 'Liminal Spaces', p.120.
81 Simmonds-Moore, 'Liminal Spaces', p.123.
82 Simmonds-Moore, 'Liminal Spaces', pp.120–21.
83 Simmonds-Moore, 'Liminal Spaces', p.125.
84 Fulbright, 'Graffiti as Ritual Transgression'.
85 Simmonds-Moore, 'Liminal Spaces', p.125.

12

HIVE MINDS: EXPLORING THE SPIRITUAL CONNECTIONS BETWEEN BEEKEEPERS AND BEES

Jake Eshelman

As some of most prolific pollinators on the planet, bees have played a fundamental role in creating the ecological conditions in which humanity could take root and grow.[1] Archaeological evidence suggests that people have been harvesting bee products (e.g., honey, wax, propolis, etc.) for at least 10,000 years.[2] This longstanding interaction eventually led to the development and global proliferation of apiculture (the domestication of bees), which can be traced back as early as 2,600 BCE.[3] In addition to beekeeping's unfolding impact on ecological and agricultural systems around the world, beekeeping also emerged as a sacred and spiritual practice across cultures.[4] However, to date, very little ethnographic research has been conducted to better understand the spiritual relationships between beekeepers and their bees.[5] In order to contribute to this underserved area of academic inquiry, this study leverages qualitative research methods to explore the beliefs, ideologies, and practices of sacred apiculture maintained by individual members of a beekeeping collective in Houston, TX. Ultimately, this research finds that spiritual beekeeping provides practitioners with a heightened sense of ecological unity, experiences of cross-species communication, and direct encounters with the sacred.

Defining sacred agriculture

One of the key challenges of studying spiritual beekeeping is to clearly define it. Apiculture—or the practice of domesticating bees—speaks for itself. However, the associated concepts surrounding the 'sacred' and 'spiritual' tend to elude such clear-cut definitions. Because both terms conjure a breadth of complementary and competing interpretations, it is important to articulate how they are used and understood in the context of this research.

To do so, I will lean on the existing work of David Hay and Rebecca Nye, whose work with children inspired a particularly elegant definition of spirituality as the 'potential to be much more deeply aware both of ourselves and of our intimate relationship with everything that is not ourselves'.[6] In other words, spirituality is a subjective (i.e., idiosyncratic) experience of heightened consciousness and radical relationality. This definition is particularly generative in the context of spiritual beekeeping for several reasons. Firstly, it establishes that spirituality is unique to—and inclusive of—every individual's experience(s). Secondly, it demonstrates that spirituality can exist independently of ideological dogma, social strata, and devotional rites often associated with religious practice. Lastly, the deliberate omission of theurgy, orthodoxy, and orthopraxy establishes that spiritual experiences can manifest in innumerable ways—including (but not by any means limited to) beekeeping.

Similarly, it is important to pin down the swirling and elusive concept of the 'sacred.' For this, it is fruitful to borrow from multiple scholars, whose various contributions can be woven together to create a workable mosaic of meaning surrounding the sacred as it manifests in apiculture. In fact, an apiary is a fitting illustration for Durkheim's concept of the sacred as being that which we 'set apart' from everyday experiences and maintain through regular ritual and community-building.[7] However, whereas Durkheim's functionalist approach casts the sacred as a purely human construct that satisfies our social impulses, other thinkers such as German philosopher and theologian Rudolf Otto argued that it is something far greater—namely an intimate interaction with an objective, noumenal realm. Otto described the sacred as 'the Wholly Other' wherein one becomes simultaneously enraptured, terrified, and inspired in an ineffable encounter with the *mysterium tremendum* that exists outside of our everyday reality.[8] Whereas Otto sought to delineate the nature and expression of the sacred, Mircea Eliade instead considered how *we experience* such encounters. Taking a phenomenological approach, he argued that interactions with the sacred characteristically alter our normal perceptions of place and time such that we can temporarily lose our spatial and temporal bearings.[9] As Andrew von Hendy summarized, Eliade's outlook suggests that the sacred catalyses a simultaneous sense of timelessness and tunnel-vision that momentarily suspends our foothold in quotidian life.[10]

While there are notable differences between the respective pathways into the sacred carved out by Durkheim, Otto, and Eliade, their collective contributions nonetheless work largely in tandem to create a three-fold assemblage of the sacred—namely that which is separated from mundane reality, temporarily re-writes the rules of our time-space continuum, and confronts us with an experience of the ineffable.

Apiculture in Academia

In context of anthropogenic climate change, the evolving relationships between people and bees has become an increasingly important area of inquiry, particularly regarding human spirituality. In her work exploring bee mythology and folklore, Hilda M. Ransome noted that sacred apiculture is well established amongst contemporary beekeepers throughout Euro-American culture.[11] Furthermore, she traced similar practices and beliefs back to beekeeping's early origins in ancient Egypt.[12] Focusing on beekeepers in the United States, Tammy Horn's anthropological research found that spiritual beekeeping is prevalent in apiaries and communities throughout America.[13] However, despite being a common practice, ethnographers have yet to meaningfully study sacred apiculture and the associated beliefs and ideologies held by these beekeepers. While various forms of bee-centred shamanistic practice can be located across time and around the globe, writer and shaman Simon Buxton suggests that these traditions remain resolutely oral and highly esoteric—in large part to protect practitioners against persecution.[14] He elaborated:

> where powerful, arcane information is being transmitted from one person to another, the oral tradition is usually the safest way of protecting this knowledge from those who might put themselves and others at risk by using it.[15]

This reluctance to share one's insight into their spiritual relationships with bees echoes the lingering distrust of anthropologists held by certain indigenous groups who suffered at the hands of anthropology's sordid colonial history.[16] Working among various communities in her native New Zealand, indigenous scholar Linda Tuhiwai Smith articulated that 'research [is] one of the dirtiest words in the indigenous world's vocabulary' as it conjures painful memories of 'the worst excesses of colonialism'.[17] However, while spiritual beekeeping may have deliberately flown under academia's radar, it also may be the case that ethnographers—for one reason or another—simply have not been interested. Regardless of the root cause(s), it nonetheless remains a considerable opportunity to ethically investigate sacred apiculture as it exists today.

Methodology

In order to explore the spiritual beliefs and experiences of contemporary beekeepers, this research employs a phenomenological approach, which David Woodruff Smith outlined as the study of how things 'appear in our experience, or the ways we experience things' from a first-person point of view in order to better articulate their subjective meaning(s) unique to each individual.[18] To do so, I employed qualitative research methods, as they are especially useful in simultaneously harnessing broad insights into a group's collective cosmology as well as the dynamic and nuanced ideologies held by individual participants.[19]

Given the highly personal and subjective nature of spiritual belief, the success of this research relies on establishing trust. To do so, I approached the founder of a local beekeeping collective, which itself is comprised of fifty-four members ranging from backyard hobbyists to established professionals. I had also previously cultivated professional rapport with several members of the collective while conducting similar visual research with them over the last four years.[20] Given these relationships, the founder granted me access to conduct this new research within the collective.

I developed a brief online questionnaire (and consent statement), which included a brief explanation of the project, information about how I would use and protect their data, a short series of closed- and open-ended questions, and an opt-in box where individuals could indicate their interest in participating in a one-to-one interview. This questionnaire was then reviewed and approved by the gatekeeper before being shared with the collective. As was noted both in the questionnaire and across all correspondences, participation in this research was strictly voluntary. Indeed, the questionnaire was designed to be optional and open-ended such that each participant could maintain agency throughout the research process.

The questionnaire served several purposes. In addition to confirming the existence of sacred apiculture within the collective, the survey also revealed key themes regarding the associated beliefs and practices. However, the primary objective of this questionnaire was to identify individuals who actively nurture spiritual relationships with their hives. This form also enabled me to identify willing participants for follow-up discussions in order to garner deeper insights into the nature, qualities, and experiences of sacred apiculture amongst actual practitioners.

From the pool of spiritual beekeepers, I selected three participants for loosely structured, one-on-one interviews, which we conducted (with their permission) in their respective apiaries. This choice of location served vital research functions. Firstly, it provided a safe, familiar, and private setting in which respondents could feel comfortable—even inspired—when sharing personal insights into their spiritual connection(s) with bees.[21] Secondly, this proximity to their bees opened up the possibility for their hives to be implicated—if not directly included—in the conversation.

Like any type of ethnographic research, this research may be influenced by certain limitations and caveats. Firstly, despite obtaining informed consent, respondents may have felt social or professional pressure to participate due to their relationship with the gatekeeper, as well as any previous interactions with me. Secondly, this relatively small sample of seventeen questionnaire respondents (out of fifty-four collective members) may not be representative of the broader beekeeping community across the city, the state, or the country. For example, it is possible that beekeepers who share certain ideologies or demographics may seek out a collective whose values mirror their own. Subsequent and broader research of this kind would be required to assess whether these considerations influence the findings from this study.

Though not a beekeeper myself, my ongoing interest, familiarity with, and research into apiculture allowed me a heightened ability to understand a beekeeper's cosmology, which may otherwise be lost to a layperson. Furthermore, such 'insider' knowledge helps pre-empt some of the concerns previously mentioned by Buxton and Linda Tuhiwai Smith regarding the perceived and potential dangers of sharing with those outside of the given community.[22] However, such privileged knowledge is not without its own hurdles. I of course have my own relationship to bees which evolved from childhood terror into an ongoing conceptual, ethical, and aesthetic fascination. This cognitive and sympathetic evolution of the researcher is particularly well articulated by E.E. Evans-Prichard, who, despite his colonial leanings, was far from impervious to the shifting sands of changing personal cosmologies. Reflecting on the tension between his own cultural conditioning and his experiences amongst the Azande people, he wrote:

> in the climate of thought I was born into and brought up in and have been conditioned by, I rejected, I reject, Zande notions of witchcraft. In [Azande] culture, in the set of ideas I then lived in, I accepted them; in a kind of way I believed them.[23]

Here, Evans-Prichard illuminated one of many ways an ethnographer can be shaped by their research. As such, I've attempted to suppress any impulse to project my own interests and experiences onto those shared by my research participants.

Sacred beekeeping: insights and ideologies

In investigating the spiritual beliefs and experiences of beekeepers in relationship with their hives, several common elements emerged that help clarify the nature of sacred apiculture as it is understood and practised today. While spirituality is an inherently individual experience, the collective accounts shared by research participants start to give shape to sacred apiculture by reinforcing and elucidating several common characteristics—specifically a sense of heightened ecological harmony, a capacity for interspecies communication, and direct interactions with the ineffable 'other'.

Heightened Ecological Harmony

Each interviewee's path to sacred apiculture suggests that beekeeping serves as a means by which one can build more meaningful, ethical, and intimate relationships to nature. In fact, each respondent cited the unfolding ecological crisis and the global decline of bee populations as prominent factors that inspired them to begin beekeeping. Recalling her own journey to sacred apiculture, Melissa shares that:

> a lot of people get into beekeeping because they feel like they're saving the world and saving the bees. I don't believe that at all anymore. It's taken me a long time to come to terms with that. I feel like honey bees are a gateway bug that will help you get interested more in other insects, native bees, and other pollinators. It gets you more in-tune with a whole new perspective on nature and your place in it.[24]

Despite being a limited and imperfect attempt to support ecological health, Melissa maintains that apiculture is nonetheless a generative practice because it leads to more constructive and holistic actions to benefit the entire natural community.

Regardless of how one finds their way into beekeeping, intimate interactions with bees catalyse deeper ecological relationships. For Beckett, spiritual connections with bees bring about a heightened appreciation for such relationships, offering that beekeeping 'reminds me of my place in the world because it helps me feel closer to our existence—our *ecosystem*... the true depth of life'.[25] Here, Beckett's experience recalls Eliade's phenomenological concept of the sacred, in that beekeeping prompts an enhanced awareness of our ontological and ecological connections.[26] This is particularly evident for another beekeeper, who found that beekeeping helped to situate themselves and build relationships in an unfamiliar place. Discussing such interactions with bees, Deborah recalls that:

being a recent transplant to this area from a place that has four seasons, the bees have definitely taught me how to adjust and connect to this new environment. By interacting with them, I've learned how to situate myself here. And wherever I go next, I'll start a hive there too so the bees can help me orient myself within that new ecosystem.[27]

The heightened ability to locate or 'find oneself' within an ecological context elegantly embodies Hay and Nye's collective understanding of spirituality as a reflexive process that blurs the relational distinctions between the self and other.[28]

In addition to helping forge new relationships with one's environment, spiritual beekeeping also inspires more ecologically oriented behaviours. Melissa recounts that 'bees change your life in so many ways', particularly by shifting one's perspective and lifestyle to be more intentional about how—and what— we consume.[29] Ultimately, a beekeeper's heightened sense of stewardship and spiritual connection may precipitate a deepening of one's ecological conscience, which is then expressed through environmentally friendly behaviours, values, and purchasing habits. This is supported by Christopher Thoms' 2018 qualitative study, which finds that the fulfilment of caregiving, increased time spent outdoors, and other latent benefits of apiculture stimulate deeper stewardship commitments amongst individual commitments—both toward their hives and the surrounding ecosystem.[30]

Other interviewees report similar senses of expanded awareness to galvanize a stronger ecological identity. For Beckett, this directly challenges the basis of human chauvinism, which Attfield described as an ideology in which people see themselves as somehow separate or superior to the rest of the natural world.[31] In directly addressing anthropocentrism, Beckett asserts that the spiritual potential of beekeeping maintains one's humility by revealing the interconnection of all experiences.[32] They go further to suggest that this ecological kinship is a fundamental aspect of being human, quipping that 'if someone thinks that the plants and animals and bees were just "put here" to support us, they need to revisit some basic biology classes'.[33] Beckett's pointed critique nonetheless reveals a reflexive celebration of their own experience of kinship and connection with the broader ecology as a result of interacting with bees.

Whereas some people privilege human experiences and values over all else, spiritual beekeepers learn other lessons through direct interactions with the superorganism. Melissa recounts that it can be difficult 'to grasp that a hive is one being' with its own collective consciousness.[34] By comparison, Melissa suggests that although humans have the capacity to act as a superorganism, people nonetheless tend to privilege the illusion of isolated and independent individual identities, which effectively separated us from ourselves and our surroundings. Ultimately, Melissa concludes that 'really, if some of us are upset, we're all a little upset. And that's what the bees teach us'.[35] In other words, bees teach us—or rather remind us—of the shared experiences and relational principles that implicate us all in our ecological networks, for better and worse.

Interspecies Communication

Of the many mechanisms by which beekeepers can share spiritual experiences with their bees, cooperative interspecies communication which emerged as a common and generative expression of sacred apiculture. Yet, communication between people and bees is far from a new phenomenon, as evidenced by the longstanding tradition of 'Telling the Bees', in which a beekeeper informs their hive of important developments in the household such as births, marriages, and deaths [see Figure 1]. In tracing the development of this particular practice, Ransome posited that the emergence and proliferation of interspecies dialogue indicates a spiritual resonance between people and bees, writing that this tradition 'would not have arisen had [bees] not been credited with almost supernatural powers'.[36] Throughout her work, she followed the history of similar associations back to antiquity, suggesting that the germ of sacred communications with bees is evidenced in ancient Egypt, Greece, Medieval Europe, and throughout contemporary Euro-American cultures.[37]

But how exactly do modern-day beekeepers communicate with their hives? Reinforcing my own observations while conducting similar visual research during the past four years, the vast majority (14 out of 17) of questionnaire respondents speak to their bees. Granted, this does not necessarily indicate a spiritual connection. As one respondent clarifies, 'I basically chat at them', suggesting a one-way communication rather than a dialogue.[38] However, many beekeepers report that they 'speak' to their bees using non-verbal communication strategies, such as intention-setting, telepathy, and meditation [see Figure 2]. In describing their own approach to communicating with bees, Melissa shares that 'I definitely *think-talk* to them [by] speaking out loud and in my head. I'll greet them, apologise, and ask them questions like "what's going on?" or "oh, hey, sorry!" '.[39] Beyond illuminating a multivalent communication strategy, Melissa's questions and apologies suggest a rhetorical possibility that the bees can respond. However, this possibility should not be misconstrued as an expectation that bees speak our language. Deborah articulates this point rather succinctly, stating that 'I can connect and communicate with my bees, but I can never communicate *in the way they do* with one another' [emphasis added].[40]

Figure 1: Hans Thoma, *Der Bienenfreund*, 1863.
Translated to 'The Bee Friend', this oil painting depicts the once common practice of Telling the Bees, or notifying the hive of notable events in the household.
Hans Thoma, Public domain, via Wikimedia Commons.

Though acknowledging the schism that distinguishes the respective communication strategies of people and bees, interviewees tend to find this divergence inspirational rather than insurmountable. For Beckett, bees have a far greater capacity for communication than humans because:

> we are so limited by reading, writing, and speaking. Sure, we have a sixth sense once in a blue moon, like when you think about someone and they call you. But these bees are communicating in this way every single second in their life. That's how they were born—and they don't go to school to learn it.[41]

In highlighting these differences in how people and bees interact, Beckett demonstrates a profound sense of appreciation for bees' inexplicable natural capacities, which are at once deeply mysterious nonetheless accessible to humans in certain contexts. Beckett elucidates this further by attributing this to bees' ability to initiate us into the collective power of community. She elaborates:

Figure 2: After lighting a saining bundle to consecrate and smoke-cleanse the apiary, a beekeeper shares an early morning meditation with her bees. In addition to communing with the bees, she also maintains a notebook where she writes sacred wisdom she receives from the bees—or the broader genius loci—during this process. ©Jake Eshelman

> When the bees are talking to me, it's not just one; it's the entire group through their reactions, the way they crawl, the way they fly around me, buzzing in my ear loudly. In this way, they'll tell me that the rain is coming, because they don't need to watch the news to know it. But if you don't spend enough time with them—if you're not receptive to them, if you go into the hive without paying attention—you're not going to be able to grasp what they're telling you.[42]

For Beckett and others, communication with bees is a mutual dance of intention and interpretation that enables beekeepers to cultivate heightened awareness of their surroundings, greater appreciation for ecological kinship, and increased capacity for obtaining spiritual knowledge.

Though it is widely held amongst interviewees that humans are innately unable to fully communicate as bees do, there is nonetheless a bit of wiggle room along this spectrum. In a particularly charming account of applied linguistics, Melissa describes the experience of adopting honey bee vernacular. She provides the example of 'bee breath', which is part of a ritual wherein beekeepers will pause before opening a hive and signal their intentions to the bees by letting out a long, audible '*buzzzzzzzzzz*' sound.[43] Drawing comparisons to Buddhist meditative practice of chanting '*Om*', Melissa recognizes that bee breath has a palpable 'calming and cleansing effect'.[44] Indeed, recent studies in bioacoustics have revealed that individual bee species can identify one another based on the unique buzzing sounds they produce during flight and pollination.[45] In the context of this research, the spiritual practice of 'bee breath' can be interpreted as a gesture and greeting to the hive in which beekeepers identify themselves through a mutually-accessible language.

Encounters with the sacred

While beekeepers interact with their hives in different ways, direct communication is not necessarily a prerequisite to encountering the sacred through apiculture. As established earlier, one commonly held characteristic of the sacred is that which is set apart. At its most fundamental level, the apiary itself is a constructed space commonly placed away from the everyday activity of a household, such as the corner of the garden or along the outer reaches of a fence line. While this of course has practical reasons (e.g., not getting stung, allowing bees to flourish uninterrupted, etc.), these spaces can also be consecrated, either by default or with active spiritual intention [see Figure 3]. Recounting a telling example of the latter, Melissa shares an experience of sanctifying an apiary alongside a Catholic beekeeper, who:

> made it a ritual. She opened up a book and said the prayer of St. Benedict—one of many patron saints of bees. And then we smoke cleansed the hive to set the space and welcome the bees before we put them in. Five years later, that hive has never died, never had any problems, and has been the best honey producer throughout the collective. Always. It is a rockstar. I don't know if it's because she talks to her bees every day or if it's because we did that prayer and blessing, but I thank her for that. It must have done something.[46]

While there are many factors that influence the health and success of a hive, Melissa's experience of consecrating an apiary alongside a fellow beekeeper embodies three essential elements of the sacred as articulated by Durkheim—namely designating an area apart from everyday spheres, maintaining it through a ritual practice, and building community through collective engagement in that space.[47] Additionally, the beekeeper's devotional practice of reciting the Blessing of the Bees every year on St. Benedict's Day [see Figure 4] directly invokes the divine into the apiary: 'May thy holy blessing descend on these bees and this hive, so that they may multiply, be fruitful and be preserved from all ills, and that the fruits coming forth from them may be distributed for thy praise and that of thy Son and the Holy Spirit and of the most blessed Virgin Mary.'

Figure 3: Smoke billows from a hive smoker used to calm honey bees during hive inspections. In addition to its practical use in managing the apiary, smoke is also used in a spiritual context to cleanse or consecrate a hive. ©Jake Eshelman

Figure 4: Under the gaze of a Green Man votive, a backyard beehive in Houston, TX is also consecrated at the base with a cross depicting St. Benedict—the patron saint of bees.
©Jake Eshelman

Any act of group-building inherently implies some level of initiation. Yet amongst spiritual practitioners, this is not always limited to the human beekeeping community. Rather, some interviewees report a sense of belonging to bee society, albeit in an asymptotic sense. Citing the responsibilities of maintaining a safe environment for the bees (e.g., providing their physical living structure, protecting them from threats, etc.) and the ability to communicate with the hives, Melissa muses that 'I've never really considered myself to be a part of the superorganism, but technically I think I already am'.[48] By implication, it follows that Melissa does in fact occupy a place in this 'other' world beyond everyday human experience.

This glimpse into what Otto might describe as the noumenal realm of the bee-superorganism underlies a common experience amongst spiritual beekeepers.[49] In discussing such encounters, Beckett recounts how 'when I go into the beehive, the world disappears. There are no dogs, no husband, no work, no school, no nothing. Just the bees'.[50] This experience of the everyday, profane reality fading to the background elegantly embodies Eliade's position that sacred encounters often alter our sense of time and space.[51] Additionally, Beckett further verifies this slippage by experiencing 'how fast everything goes back to normal after I close the hive'.[52]

As previously established, much of what characterizes sacred experience is its highly inexplicable nature. Even amongst practising beekeepers who interact with their hives on a frequent and regular basis, such ineffable encounters with bees are common nonetheless. Much of this stems from the lingering mysteries surrounding bee behaviour. Beckett puts it bluntly, 'I don't think a single person in this world fully understands the bees, the colonies, the way they live, and work, and die, and are born, and all they do'.[53] By implication, Beckett suggests that we all have much yet to learn about—and from—bees.

Beyond unearthing the otherwise esoteric intricacies of bee biology and ecology, sacred apiculture seeks to obtain spiritual knowledge from interactions with their hives. This of course largely manifests in experiences of the ineffable. To this effect, Melissa asserts that:

> I often receive spiritual knowledge from bees, especially in every 'first'. The first swarm you see… it's a very intense, spiritual moment. It is such a majestic, just unimaginable experience. It's breath-taking and immense and loud and beautiful. I was shocked by the first swarm I saw, but it was magnificent at the same time to see them all acting as one.[54]

This account of the overwhelming and inexplicable encounter aligns with Otto's *heirophany*, where a person finds themselves confounded by the gravity of the *mysterium tremendum*, which challenges existing sense of the world.[55] Though suspended in intense bouts of awe, wonder, terror, and enchantment, insights into sacred apiculture practices suggest that this glimpse into the noumenal can also evolve into a consistent spiritual practice. Illustrating this shift, Melissa shares that nurturing spiritual relationships with bees precipitates 'a sort of inexplicable synchronicity and serendipity' in one's life wherein a person feels guided and supported.[56] Though admitting that the correlation is difficult to articulate, this nonetheless reveals a deeply held understanding that sacred relationships with bees can be beneficial and—more importantly—*felt*.

Conclusion

This research finds that a phenomenological investigation of sacred apiculture provides a rich, nuanced, and generative lens into the spiritual connections between contemporary beekeepers and their bees. Furthermore, this chapter begins to illuminate some of the individual beliefs, practices, and experiences amongst a small sample of beekeepers who nurture sacred relationships with their bees. Largely through in-depth interviews, this research contextualises spiritual beekeeping within the ongoing academic study of the sacred by employing the respective work of Durkheim, Otto, and Eliade to elucidate key themes that characterise sacred apiculture as it is practised today—namely a heightened ecological consciousness, the capacity for interspecies communication, and direct interactions with the ineffable 'other'. While this research offers an initial glimpse into the spiritual beliefs and practices held by contemporary beekeepers, it nonetheless warrants further exploration across a wider sample in order to delve deeper into the nuances and intricacies of sacred apiculture as it is practised today.

Notes

1 Wilson, Noah, *The Bee: A Natural History*, (Princeton, New Jersey, Princeton University Press, 2014), pp. 15–16

2 Roffet-Salque, Melanie, et al., 'Widespread Exploitation of the Honeybee by Early Neolithic Farmers' in *Nature*, Issue 527, pp. 226–230 (2015). <https://doi.org/10.1038/nature15757>

3 Kritsky, Gene, *The Tears of Re: Beekeeping in Ancient Egypt*, (Oxford, Oxford University Press, 22015), p. 26

4 Ransome, Hilda A., *The Sacred Bee in Ancient Times and Folklore*, (Mineola, New York, Dover Publications Inc., 2004), p. 218

5 Buxton, Simon. *The Shamanic Way of the Bee: Ancient Wisdom and Healing Practices of the Bee Masters,* (Rochester, Vermont, Inner Traditions, 2004), pp. 9–10

6 Hay, David and Rebecca Nye, *The Spirit of the Child.* (London: Jessica Kingsley Publishing, 2006), pp. 21–22

7 Durkheim, Emile, *The Elementary Forms of Religious Life,* Translated by Karen E. Fields, (New York, The Free Press, 1995), p. 118

8 Otto, Rudolf, *The Idea of the Holy,* Reprint (Oxford, Oxford University Press, 1978), p.26

9 Eliade, Mircea, *The Sacred and the Profane: The Nature of Religion,* (New York, Pantheon, 1957), pp. 68–70

10 Von Hendy, Andrew, *The Modern Construction of Myth,* (Bloomington, Indiana, Indiana University Press, 2002), p. 184

11 Ransome, *The Sacred Bee in Ancient Times and Folklore,* p. 218

12 Ransome, *The Sacred Bee in Ancient Times and Folklore,* p. 218

13 Horn, Tammy, *Bees in America: How the Honey Bee Shaped a Nation,* (Lexington, Kentucky, University Press of Kentucky, 2006), pp. 406–407

14 Buxton, *The Shamanic Way of the Bee,* p. 10

15 Buxton, *The Shamanic Way of the Bee,* p. 11

16 Smith, Linda Tuhiwai, *Decolonizing Methodologies: Research And Indigenous Peoples,* 2nd edn, (London, Zed Books Ltd, 2012), p. 2

17 Smith, *Decolonizing Methodologies,* p. 1

18 Smith, David Woodruff, "Phenomenology", The Stanford Encyclopedia of Philosophy (Summer 2018 Edition), Edward N. Zalta (ed.), https://plato.stanford.edu/archives/sum2018/entries/phenomenology/ [accessed May 2, 2022]

19 Hennink, *Qualitative Research Methods,* p. 42

20 See Jake Eshelman, *Telling of the Bees.* <www.jakeeshelman.com/Telling-of-the-Bees> [Accessed 1 May, 2023]

21 Hennink, *Qualitative Research Methods,* p. 11

22 Smith, *Decolonizing Methodologies,* pp. 1–2; Buxton, *The Shamanic Way of the Bee,* pp. 9–10

23 Evans-Pritchard, E.E. *Witchcraft, Oracles, And Magic Among The Azande,* (Oxford: Clarendon Press, 1976), p. 244

24 Interviewee A (pseudonym: Melissa), interviewed 3 Apr, 2022

25 Interviewee B (pseudonym: Beckett), interviewed 6 Apr, 2022

26 Eliade, *The Sacred and the Profane,* pp. 68–70

27 Interviewee C (pseudonym: Deborah), interviewed 8 Apr, 2022

28 Hay and Nye, *The Spirit of the Child.* pp. 21–22

29 Interviewee A (pseudonym: Melissa), interviewed 3 Apr, 2022

30 Thoms, Christopher A., Kristen C. Nelson, Andrew Kubas, Nathalie Steinhauer, Michael E. Wilson, and Dennis van Engelsdorp, 'Beekeeper Stewardship, Colony Loss, and Varroa Destructor Management' in *AMBIO,* (The Royal Swedish Academy of Sciences, 2018), pp. 1–10]

31 Attfield, Robin, *Environmental Ethics: An Overview for the Twenty-First Century,* 2nd edn. (Cambridge, Polity Press, 2014), pp. 30–31

32 Interviewee B (pseudonym: Beckett), interviewed 6 Apr, 2022

33 Interviewee B (pseudonym: Beckett), interviewed 6 Apr, 2022

34 Interviewee A (pseudonym: Melissa), interviewed 3 Apr, 2022

35 Interviewee A (pseudonym: Melissa), interviewed 3 Apr, 2022

36 Ransome, *The Sacred Bee,* pp. 19–20

37 Ransome, *The Sacred Bee,* p. 218

38 Questionnaire respondent 4, submitted Apr 10, 2022

39   Interviewee A (pseudonym: Melissa), interviewed 3 Apr, 2022
40   Interviewee C (pseudonym: Deborah), interviewed 8 Apr, 2022
41   Interviewee B (pseudonym: Beckett), interviewed 6 Apr, 2022
42   Interviewee B (pseudonym: Beckett), interviewed 6 Apr, 2022
43   Interviewee A (pseudonym: Melissa), interviewed 3 Apr, 2022
44   Interviewee A (pseudonym: Melissa), interviewed 3 Apr, 2022
45   Ribeiro AP, da Silva NFF, Mesquita FN, Araújo PdCS, Rosa TC, et al. 'Machine Learning Approach for Automatic Recognition of Tomato-Pollinating Bees Based on Their Buzzing-Sounds', in *PLOS Computational Biology 17(9): e1009426*. 2021
46   Interviewee A (pseudonym: Melissa), interviewed 3 Apr, 2022
47   Durkheim, *The Elementary Forms of Religious Life*, p. 118
48   Interviewee A (pseudonym: Melissa), interviewed 3 Apr, 2022
49   Otto, *The Idea of the Holy*, p.26
50   Interviewee B (pseudonym: Beckett), interviewed 6 Apr, 2022
51   Eliade, *The Sacred and the Profane*, pp. 68–70
52   Interviewee B (pseudonym: Beckett), interviewed 6 Apr, 2022
53   Interviewee B (pseudonym: Beckett), interviewed 6 Apr, 2022
54   Interviewee A (pseudonym: Melissa), interviewed 3 Apr, 2022
55   Otto, *The Idea of the Holy*, p.26
56   Interviewee A (pseudonym: Melissa), interviewed 3 Apr, 2022

INDEX

Word by word alphabetisation

Abram, David, 29, 75, 146, 154
Ackerman, Joy Whiteley, 93, 100
Albrecht, Glenn, 189
Allerton, Catherine, 159
Altman, Irwin and Low, Setha M., 94
Aluna 31
Amerindian cosmological models *see* cosmology
Ammerman, Albert J., 40
ancestral knowledge, 35
animacy, 17, 19
animism, 14, 17, 18, 146
Animism, New, 145, 154
Aporta, Caludio, 76
archaeoastronomy, brown, 3
archaeoastronomy, green, 3
Aristotle, 5, 6, 7, 8, 39, 41, 42, 43, 45, 81, 113, 130, 132, 186
    Aristotelian, 4, 5, 6, 81, 84, 191
attachment to place *see* place
Attfield, Robin, 209
auto-ethnography, 57
Aveni, Anthony, 3
axis mundi, 43, 44, 46, 47, 49, 51, 73, 80, 81, 85, 165, 176, 179, 183
Badia, Lynn, 56, 57, 65, 68
Bath Royal Circus, 3
bee breath, 212, 213
Bell, Judith and Waters, Stephen, 159, 160, 168
Bell, Sarah and Instone, Leslie, 128, 134, 135, 139
Bender, Barbara, 55, 57, 59, 64, 68, 176, 180, 181, 182
Berger, Alan, 185, 187, 193
Bergmann, Sigurd, 2, 4

Bernbaum, Edwin, 74, 82
Berry, Thomas, 146, 152
Beyond the Mushroom Cloud, 177
Bhattacharjee, Amit and Mogilner, Cassie, 26
Black Stone of Festus, 50
Boni, Giacomo, 40, 41, 45, 47, 48, 50
Book of Burial, 118
boundary thinness, 186
Box of Delights, 191
Brady, Bernadette, 11, 42, 91, 97, 130, 132, 134
Brown, Barbara B.; Altman, Irwin; and Werner, Carol M., 91
Buddhist, 76, 79, 112, 115, 120, 122, 180, 181, 212
Budka, Julia, 92, 103
Buhner, Stephen Harrod, 28, 30
Burkert, Walter, 121
Buxton, Simon, 205, 207
Byrne, Denis, 159
Cambridge Declaration on Consciousness, 15
Cameron-Daum, Kate, 57, 95, 104, 130, 132, 134, 159
Campbell, Elaine, 159
cannabis sativa, 33
Cannon, Jon, 41, 43, 80
cardinal points, 41
Casey, Edward, 4, 5, 42, 81, 162, 163, 186, 191, 198
Cassiopeia, 122
cathedrals, 2 159
centre of the world *see* axis mundi
Cézanne, Paul, 84
Chevrier, Marie-Hélène, 96, 106

chora, 43, 49, 112, 113, 116, 117, 123
Christian
    context, 1, 2, 30
    missionaries, 32
    theology, 4
chronos *see* time
Cicero, 48
Clandinin, Jean D., and Murphy Shaun M., 90
communication
    attuned, 31, 32
    plant, 32, 33, 36
consciousness
    collective, 42, 43, 74, 80, 85, 161, 209
    mystical, 35
    non-human, 15, 16
Cooper, David, 28, 131, 139
Cop 26 United Nations Climate Change Conference, 188
Corbin, Henry, 43
cosmic order, 2
cosmic pole, 179
cosmology
    Amerindian, 19
    Daoist, 111, 121, 122, 123
Crayone, 192, 198
Cross, Jennifer, 89, 91, 92
Cuba, Lee and Hummon, David M., 92
Cunningham, Paul, 29
Curry, Patrick, 1, 130, 137, 138, 139
Dagnall, Neil, 13
darkness, 96, 97, 105, 106
Darwin, Charles, 17
Davis, Annie Rischard, 94, 102
de Castro, Eduardo Viveiros, 19
De Orellana, Margarita, 33

219

INDEX

della Dora, Veronica, 162
developmentalism, 17
Devereux, Paul, 22, 74, 77, 81, 92, 98, 99, 100, 102
Digance, Justine, 73, 77
Dionysius of Halicarnassus, 48
dreams, 17, 29, 188
drosscape, 185, 186, 187, 192, 193, 198
Dumézil, Georges, 48, 49
Durkheim, Émile, 6, 11, 25, 39, 41, 42, 43, 44, 48, 51, 55, 56, 57, 68, 73, 74, 80–86, 91, 95, 97, 112, 113, 118, 121, 127, 129, 134, 144, 147, 148, 154, 157, 158, 159, 160, 161, 162, 165, 166, 167, 169, 170, 176, 177, 179, 181, 182, 186, 204, 213, 216
Durkheimian, 8, 11, 12, 22, 49, 57, 65, 68, 74, 75, 81, 84, 114, 118, 119, 147, 179, 196, 197
dwelling perspective, 57, 58, 59
Eagleton, Terry, 121
Earth
  Community, 146, 152
  living organism, 20, 146
earthing sacredness, 2, 4
Eastman Attebury, Jennifer, 195
Eaton, Gary, 120
Edgelands, 188
elements, 42, 49, 127, 140
  five, 122
  four, 45
  nature, three, 118
  sacred, 213
  theory of, 5
Eliade, Mircea, 5, 9, 12, 22, 39, 41, 42, 43, 46, 47, 51, 73, 74, 80, 82, 85, 86, 91, 94, 97, 102, 112, 113, 114, 115, 118, 119, 127, 129, 132, 134, 145, 147, 148, 151, 154, 157, 158, 160, 161, 162, 164, 165, 166, 169, 170, 175, 176, 177, 178, 179, 182, 186, 193, 194, 204, 208, 215, 216
enchantment, 62, 96, 127, 138, 139, 140, 216
encultured landscapes, 43

Endsjo, Dag Oistein, 187, 192, 198
entheogen, 32, 33
Ereira, Alan, 31
Estaroth, Anna, 80
Etherington, Kim, 129
Evans-Prichard, E. E., 207
experience
  extraordinary, 13, 25–30, 31, 33–35
  extrovertive, 13, 14
  mystical, 14, 27, 28, 35, 106
  near death, 26, 29
  out-of-body, 26, 29
Fagetti, Antonella, 32
Farley, Paul and Roberts, Michael Symmons, 188, 192
Fields, Karen, 176
folklore, 3, 16, 55, 56, 57, 62, 66, 68, 69, 81, 205
Fort, Charles, 20
Foucault, Michel, 55, 57, 59, 63
Foucauldian, 69
Fulbright, John, 188
Gagliano, Monica, 33
Gaia
  Foundation, 145
  theory, 20, 146, 152, 154
Gaiman, Neil, 195
Garuba, Harry Olúdáre, 17
gathering, 130–135, 140
Geertz, Clifford, 114
Giamo, Benedict, 173
Gilhus, Ingvild, 121
Glastonbury, 2
Glockner, Julio, 32
Goethe, Johann Wolfgang, 4
González-González, José-Manuel; Franco-Calvo, and Jesús Gerardo, 160
Gonzalez, Lilian, 32
Goodwin, Brian, 146, 152, 153
Gosden, Chris and Lock, Gary, 56, 69
Govinda, Lama, 79
graffiti, 58, 67, 68, 69, 188, 191, 192, 193, 198
Grahame, Kenneth, 8
Grant, Michael, 48
gravity, 5, 42, 130, 134, 140, 216
Griffioen, Amber, 160, 166

Guénon, Rene, 2
Gunzburg, Darrelyn and Brady, Bernadette, 91, 97
Haberman, David L., 92, 98
Haid, Christian, 192
haiku, 119, 120
Hall, C. Michael, 188
Hallowell, Alfred Irving, 19, 95, 98, 102, 145, 151
Happold, F. C., 26, 27, 30, 34, 35
Harding, Stephan, 146, 151, 152
Hardy, Alister, 27, 34
Harvey, Graham, 14, 18, 129, 145, 149, 151, 153, 154, 196
Hashemnezhad, Hashem; Heidari, Ali Akbar; and Hoseini, Parisa Mohammad, 96, 104
haunt, 12, 13, 21, 60
Hay, David and Nye, Rebecca, 203, 209
Heart of the World, 31
heaven, 29, 80, 111, 122, 165, 176, 179
Heidegger, Martin, 111, 123, 130
Heinsch, Josef, 2, 3
Helminiak, Daniel A., 28, 29
Henare, Amira, 6
Hennink, Monique, 75, 178
heterotopia, 55, 57, 59, 63, 68, 69
Hernández, Bernardo; Hidalgo, M. Carmen; and Ruiz, Cristina, 89
Heywood, Paolo, 168
hierophany, 5, 8, 11–13, 39, 42–44, 47, 51, 73–75, 79, 81–85, 91, 113, 115, 118, 127, 129, 130, 134, 145, 147, 151, 154, 158, 160, 161, 164, 166, 170, 175, 176, 179, 181, 183, 186, 190, 196, 197, 216
Hindu, 92, 98
Holbraad, Martin, 6
holistic conception of development, 29
Horn, Tammy, 205
Hülsen, Christian, 41
Hunter, Jack, 3, 25, 27, 29, 36, 130

INDEX

Husserl, Edmund, 90, 112, 187
Hutton, Ronald, 30, 56, 61, 195, 196
Ingold, Tim, 43, 46, 50, 55, 57, 58, 59, 64, 65, 73, 75, 76, 80, 83, 85, 95, 102, 128, 130, 134, 135, 136, 139, 146, 151, 154, 176, 182
insight
 animistic, 14
 experiential, 69
 natural, 2
 religious, 25, 27–29, 77
iugues auscpicium, 48
irruption, 42, 43, 94, 130, 145, 175, 179, 186
Ivakhiv, Adrian, 22
James, William, 27, 29
Janowski, Monica, 92, 102
Jeffries, Richard, 34
kairos time *see* time
Kane, Sean, 127, 130, 138, 139
karesansui, 117
Keel, John 20, 21
Kimmerer, Robin Wall, 17, 18, 30, 31
Knobloch, Patricia J., 92, 93, 103
knowledge, ancestral, 35
Kogi of the Sierra Nevada, 31, 36
Koopman, Wilma, 168
Korpisaari, Antti and Pärssinen, Martti, 93, 103
Koyukon Indians, 95
kratophany, 12
Kuo, Alexander and Margalit, Yotam, 89, 100, 102
Kuo, Hui-Ming; Su, Jung-Yao; Wang, Cheng-Hua; and Kiatsakared, Pinyapat, 89, 94, 100, 102
Kushner, S., 90
Lane, Belden C., 4, 7, 39, 40, 43, 45, 46, 49, 50, 51, 74, 81, 90, 93, 96, 97, 100, 101, 102, 103, 105, 112, 114, 115, 117, 119, 122, 123, 124, 127, 130, 132, 141, 143, 145, 147, 148, 149, 154, 157, 158, 159, 161, 162, 163, 164, 165, 166, 167, 168, 169, 170, 176, 182, 183
Leopold, Aldo 34

Levo-Strauss, Claude 42
Levy-Bruhl, Lucien 41, 50, 92, 97, 102, 103, 113, 114, 115, 116, 118, 122, 123, 128, 139, 187, 195, 196, 197
liminal 8, 9, 44, 48, 49, 51, 74, 96, 97, 105, 185–193, 196–198
Lin, Martin 7
litter, ritual 56
locale, 95, 130, 186, 187, 188, 198
Lopez, Barry, 84
Lovelock, James, 20
Lukes, Steven, 176
Lynch, Kevin, 188
ma, 113, 116, 117, 118, 120, 121
Machamer, Peter, 81
Mazatec, 32
Mayo, James, 162
McCune, Rochelle, 129
McMartin, James, 166
Mechling, Jay, 16
memorates, 13
memory, 4, 7, 9, 27, 56, 59, 96, 98, 101, 105, 106, 144, 149, 160, 187, 198, 205
Merleau-Ponty, Maurice, 41, 143
Milky Way, 122
Miyamoto, Yuki, 177, 178, 179, 181
Monet, Claude, 30
Mooney, Patrick, 91
Morrison, Kenneth, 19
Moyes, Holley, 96, 106
Mundus Imaginalis, 43, 46, 50, 51
music of the spheres, 15
Myers, F. W. H., 20, 27
mysterium tremendum, 42, 49, 51, 144, 147, 204, 216
myth, 4, 39, 40, 43, 47, 51, 62, 63, 68, 69, 121, 123, 130, 195
Naess, Arne, 13
nature-mysticism, 34
Navaho, 93
Naydler, Jeremy, 30
Nelis, Damien P., 187, 192, 198
Nichols, Tom, 177
non-human, 11

intelligence, 30
relationships, 3
Nordstrom, Ralph, 129
numen loci, 13, 15
numinous, 12, 13, 27, 42, 50, 51, 61, 63, 65, 74, 82, 84, 85, 94, 96–98, 102, 103, 105, 106, 144, 154, 158, 159, 161, 168
Ojibwa, 19, 95, 98, 102
ontologies
 animistic, 92
 relational, 18, 19
orchestration, 22
otherworlds, 74
Otto, Rudolf, 12, 13, 22, 27, 42, 50, 74, 82, 144, 147, 148, 154, 158, 168, 204, 215, 216
Otomi, 33
ownership, 64, 93–96, 100–103, 180
Paden, William, 158
pagan
 practice, 56, 65, 67
 ritual, 30
participatory ecoconsciousness, 186
Pearson, Jo, 168
Pearson, Mike Parker, 190
Pickering, William, 159
phenomenology, 4, 41, 57, 58, 73, 182, 183
pink noise, 197
plant communication *see* communication
place
 as a vessel, 5, 186
 attachment, 89, 91, 92, 94, 95, 96, 101, 104, 105, 106, 107
 high, 74, 79, 84
 names, 4, 48, 61
 song of, 127, 138, 139, 141
 storied, 43, 47, 80, 149
 thin, 12
Plato, 42, 43, 113
Plumwood, Val, 189
Plutarch, 46, 47, 51
pot breaking, 92, 101, 103
Prendergast, Frank, 79
Pronko, Leonard, 195
qi, 118
Ransome, Hilda M., 205, 210
ratios, sacred, 2

INDEX

Rennie, Bryan, 177
Reynolds, Mary, 128
Rios, Maria and Cubero, Maria, 33
ritual, 14, 25, 31, 32, 34, 39, 42, 43, 46, 48, 49, 51, 56, 58, 59, 61, 63, 65– 69, 92, 96, 99, 103, 106, 115, 118, 119, 123, 147, 158, 161–167, 169, 170, 188, 192, 196–198, 204, 212, 213
Romanelli, 45
rootedness, 94, 101
Roszak, Theodore, 18
Rowlinson, Col., 1, 2
Royal Geographical Society, 1
sacred geography
  brown, 3, 4, 6
  definition, 1
  green, 3, 4
  origin of term, 1
  prehistoric, 2, 3, 185
sacred-profane dichotomy, 74
Sakuteki, 116, 123
Scannell, Lelia and Gifford, Robert, 89, 94, 100, 101, 102
Sepie, Amba J., 31
shakkei, 115
shamanism, 32, 33, 76, 93, 103
Shaw, Martin, 187, 196
Shepherd, Nan, 91, 99
shimenawa, 119
Shintoism, 173, 180
Shinzō, Hamai, 179
Shuoshi, Mizuhara, 120
Silla people, 76
Simmonds-Moore, Christine, 186, 187, 196, 197, 198, 202
Smith, David Woodruff, 205
Smith, Jonathan Z., 44, 147
Smith, Linda Tuhiwai, 205, 207
Society for Psychical Research, 27
solastalgia, 189, 197
song of the place see place
solstice, 47, 58, 65, 148
space
  neutrality of, 4
  differentiated, 80
Spinoza, Barcuh de, 7
Stace, Walter T., 13

Stonehenge, 3, 57, 64, 68, 180, 182
Stow, John, 30
Straight Track Club, 3
Studstill, Randall, 175
subtle ecologies, 21
sun, movement of, 47
Sundarum, Usha, 93, 103
supernatural, 11, 12, 13, 20, 25, 26, 27, 29, 113, 114, 115, 119, 123, 195, 210
supernormal, 20
Svendsen, Erika and Campbell, Lindsay, 162, 165, 166
symbolic world centre see axis mundi
sympatheia, 122, 123
synaesthesia, 188
synchronicity, 168, 216
Telling the Bees, 210, 211
theophany, 176, 178, 179, 183
Thomassen, Bjørn, 185, 187, 190, 196, 197, 198
Thoms, Christopher, 209
Thorley, Anthony and Gunn, Celia, 145, 159
Thorley, Anthony, 1, 22, 153
Tilley, Christopher, 4, 7, 39, 43, 46, 48, 50, 55, 57, 58, 59, 62, 65, 73, 74, 77, 79, 80, 84, 85, 89, 90, 93, 95, 97, 99, 100, 104, 106, 128, 130, 132, 134, 143, 146, 149, 152, 154, 159, 186, 187, 188
time
  chronos, 113
  kairos, 113, 116, 117
  liminal, 9, 197
  social, 57
  tenseless, 7
timelessness, atemporal, 7
topophilia, 91
topos, 43, 112, 113, 186
threshold, 44, 49, 51, 97, 99, 104, 105, 132, 134, 140, 176, 193, 194
Trahar, Sheila, 90
Traherne, Thomas, 35
troll, 195–197
Trubshaw, Robert, 129, 134
Tuan, Yi-Fu, 91, 93, 94, 101, 104
Turner, Victor, 187, 192
Tweed, Thomas, 80

Tylor, Edward Burnett, 17
UFOs, 20–21
Ujang, Norsidah and Zakariya, Khalilah, 94, 103, 104
ultraterrestrials, 19, 20, 21
underworld, 106, 165, 179, 186
urban planning, 2, 3
Ursa Major, 122
Valens Varro, 48
van Gennep, Arnold, 187, 192
von Hendy, Andrew, 204
wabi sabi, 119, 120
Wain, Louis, 8
Wallis, Robert J and Blain, Jenny, 56, 65, 66, 67, 68
Wari people, 93, 103
Wastell, Sari, 6
Weil, Simone, 83
Whitehead, Amy, 147, 150
Whittle, Alasdair, 55, 59, 60
Whyte, Nicola 57, 58, 61
Wind in the Willows, 8
Wissers, Nancy, 187, 194, 196
Woldoff, R. A., 92
Wood, John, 3
Woods, Angela, 129
Wright, Julia, 21
yard, megalithic, 3
Zangshu (see *Book of Burial*)
Zolberg, Vera, 176